# PUBLIC SPEAKING AND
# INFLUENCING MEN IN BUSINESS
# by

*Dale Carnegie*

데일카네기 성공대화론

Public Speaking and Influencing Men In Business

Copyright ⓒ by THE INTERNATIONAL COMMITTEE
OF YOUNG MEN'S CHRISTIAN ASSOCIATIONS
Korean Translation Copyright ⓒ 2007 by LIBER BOOKS.

Public Speaking and
Influencing Men In Business

1판 4쇄 발행 2010년 7월 19일
개정판 1쇄 발행 2012년 5월 16일
개정판 2쇄 발행 2012년 9월 10일

지은이 | Dale Carnegie
주석 | 강성복, 권오열
펴낸이 | 박찬영
기획편집 | 박시내, 김혜경, 한미정
마케팅 | 이진규, 장민영
디자인 | 이창욱

발행처 | 리베르
주소 | 서울시 용산구 용산동5가 24번지 용산파크타워 103동 505호
등록번호 | 제2003-43호
전화 | 02-790-0587, 0588
팩스 | 02-790-0589

홈페이지 | www.리베르.com
커뮤니티 | blog.naver.com/liber_book(블로그)
          cafe.naver.com/talkinbook(카페)
e-mail | skyblue7410@hanmail.net

ISBN | 978-89-6582-033-8 (14740)

리베르(Liber 전원의 신)는 자유와 지성을 상징합니다.

# PUBLIC SPEAKING
# AND
# INFLUENCING MEN
# IN BUSINESS
by
*Dale Carnegie*

## 데일카네기 성공대화론

리베르

# 머리말

그 동안 한국에서는 구하기 힘들었던 '데일카네기 성공대화론 (Public Speaking and Influencing Men In Business)' 원본 텍스트가 완역본과 동시에 출간됐다. 원본을 읽고 싶었던 독자들에게는 더 없이 좋은 기회가 될 것이다. 더구나 이 책의 역서는 원본을 기본 텍스트로 삼았고 원본의 완역을 목표로 했기 때문에 원본과 대조하면서 읽고 싶은 사람들에게는 더 많은 도움이 되리라 생각한다. 해설판 원본 텍스트와 완역본은 완벽한 영한 대역본 역할을 할 수 있을 것이다.

데일 카네기의 글은 고등학교 영어 교과서에도 수록될 정도로 영어를 배우는 사람들에게는 훌륭한 교재로 알려져 있다. 카네기의 책은 이론 중심이 아닌 사례 중심으로 구성돼 있어 예나 지금이나 많은 사람들에게 감동을 준다. 이 책이 훌륭한 영어 교재가 될 수 있는 것은 바로 이 점 때문이다. 원본 텍스트와 완역본을 통해 세상사의 이치와 영어라는 두 마리 토끼를 잡을 수 있다면 더 이상 바랄 것이 없겠다.

『데일 카네기 성공 대화론』 역자 강성복 씀

# Contents

**머리말** · 5

**CHAPTER I**

DEVELOPING COURAGE AND SELF-CONFIDENCE · 9

**CHAPTER II**

SELF-CONFIDENCE THROUGH PREPARATION · 37

**CHAPTER III**

HOW FAMOUS SPEAKERS PREPARED THEIR ADDRESSES · 71

**CHAPTER IV**

THE IMPROVEMENT OF MEMORY · 105

**CHAPTER V**

KEEPING THE AUDIENCE AWAKE · 141

**CHAPTER VI**

ESSENTIAL ELEMENTS IN SUCCESSFUL SPEAKING · 169

**CHAPTER VII**

THE SECRET OF GOOD DELIVERY · 189

**CHAPTER VIII**

PLATFORM PRESENCE AND PERSONALITY · 219

**CHAPTER IX**

HOW TO OPEN A TALK • 253

**CHAPTER X**

CAPTURING YOUR AUDIENCE AT ONCE • 285

**CHAPTER XI**

HOW TO CLOSE A TALK • 317

**CHAPTER XII**

HOW TO MAKE YOUR MEANING CLEAR • 343

**CHAPTER XIII**

HOW TO BE IMPRESSIVE AND CONVINCING • 373

**CHAPTER XIV**

HOW TO INTEREST YOUR AUDIENCE • 407

**CHAPTER XV**

HOW TO GET ACTION • 437

**Words & Phrases** • 471

**CHAPTER ONE**

# DEVELOPING COURAGE AND SELF-CONFIDENCE

"Courage is the chief attribute to manliness."
—Daniel Webster.

"It is never safe to look into the future with eyes of fear." —E. H. Harriman.

"Never take counsel of your fears."
—Motto of Stonewall Jackson.

"If you persuade yourself that you can do a certain thing, provided this thing be possible, you will do it, however difficult it may be. If, on the contrary, you imagine that you cannot do the simplest thing in the world, it is impossible for you to do it, and molehills become for you unscalable mountains."
—Emile Coué.

# DEVELOPING COURAGE AND SELF-CONFIDENCE

More than eighteen thousand business men, since 1912, have been members of the various public speaking courses conducted by the author. Most of them have, at his request, written stating why they had enrolled for this training and what they hoped to obtain from it. Naturally, the phraseology varied; but the central desire in these letters, the basic want in the vast majority, remained surprisingly the same: "When I am called upon to stand up and speak," man after man wrote, "I become so self-conscious, so frightened, that I can't think clearly, can't concentrate, can't remember what I had intended to say. I want to gain self-confidence, poise, and the ability to think on my feet. I want to get my thoughts together in logical order and I want to be able to say my say clearly and convincingly before a business group or audience." Thousands of their confessions sounded about like that. To cite a concrete case: Years ago, a gentleman here called Mr. D. W. Ghent, joined my public speaking course in Philadelphia. Shortly after the opening session, he invited me to lunch with him in the Manufacturers' Club. He was a man of middle age and had always led an active life; was head of his own manufacturing establishment, a leader in church work and civic activities. While we were having lunch that day, he leaned across the table and said: "I have been asked many times to talk before various gatherings, but I have never been able to do so. I get so fussed, my mind becomes an utter blank: so I have sidestepped it all my life. But I am chairman now of a board of college trustees. I must preside at their meetings. I simply have to do some talking······ Do you think it will be possible for me to learn to speak at this late date in my life?"

"Do I think, Mr. Ghent?" I replied. "It is *not* a question of my *thinking*. I *know you can*, and I *know you will* if you will only practise and follow the directions and instructions."

He wanted to believe that, but it seemed too rosy, too optimistic. "I am afraid you are just being kind," he answered, "that you are merely trying to encourage me."

After he had completed his training, we lost touch with each other for a while. In 1921, we met and lunched together again at the Manufacturers' Club. We sat in the same corner and occupied the same table that we had had on the first occasion. Reminding him of our former conversation, I asked him if I had been too sanguine then. He took a little red-backed note book out of his pocket and showed me a list of talks and dates for which he was booked. "And the ability to make these," he confessed, "the pleasure I get in doing it, the additional service I can render to the community—these are among the most gratifying things in my life."

The International Conference for the Limitation of Armaments had been held in Washington shortly before that. When it was known that Lloyd George was planning to attend it, the Baptists of Philadelphia cabled, inviting him to speak at a great mass meeting to be held in their city. Lloyd George cabled back that, if he came to Washington, he would accept their invitation. And Mr. Ghent informed me that he himself had been chosen, from among all the Baptists of that city, to introduce England's premier to the audience.

And this was the man who had sat at that same table

less than three years before and solemnly asked me if I thought he would ever be able to talk in public!

Was the rapidity with which he forged ahead in his speaking ability unusual? Not at all. There have been hundreds of similar cases. For example—to quote one more specific instance—years ago, a Brooklyn physician, whom we will call Dr. Curtis, spent the winter in Florida near the training grounds of the Giants. Being an enthusiastic baseball fan, he often went to see them practise. In time, he became quite friendly with the team, and was invited to attend a banquet given in their honor.

After the coffee and nuts were served, several prominent guests were called upon to "say a few words." Suddenly, with the abruptness and unexpectedness of an explosion, he heard the toastmaster remark: "We have a physician with us tonight, and I am going to ask Dr. Curtis to talk on a Baseball Player's Health."

Was he prepared? Of course. He had had the best preparation in the world: he had been studying hygiene and practising medicine for almost a third of a century. He could have sat in his chair and talked about this subject all night to the man seated on his right or left. But to get up and say the same things to even a small audience—that was another matter. That was a paralyzing matter. His heart doubled its pace and skipped beats at the very contemplation of it. He had never made a public speech in his life, and every thought that he had had now took wings.

What was he to do? The audience was applauding. Every one was looking at him. He shook his head. But that served only to heighten the applause, to increase the demand. The cries of "Dr. Curtis! Speech! Speech!" grew louder and more insistent.

He was in positive misery. He knew that if he got up he would fail, that he would be unable to utter half a dozen sentences. So he arose, and, without saying a word, turned his back on his friends and walked silently out of the room, a deeply embarrassed and humiliated man.

Small wonder that one of the first things he did after getting back to Brooklyn was to come to the Central Y. M. C. A. and enroll in the course in Public Speaking. He didn't propose to be put to the blush and be stricken dumb a second time.

He was the kind of student that delights an instructor: he was in dead earnest. He wanted to be able to talk, and there was no half-heartedness about his desires. He prepared his talks thoroughly, he practised them with a will, and he never missed a single session of the course.

He did precisely what such a student always does: he progressed at a rate that surprised him, that surpassed his fondest hopes. After the first few sessions his nervousness subsided, his confidence mounted higher and higher. In two months he had become the star speaker of the group. He was soon accepting invitations to speak elsewhere; he now loved the feel and exhilaration of it, the distinction and the additional friends it brought him.

A member of the New York City Republican Campaign Committee, hearing one of his public addresses, invited Dr. Curtis to stump the city for his party. How surprised that politician would have been had he realized that, only a year before, the speaker had gotten up and left a public banquet hall in shame and confusion because he was tongue-tied with audience-fear!

The gaining of self-confidence and courage, and the ability to think calmly and clearly while talking to a group is not one-tenth as difficult as most men imagine. It is not a gift bestowed by Providence on only a few rarely endowed individuals. It is like the ability to play golf. Any man can develop his own latent capacity if he has sufficient desire to do so.

Is there the faintest shadow of a reason why you should not be able to think as well in a perpendicular position before an audience as you can when sitting down? Surely, you know there is not. In fact, you ought to think better when facing a group of men, their presence ought to stir you and lift you. A great many speakers will tell you that the presence of an audience is a stimulus, an inspiration, that drives their brains to function more clearly, more keenly. At such times, thoughts, facts, ideas, that they did not know they possessed, drift smoking by, as Henry Ward Beecher said; and they have but to reach out and lay their hands hot upon them. That ought to be your experience. It probably will be if you practise and persevere.

Of this much, however, you may be absolutely sure: training and practise will wear away your audience-fright and give you self-confidence and an abiding courage.

Do not imagine that your case is unusually difficult. Even those who afterwards became the most eloquent representatives of their generation were, at the outset of their careers, afflicted by this blinding fear and self-consciousness.

William Jennings Bryan, battle-marked veteran that

he was, admitted that, in his first attempts, his knees fairly smote together.

Mark Twain, the first time he stood up to lecture, felt as if his mouth were filled with cotton and his pulse were speeding for some prize cup.

Grant took Vicksburg and led to victory one of the greatest armies the world had ever seen up to that time; yet, when he attempted to speak in public, he admitted he had something very like locomotor ataxia.

The late Jean Jaurès, the most powerful political speaker that France produced during his generation, sat, for a year, tongue-tied in the Chamber of Deputies before he could summon up the courage to make his initial speech.

"The first time I attempted to make a public talk," confessed Lloyd George, "I tell you I was in a state of misery. It is no figure of speech, but literally true, that my tongue clove to the roof of my mouth: and, at first, I could hardly get out a word."

John Bright, the illustrious Englishman, who, during the civil war, defended in England the cause of union and emancipation, made his maiden speech before a group of country folk gathered in a school building. He was so frightened on the way to the place, so fearful that he would fail, that he implored his companion to start applause to bolster him up whenever he showed signs of giving way to his nervousness.

Charles Stewart Parnell, the great Irish leader, at the outset of his speaking career, was so nervous, according to the testimony of his brother, that he frequently clenched his fists until his nails sank into his flesh and his palms bled.

Disraeli admitted that he would rather have led a cavalry charge than to have faced the House of Commons for the first time. His opening speech there was a ghastly failure. So was Sheridan's.

In fact, so many of the famous speakers of England have made poor showings at first that there is now a feeling in Parliament that it is rather an inauspicious omen for a young man's initial talk to be a decided success. So take heart.

After watching the careers and aiding somewhat in the development of so many speakers, the author is always glad when a student has, at the outset, a certain amount of flutter and nervous agitation.

There is a certain responsibility in making a talk, even if it is to only two dozen men in a business conference—a certain strain, a certain shock, a certain excitement. The speaker ought to be keyed up like a thoroughbred straining at the bit. The immortal Cicero said, two thousand years ago, that all public speaking of real merit was characterized by nervousness.

Speakers often experience this same feeling even when they are talking over the radio. "Microphone fright," it is called. When Charlie Chaplin went "on the air," he had his speech all written out. Surely he was used to audiences. He toured this country back in 1912 with a vaudeville sketch entitled "A Night in a Music Hall." Before that he was on the legitimate stage in England. Yet, when he went into the padded room and faced the microphone, he had a feeling in the stomach not unlike the sensation one gets when he crosses the Atlantic during a stormy February.

James Kirkwood, a famous motion picture actor and director, had a similar experience. He used to be a star on the speaking stage; but, when he came out of the sending room after addressing the invisible audience, he was mopping perspiration from his brow. "An opening night on Broadway," he confessed, "is nothing in comparison to that."

Some men, no matter how often they speak, always experience this self-consciousness just before they commence but, in a few seconds after they have gotten on their feet, it disappears.

Even Lincoln felt shy for the few opening moments. "At first he was very awkward," relates his law partner, Herndon," and it seemed a real labor to adjust himself to his surroundings. He struggled for a time under a feeling of apparent diffidence and sensitiveness, and these only added to his awkwardness. I have often seen and sympathized with Mr. Lincoln during these moments. When he began speaking, his voice was shrill, piping and unpleasant. His manner, his attitude, his dark, yellow face, wrinkled and dry, his oddity of pose, his diffident movements —everything seemed to be against him, but only for a short time." In a few moments he gained composure and warmth and earnestness, and his real speech began.

Your experience may be similar to his.

In order to get the most out of this training, and to get it with rapidity and dispatch, four things are essential:

## FIRST: START WITH A STRONG AND PERSISTENT DESIRE

This is of far more importance than you probably realize. If your instructor could look into your mind and heart now and ascertain the depth of your desires, he could foretell, almost with certainty, the swiftness of the progress you will make. If your desire is pale and flabby, your achievements will also take on that hue and consistency. But, if you go after this subject with persistence, and with the energy of a bulldog after a cat, nothing underneath the Milky Way will defeat you.

Therefore, arouse your enthusiasm for this study. Enumerate its benefits. Think of what additional self-confidence and the ability to talk more convincingly in business will mean to you. Think of what it may mean and what it ought to mean, in dollars and cents. Think of what it may mean to you socially; of the friends it will bring, of the increase of your personal influence, of the leadership it will give you. And it will give you leadership more rapidly than almost any other activity you can think of or imagine.

"There is no other accomplishment," stated Chauncey M. Depew, "which any man can have which will so quickly make for him a career and secure recognition as the ability to speak acceptably."

Philip D. Armour, after he had amassed millions, said: "I would rather have been a great speaker than a great capitalist."

It is an attainment that almost every person of education longs for. After Andrew Carnegie's death there was found, among his papers, a plan for his life drawn up when he was thirty-three years of age. He then felt that in two more years he could so arrange his business as to have an annual income of fifty thousand; so he proposed to retire at thirty-five, go to Oxford and get a thorough education, and *"pay special attention to speaking in public."*

Think of the glow of satisfaction and pleasure that will accrue from the exercise of this new power. The author has traveled around over no small part of this terrestrial ball; and has had many and varied experiences; but for downright, and lasting inward satisfaction, he knows of few things that will compare to standing before an audience and making men think your thoughts after you. It will give you a sense of strength, a feeling of power. It will appeal to your pride of personal accomplishment. It will set you off from and raise you above your fellow-men. There is magic in it and a never-to-be-forgotten thrill. "Two minutes before I begin," a speaker confessed, "I would rather be whipped than start; but two minutes before I finish, I would rather be shot than stop."

In every course, some men grow faint-hearted and

fall by the wayside; so you should keep thinking of what this course will mean to you until your desire is white hot. You should start this program with an enthusiasm that will carry you through every session, triumphant to the end. Tell your friends that you have joined this course. Set aside one certain night of the week for the reading of these lessons and the preparation of your talks. In short, make it as easy as possible to go ahead. Make it as difficult as possible to retreat.

When Julius Caesar sailed over the channel from Gaul and landed with his legions on what is now England, what did he do to insure the success of his arms? A very clever thing: he halted his soldiers on the chalk cliffs of Dover, and, looking down over the waves two hundred feet below, they saw red tongues of fire consume every ship in which they had crossed. In the enemy's country, with the last link with the Continent gone, the last means of retreating burned, there was but one thing left for them to do: to advance, to conquer. That is precisely what they did.

Such was the spirit of the immortal Caesar. Why not make it yours, too, in this war to exterminate your foolish fear of audiences.

## SECOND: KNOW THOROUGHLY WHAT YOU ARE GOING TO TALK ABOUT

Unless a man has thought out and planned his talk and knows what he is going to say, he can't feel very comfortable when he faces his auditors. He is like the blind leading the blind. Under such circumstances, your speaker ought to be self-conscious, ought to feel repentant, ought to be ashamed of his negligence.

"I was elected to the Legislature in the fall of 1881," Teddy Roosevelt wrote in his *Autobiography,* "and found myself the youngest man in that body. Like all young men and inexperienced members, I had considerable difficulty in teaching myself to speak. I profited much by the advice of a hard-headed old countryman—who was unconsciously paraphrasing the Duke of Wellington, who was himself doubtless paraphrasing somebody else. The advice ran: 'Don't speak until you are sure you have something to say, and know just what it is; then say it, and sit down.'"

This "hard-headed old countryman" ought to have told Roosevelt of another aid in overcoming nervousness. He ought to have added: "It will help you to throw off your embarrassment if you can find something to do before an audience—if you can exhibit something, write a word on the blackboard or point out a spot on the map or move a table or throw open a window or shift some books and papers—any physical action with a purpose behind it may help you to feel more at home."

True, it is not always easy to find an excuse for doing such things; but there is the suggestion. Use it if you can; but use it the first few times only. A baby does not cling to chairs after it once learns to walk.

## THIRD: ACT CONFIDENT

The most famous psychologist that America has produced, Professor William James, wrote as follows:

"Action seems to follow feeling, but really action and feeling go together; and by regulating the action, which is under the more direct control of the will, we can indirectly regulate the feeling, which is not.

Thus the sovereign voluntary path to cheerfulness, if our spontaneous cheerfulness be lost, is to sit up cheerfully and to act and speak as if cheerfulness were already there. If such conduct does not make you feel cheerful, nothing else on that occasion can.

So, to feel brave, act as if we were brave, use all of our

will to that end, and a courage-fit will very likely replace the fit of fear."

Apply Professor James' advice. To develop courage when you are facing an audience, act as if you already had it. Of course, unless you are prepared, all the acting in the world will avail but little. But granted that you know what you are going to talk about, step out briskly and take a deep breath. In fact, breathe deeply for thirty seconds before you ever face your audience. The increased supply of oxygen will buoy you up and give you courage. The great tenor, Jean de Reszke, used to say that, when you had your breath so you "could sit on it," nervousness vanished.

When a youth of the Peuhl tribe in Central Africa attains manhood and wishes to take unto himself a wife, he is compelled to undergo the ceremony of flagellation. The women of the tribe foregather, singing and clapping their hands to the rhythm of tom-toms. The candidate strides forth stripped naked to the waist. Suddenly a man armed with a cruel whip, sets upon the lad, beating his bare skin, lashing him, flogging him like a fiend. Welts appear; often the skin is cut, blood flows; scars are made that last a lifetime. During this scourging, a venerable judge of the tribe crouches at the feet of the victim to see if he moves or exhibits the slightest evidence of pain. To pass the test successfully the tortured aspirant must not only endure the ordeal, but, as he endures it, he must sing a paean of praise.

In every age, in every clime, men have always admired courage; so, no matter how your heart may be pounding inside, stride forth bravely, stop, stand still like the scourged youth of Central Africa, and, like him, act as if you loved it.

Draw yourself up to your full height and look your audience straight in the eyes, and begin to talk as confidently as if every one of them owed you money. Imagine that they do. Imagine that they have assembled there to beg you for an extension of credit. The psychological effect on you will be beneficial.

Do not nervously button and unbutton your coat, and fumble with your hands. If you must make nervous movements, place your hands behind your back and twist your fingers there where no one can see the performance—or wiggle your toes.

As a general rule, it is bad for a speaker to hide behind furniture; but it may give you a little courage the first few times to stand behind a table or chair and to grip them tightly—or hold a coin firmly in the palm of your hand.

How did Roosevelt develop his characteristic courage and self-reliance? Was he endowed by nature with a venturesome and daring spirit? Not at all. "Having been a rather sickly and awkward boy," he confesses in his *Autobiography,* "I was, as a young man, at first both nervous and distrustful of my own prowess. I had to train myself painfully and laboriously not merely as regards my body but as regards my soul and spirit."

Fortunately, he has told us how he achieved the transformation: "When a boy," he writes, "I read a passage in one of Marryat's books which always impressed me. In this passage the captain of some small British man-of-war is explaining to the hero how to acquire the quality of fearlessness. He says that at the outset almost every man is frightened when he goes into action, but that the course to follow is for the man to keep such a grip on himself that he can act just as if he were not frightened. After this is kept up long enough, it changes from pretense to reality, and the man does in very fact become fearless by sheer dint of practising fearlessness when he does not feel it. (I am using my own language, not Marryat's.)

"This was the theory upon which I went. There were

all kinds of things of which I was afraid at first, ranging from grizzly bears to 'mean' horses and gun-fighters; but by acting as if I was not afraid I gradually ceased to be afraid. Most men can have the same experience if they choose."

You can have that very experience in this course, if you wish. "In war," said Marshal Foch, "the best defensive is an offensive." So take the offensive against your fears. Go out to meet them, battle them, conquer them by sheer boldness at every opportunity.

Have a message, and then think of yourself as Western Union boy instructed to deliver it. We pay slight attention to the boy. It is the telegram that we want. The message—that is the thing. Keep your mind on it. Keep your heart in it. Know it like the back of your hand. Believe it feelingly. Then talk as if you were determined to say it. Do that, and the chances are ten to one that you will soon be master of the occasion and master of yourself.

## FOURTH: PRACTISE! PRACTISE! PRACTISE!

The last point we have to make here is emphatically the most important. Even though you forget everything you have read so far, do remember this: the first way, the last way, the never-failing way to develop self-confidence in speaking is —to speak. Really the whole matter finally simmers down to but one essential; practise, practise, practise. That is the *sine quo non* of it all, "the without which not."

"Any beginner," warned Roosevelt, "is apt to have 'buck fever.' 'Buck fever' means a state of intense nervous excitement which may be entirely divorced from timidity. It may affect a man the first time he has to speak to a large audience just as it may affect him the first time he sees a buck or goes into battle. What such a man needs is not courage, but nerve control, cool headedness. *This he can get only by actual practice. He must, by custom and repeated exercise of self-mastery, get his nerves thoroughly under control. This is largely a matter of habit; in the sense of repeated effort and repeated exercise of will power. If the man has the right stuff in him, he will grow stronger and stronger with each exercise of it.*"

So, persevere. Don't remain away from any session of the course because the business duties of the week have rendered it impossible for you to prepare something. Prepared or unprepared, come. Let the instructor, the class, suggest a topic for you after you have come before them.

You want to get rid of your audience fear? Let us see what causes it.

"Fear is begotten of ignorance and uncertainty," says Professor Robinson in *The Mind in the Making*. To put it another way: it is the result of a lack of confidence.

And what causes that? It is the result of not knowing what you can really do. And not knowing what you can do is caused by a lack of experience. When you get a record of successful experience behind you, your fears will vanish; they will melt like night mists under the glare of a July sun.

One thing is certain: the accepted way to learn to swim is to plunge into the water. You have been reading this book long enough. Let us toss it aside now, and get busy with the real work in hand.

Choose your subject, preferably one on which you have some knowledge, and construct a three-minute talk. Practise the talk by yourself a number of times. Then give it, if possible, to the group for whom it is intended, or before your class, putting into the effort all your force and power.

# SUMMARY

1. A few thousand students of this course have written the author stating why they enrolled for this training and what they hoped to obtain from it. The prime reason that almost all of them gave was this: they wanted to conquer their nervousness, to be able to think on their feet, and to speak with self-confidence and ease before a group of any size.
2. The ability to do this is not difficult to acquire. It is not a gift bestowed by Providence on only a few rarely endowed individuals. It is like the ability to play golf: any man—every man—can develop his own latent capacity if he has sufficient desire to do so.
3. Many experienced speakers can think better and talk better when facing a group than they can in conversation with an individual. The presence of the larger number proves to be a stimulus, an inspiration. If you faithfully follow this course, the time may come when that will be your experience, too; and you will look forward with positive pleasure to making an address.
4. Do not imagine that your case is unusual. Many

men who afterwards became famous speakers were, at the outset of their careers, beset with self-consciousness and almost paralyzed with audience fright. This was the experience of Bryan, Jean Jaurès, Lloyd George, Charles Stewart Parnell, John Bright, Disraeli, Sheridan and a host of others.

5. No matter how often you speak, you may always experience this self-consciousness just before you begin; but, in a few seconds after you have gotten on your feet, it will vanish completely.

6. In order to get the most out of this course and to get it with rapidity and dispatch, do these four things:

    a. Start this course with a strong and persistent desire. Enumerate the benefits this training will bring you. Arouse your enthusiasm for it. Think what it can mean to you financially, socially and in terms of increased influence and leadership. Remember that upon the depth of your desire will depend the swiftness of your progress.

    b. Prepare. You can't feel confident unless you know what you are going to say.

    c. Act confident. "To feel brave," advises

Professor William James, "act as if we were brave, use all of our will to that end, and a courage fit will very likely replace the fit of fear." Roosevelt confessed that he conquered his fear of grizzly bears, mean horses and gunfighters by that method. You can conquer your fear of audiences by taking advantage of this psychological fact.

d. Practise. This is the most important point of all. Fear is the result of a lack of confidence; and a lack of confidence is the result of not knowing what you can do: and that is caused by a lack of experience. So get a record of successful experience behind you, and your fears will vanish.

# CHAPTER TWO

# SELF-CONFIDENCE THROUGH PREPARATION

"The best way for you to gain confidence is to prepare so well on something that you really want to say that there can be little chance to fail."

— 『Public Speaking Today』, Lock-wood-Thorpe.

"'To trust to the inspiration of the moment'—that is the fatal phrase upon which many promising careers have been wrecked. The surest road to inspiration is preparation. I have seen many men of courage and capacity fail for lack of industry. Mastery in speech can only be reached by mastery in one's subject."

—Lloyd George.

"Before a speaker faces his audience, he should write a letter to a friend and say: 'I am to make an address on a subject, and I want to make these points.' He should then enumerate the things he is going to speak about in their correct order. If he finds that he has nothing to say in his letter, he had better write to the committee that invited him and say that the probable death of his grandmother will possibly prevent his being present on the occasion."

—Dr. Edward Everett Hale.

**CHAPTER 2**

# SELF-CONFIDENCE
# THROUGH PREPARATION

It has been the author's professional duty as well as his pleasure to listen to and criticize approximately six thousand speeches a year each season since 1912. These were made, not by college students, but by mature business and professional men. If that experience has engraved on his mind any one thing more deeply than another, surely it is this: the urgent necessity of preparing a talk before one starts to make it and of having something clear and definite to say, something that has impressed one, something that won't stay unsaid. Aren't you unconsciously drawn to the speaker who, you feel, has a real message in his head and heart that he zealously desires to communicate to your head and heart? That is half the secret of speaking.

When a speaker is in that kind of mental and

emotional state he will discover a significant fact: namely, that his talk will almost make itself. Its yoke will be easy, its burden will be light. A well prepared speech is already nine-tenths delivered.

The primary reason why most men take this course, as was recorded in Chapter 1, is to acquire confidence and courage and self-reliance. And the one fatal mistake many make is neglecting to prepare their talks. How can they even hope to subdue the cohorts of fear, the cavalry of nervousness, when they go into the battle with wet powder and blank shells, or with no ammunition at all? Under the circumstances, small wonder that they are not exactly at home before an audience. "I believe," said Lincoln in the White House, "that I shall never be old enough to speak without embarrassment when I have nothing to say."

If you want confidence, why not do the things necessary to bring it about? "Perfect love," wrote the Apostle John, "casteth cast out fear." So does perfect preparation. Webster said he would as soon think of appearing before an audience half-clothed as half-prepared.

Why don't those enrolled in this course prepare their talks more carefully? Why? Some don't clearly understand what preparation is nor how to go about it wisely; others plead a lack of time. So we shall discuss these problems rather fully—and we trust lucidly and profitably—in this chapter.

## THE RIGHT WAY TO PREPARE

What is preparation? Reading a book? That is one kind, but not the best. Reading may help; but if one attempts to lift a lot of "canned" thoughts out of a book and to give them out immediately as his own, the whole performance will be lacking in something. The audience may not know precisely what is lacking, but they will not warm to the speaker.

To illustrate: some time ago, the writer conducted a course in public speaking for the senior officers of New York City banks. Naturally, the members of such a group, having many demands upon their time, frequently found it difficult to prepare adequately, or to do what they conceived of as preparing. All their lives they had been thinking their own individual thoughts, nurturing their own personal convictions, seeing things from their own distinctive angles, living their own original experiences. So, in that fashion, they had spent forty years storing up material for speeches. But it was hard for some of them to realize that. They could not see the forest for "the murmuring pines and the hemlocks."

This group met Friday evenings from five to seven. One Friday, a certain gentleman connected with an uptown bank—for our purposes here, we shall designate him as Mr. Jackson—found four-thirty had arrived, and, what was he to talk about? He walked out of his office, bought a copy of *Forbes' Magazine* at a news stand and, in the subway coming down to the Federal Reserve Bank where the class met, he read an article entitled, "You Have Only Ten Years To Succeed." He read it, not because he was interested in the article especially: but because he must speak on something, on anything, to fill his quota of time.

An hour later, he stood up and attempted to talk convincingly and interestingly on the contents of this article.

What was the result, the inevitable result?

He had not digested, had not assimilated what he was trying to say. "Trying to say"—that expresses it precisely. He was *trying*. There was no real message in him seeking for an outlet; and his whole manner and tone revealed it unmistakably. How could he expect the audience to be any more impressed than he himself was? He kept referring to the article saying the author said so and so. There was a surfeit of *Forbes' Magazine* in it; but regrettably little of Mr. Jackson.

So the writer addressed him somewhat in this fashion: "Mr. Jackson, we are not interested in this shadowy personality who wrote that article. He is not here. We can't see him. But we are interested in you and your ideas. Tell us what you think, personally, not what somebody else said. Put more of Mr. Jackson in this. Why not take this same subject for next week? Why not read this article again, and ask yourself whether you agree with the author or not? If you do, think out his suggestions and illustrate them with observations from your own experience. If you don't agree with him, say so and tell us why. Let this article be merely the starting point from which you launch your own speech."

Mr. Jackson accepted the suggestion, reread the article and concluded that he did not agree with the author at all. He did not sit down in the subway and try to prepare this next speech to order. He let it grow. It was a child of his own brain; and it developed and expanded and took on stature just as his physical children had done. And like his daughters, this other child grew day and night when he was least conscious of it. One thought was suggested to him while reading some item in the newspaper; another illustration swam into his mind unexpectedly when he was discussing the subject with a friend. The thing deepened and heightened, lengthened and thickened as he thought over it during the odd moments of the week.

The next time Mr. Jackson spoke on this subject, he had something that was his, ore that he dug out of his own mine, currency coined in his own mint. And he spoke all the better because he was disagreeing with the author of the article. There is no spur to rouse one like a little opposition.

What an incredible contrast between these two speeches by the same man, in the same fortnight, on the same subject. What a colossal difference the right kind of preparation makes!

Let us cite another illustration of how to do it and how not to do it. A gentleman, whom we shall call Mr. Flynn, was a student of this course in Washington, D. C. One afternoon he devoted his talk to eulogizing the capital city of the nation. He had hastily and superficially gleaned his facts from a booster booklet issued by the *Evening Star*. They sounded like it—dry, disconnected, undigested. He had not thought over his subject adequately. It had not elicited his enthusiasm. He did not feel what he was saying deeply enough to make it worth while expressing. The whole affair was flat and flavorless and unprofitable.

## A SPEECH THAT COULD NOT FAIL

A fortnight later, something happened that touched Mr. Flynn to the core: a thief stole his Cadillac out of a public garage. He rushed to the police and offered rewards, but it was all in vain. The police admitted that it was well nigh impossible for them to cope with the crime situation; yet, only a week previously, they had found time to walk about the street, chalk in hand, and fine Mr. Flynn because he had parked his car fifteen minutes overtime. These "chalk cops," who were so busy annoying respectable citizens that they could not catch criminals, aroused his ire. He was indignant. He had something now to say, not something that he had gotten out of a book issued by the *Evening Star*, but something that was leaping hot out of his own life and experience. Here was something that was part and parcel of the real man—something that had aroused his feelings and convictions. In his speech eulogizing the city of Washington, he had laboriously pulled out sentence by sentence; but now he had but to stand on his feet and open his mouth, and his condemnation of the police welled up and boiled forth like Vesuvius in action. A speech like that is almost foolproof. It can hardly fail. It was experience plus reflection.

## WHAT PREPARATION REALLY IS

Does the preparation of a speech mean the getting together of some faultless phrases written down or memorized? No. Does it mean the assembling of a few casual thoughts that really convey very little to you personally? Not at all. It means the assembling of *your* thoughts, *your* ideas, *your* convictions, *your* urges. And you have such thoughts, such urges. You have them every day of your waking life. They even swarm through your dreams. Your whole existence has been filled with feelings and experiences. These things are lying deep in your subconscious mind as thick as pebbles on the seashore. Preparation means thinking, brooding, recalling, selecting the ones that appeal to you most, polishing them, working them into a pattern, a mosaic of your own. That doesn't sound like such a difficult program, does it? It isn't. Just requires a little concentration and thinking to a purpose.

How did Dwight L. Moody prepare those addresses of his which made spiritual history during the last generation? "I have no secret," he replied in answer to that question.

"When I choose a subject, I write the name of it on the outside of a large envelope. I have many such envelopes. If, when I am reading, I meet a good thing on any subject I am to speak on, I slip it into the right envelope, and let it lie there. I always carry a notebook, and if I hear anything in a sermon that will throw light on that subject, I put it down, and slip it into the envelope. Perhaps I let it lie there for a year or more. When I want a new sermon, I take everything that has been accumulating. Between what I find there and the results of my own study, I have material enough. Then, all the time I am going over my sermons, taking out a little here, adding a little there. In that way they never get old."

## THE SAGE ADVICE OF DEAN BROWN OF YALE

A few years ago the Yale Divinity School celebrated the one hundredth anniversary of its founding. On that occasion, the Dean, Dr. Charles Reynold Brown, delivered a series of lectures on the Art of Preaching. These are now published in book form under that name by the Macmillan Company, New York. Dr.

Brown has been preparing addresses himself weekly for a third of a century, and also training others to prepare and deliver; so he was in a position to dispense some sage advice on the subject, advice that will hold good regardless of whether the speaker is a man of the cloth preparing a discourse on the Ninety-first Psalm, or a shoe manufacturer preparing a speech on Labor Unions. So I am taking the liberty of quoting Dr. Brown here:

"Brood over your text and your topic. Brood over them until they become mellow and responsive. You will hatch out of them a whole flock of promising ideas as you cause the tiny germs of life there contained to expand and developp……

It will be all the better if this process can go on for a long time and not be postponed until Saturday forenoon when you are actually making your final preparation for next Sunday. If a minister can hold a certain truth in his mind for a month, for six months perhaps, for a year it may be, before he preaches on it he will find new ideas perpetually sprouting out of it, until it shows an abundant growth. He may meditate on it as he walks the streets, or as he spends some hours on a train, when his eyes are too tired to read.

He may indeed brood upon it in the night-time. It is

better for the minister not to take his church or his sermon to bed with him habitually—a pulpit is a splendid thing to preach from, but it is not a good bed-fellow. Yet, for all that, I have sometimes gotten out of bed in the middle of the night to put down the thoughts which came to me, for fear I might forget them before morning······

When you are actually engaged in assembling the material for a particular sermon, write down everything that comes to you bearing upon that text and topic. Write down what you saw in the text when you first chose it. Write down all the associated ideas which now occur to you······

Put all these ideas of yours down in writing, just a few words, enough to fix the idea, and keep your mind reaching for more all the time as if it were never to see another book as long as it lived. This is the way to train the mind in productiveness. You will by this method keep your own mental processes fresh, original, creative······

Put down all of those ideas which you have brought to the birth yourself, unaided. They are more precious for your mental unfolding than rubies and diamonds and much fine gold. Put them down, preferably on scraps of paper, backs of old letters, fragments of envelopes, waste paper, anything which comes to your hand. This is much better every way than to use nice, long, clean sheets of foolscap.

It is not a mere matter of economy—you will find it easier to arrange and organize these loose bits when you come to set your material in order.

Keep on putting down all the ideas which come to your mind, thinking hard all the while. You need not hurry this process. It is one of the most important mental transactions in which you will be privileged to engage. It is this method which causes the mind to grow in real productive power……

You will find that the sermons you enjoy preaching the most and the ones which actually accomplish the most good in the lives of your people will be those sermons which you take most largely out of your own interiors. They are bone of your bone, flesh of your flesh, the children of your own mental labor, the output of your own creative energy. The sermons which are garbled and compiled will always have a kind of second-hand, warmed-over flavor about them. The sermons which live and move and enter into the temple, walking and leaping and praising God, the sermons which enter into the hearts of men causing them to mount up with wings like eagles and to walk in the way of duty and not faint—these real sermons are the ones which are actually born from the vital energies of the man who utters them."

# HOW LINCOLN PREPARED HIS SPEECHES

How did Lincoln prepare his speeches? Fortunately, we know the facts; and, as you read here of his method, you will observe that Dean Brown, in his lecture, commended several of the procedures that Lincoln had employed three-quarters of a century previously. One of Lincoln's most famous addresses was that in which he declared with prophetic vision: "'A house divided against itself cannot stand.' I believe this government cannot endure, permanently, half slave and half free." This speech was thought out as he went about his usual work, as he ate his meals, as he walked the street, as he sat in his barn milking his cow, as he made his daily trip to the butcher shop and grocery, an old gray shawl over his shoulders, his market basket over his arm, his little son at his side, chattering and questioning, growing peeved, and jerking at the long bony fingers in a vain effort to make his father talk to him. But Lincoln stalked on, absorbed in his own reflections, thinking of his speech, apparently unconscious of the boy's existence.

From time to time during this brooding and hatching process, he jotted down notes, fragments, sentences here and there on stray envelopes, scraps of paper, bits torn from paper sacks—anything that was near. These he stowed away in the top of his hat and carried them there until he was ready to sit down and arrange them in order, and to write and revise the whole thing, and to shape it up for delivery and publication.

In the joint debates of 1858, Senator Douglas delivered the same speech wherever he went; but Lincoln kept studying and contemplating and reflecting until he found it easier, he said, to make a new speech each day than to repeat an old one. The subject was forever widening and enlarging in his mind.

A short time before he moved into the White House, he took a copy of the Constitution and three speeches, and with only these for reference, he locked himself in a dingy, dusty back room over a store in Springfield; and there, away from all intrusion and interruption, he wrote out his inaugural address.

How did Lincoln prepare his Gettysburg address? Unfortunately, false reports have been circulated about it. The true story, however, is fascinating. Let us have it:

When the commission in charge of the Gettysburg cemetery decided to arrange for a formal dedication, they invited Edward Everett to deliver the speech. He had been a Boston minister, President of Harvard, governor of Massachusetts, United States senator, minister to England, secretary of state, and was generally considered to be America's most capable speaker. The date first set for the dedication ceremonies was October 23, 1863. Mr. Everett very wisely declared that it would be impossible for him to prepare adequately on such short notice. So the dedication was postponed until November 19, nearly a month, to give him time to prepare. The last three days of that period he spent in Gettysburg, going over the battlefield, familiarizing himself with all that had taken place there. That period of brooding and thinking was most excellent preparation. It made the battle real to him.

Invitations to be present were despatched to all the members of Congress, to the President and his cabinet. Most of these declined: the committee was surprised when Lincoln agreed to come. Should they ask him to speak? They had not intended to do so. Objections were raised. He would not have time to prepare. Besides, even if he did have time, had he the ability? True, he could handle himself well in a debate on slavery or in a Cooper Union address; but no one had ever heard him deliver a dedicatory address. This was a grave and solemn occasion. They ought not to take any chances. Should they ask him to speak? They wondered, wondered······But they would have wondered a thousand times more had they been able to look into the future and to see that this man, whose ability they were questioning, was to deliver on that occasion what is very generally accepted now as one of the most enduring addresses ever delivered by the lips of mortal man.

Finally, a fortnight before the event, they sent Lincoln a belated invitation to make "a few appropriate remarks." Yes, that is the way they worded it: "a few appropriate remarks." Think of writing that to the President of the United States!

Lincoln immediately set about preparing. He wrote to Edward Everett, secured a copy of the address that that classic scholar was to deliver; and, a day or two later, going to a photographer's gallery to pose for his photograph, Lincoln took Everett's manuscript with him and read it during the spare time that he had at the studio. He thought over his talk for days, thought over it while walking back and forth between the White House and the war office, thought over it while stretched out on a leather couch in the war office waiting for the late telegraphic reports. He wrote a rough draft of it on a piece of foolscap paper, and carried it about in the top of his tall silk hat. Ceaselessly he was brooding over it, ceaselessly it was taking shape. The Sunday before it was delivered he said to Noah Brooks: "It is not exactly written. It is not finished anyway. I have written it over two or three times, and I shall have to give it another lick before I am satisfied."

He arrived in Gettysburg the night before the dedication. The little town was filled to overflowing. Its usual population of thirteen hundred had been suddenly swelled to fifteen thousand. The sidewalks became clogged, impassable, men and women took to the dirt streets. Half a dozen bands were playing; crowds were singing "John Brown's Body." People foregathered before the home of Mr. Wills where Lincoln was being entertained. They serenaded him; they demanded a speech. Lincoln responded with a few words which conveyed with more clearness than tact, perhaps, that he was unwilling to speak until the morrow. The facts are that he was spending the latter part of that evening giving his speech "another lick." He even went to an adjoining house where Secretary Seward was staying and read the speech aloud to him for his criticism. After breakfast the next morning, he continued "to give it another lick," working on it until a rap came at the door informing him that it was time for him to take his place in the procession. "Colonel Carr, who rode just behind the President, stated that when the procession started, the President sat erect on his horse, and looked the part of the commander-in-chief of the army; but, as the procession moved on, his body leaned forward, his arms hung limp, and his head was bowed. He seemed absorbed in thought."

We can only guess that even then he was going over his little speech of ten immortal sentences, giving it "another lick."

Some of Lincoln's speeches, in which he had only a superficial interest, were unquestioned failures; but he was possessed of extraordinary power when he spoke of slavery and the union. Why? Because he thought ceaselessly on these problems and felt deeply. A companion who shared a room with him one night in an Illinois tavern awoke next morning at daylight to find Lincoln sitting up in bed, staring at the wall, and his first words were: "This government cannot endure permanently, half slave and half free."

How did Christ prepare His addresses? He withdrew from the crowd. He thought. He brooded. He pondered. He went out alone into the wilderness and meditated and fasted for forty days and forty nights. "From that time on," records Saint Matthew, "Jesus began to preach." Shortly after that, He delivered one of the world's most celebrated speeches: the Sermon on the Mount.

"That is all very interesting," you may protest; "but I have no desire to become an immortal orator. I merely want to make a few simple talks in business occasionally."

True, and we realize your wants fully. This course is for the specific purpose of helping you and other business men like you to do just that. But, unpretending as the talks of yours may prove to be, you can profit by and utilize in some measure the methods of the famous speakers of the past.

## HOW TO PREPARE YOUR TALK

What topics ought you to speak on during the sessions of this course? Anything that interests you. If possible, choose your own topics; you will be more fortunate still if your topic chooses you. However, you will often have topics suggested for you by your instructor.

Don't make the almost universal mistake of trying to

cover too much ground in a brief talk. Just take one or two angles of a subject and attempt to cover them adequately. You will be fortunate if you can do that in the short speeches that are necessitated by the time schedule of this course.

Determine your subject a week in advance, so that you will have time to think it over in odd moments. Think over it for seven days; dream over it for seven nights. Think of it the last thing when you retire. Think of it the next morning while you are shaving, while you are bathing, while you are riding down town, while you are waiting for elevators, for lunch, for appointments. Discuss it with your friends. Make it a topic of conversation.

Ask yourself all possible questions concerning it. If, for example, you are to speak on divorce, ask yourself what causes divorce, what are the effects economically, socially. How can the evil be remedied? Should we have uniform divorce laws? Why? Or should we have any divorce laws? Should divorce be made impossible? More difficult? Easier?

Suppose you were going to talk on why you enrolled for this course. You ought then to ask yourself such questions as these: What are my troubles? What do I hope to get out of this instruction? Have I ever made a public talk? If so, when? Where? What happened? Why do I think this training is valuable for a business man? Do I know men who are forging ahead commercially largely because of their self-confidence, their presence, their ability to talk convincingly? Do I know others who will probably never achieve a gratifying measure of success because they lack these positive assets? Be specific. Tell the stories of these men without mentioning their names.

If you stand up and think clearly and keep going for two or three minutes, that is all that will be expected of you during your first few talks. A topic, such as why you enrolled for this course, is very easy; that is obvious. If you will spend a little time selecting and arranging your material on that topic, you will be almost sure to remember it, for you will be speaking of your own observations, your own desires, your own experiences.

On the other hand, let us suppose that you have decided to speak on your business or profession. How shall you set about preparing such a talk? You already have a wealth of material on that subject. Your problem, then, will be to select and arrange it. Do not attempt to tell us all about it in three minutes. It can't be done. The attempt will be too sketchy, too fragmentary. Take one and only one phase of your topic: expand and enlarge that. For example, why not tell us how you came to be in your particular business or profession? Was it a result of accident or choice? Relate your early struggles, your defeats, your hopes, your triumphs. Give us a human interest narrative, a real life picture based on first hand experiences. The truthful, inside story of almost any man's life—if told modestly and without offending egotism—is most entertaining. It is almost sure-fire speech material.

Or take another angle of your business: what are its troubles? What advice would you give to a young man entering it?

Or tell us about the people with whom you come in contact—the honest and dishonest ones. Tell us of your problems with labor, your problems with your customers. What has your business taught you about the most interesting topic in the world: human nature? If you speak about the technical side of your business, about things, your talk may very easily prove uninteresting to others. But people, personalities—one can hardly go wrong with that kind of material.

Above all else, don't make your talk an abstract preachment. That will bore us. Make your talk a regular layer cake of illustrations and general statements. Think of concrete cases you have observed, and of the fundamental truths which you believe those specific instances illustrate. You will also discover that these concrete cases are far easier to remember than abstractions; are far easier to talk about. They will also aid and brighten your delivery.

Here is the way a very interesting writer does it. This is an excerpt from an article by B. A. Forbes on the necessity of executives delegating responsibilities to their associates. Note the illustrations—the gossip about people.

"Many of our present-day gigantic enterprises were at one time one-man affairs. But most of them have outgrown this status. The reason is that, while every great organization is 'the lengthened shadow of one man,' business and industry are now conducted on such a colossal scale that of necessity even the ablest giant must gather about him brainy associates to help in handling all the reins.

Woolworth once told me that his was essentially a one-man business for years. Then he ruined his health, and it was while he lay week after week in the hospital that he awakened to the fact that if his business was to expand as he hoped, he would have to share the managerial responsibilities.

Bethlehem Steel for a number of years was distinctly of the one-man type. Charles M. Schwab was the whole works. By and by Eugene G. Grace grew in stature and developed into an abler steel man than Schwab, according to the repeated declarations of the latter. Today Bethlehem Steel is no longer simply Schwab.

Eastman Kodak in its earlier stages consisted mainly of George Eastman, but he was wise enough to create an efficient organization long ago. All the greatest Chicago packing houses underwent a similar experience during the time of their founders. Standard Oil, contrary to the popular notion, never was a one man organization after it grew to large dimensions.

J. P. Morgan, although a towering giant, was an ardent believer in choosing the most capable partners and sharing the burdens with them.

There are still ambitious business leaders who would like to run their business on the one-man principle, but, willy-nilly, they are forced by the very magnitude of modern operations to delegate responsibilities to others."

Some men, in speaking of their businesses, commit the unforgivable error of talking only of the features that interest them. Shouldn't the speaker try to ascertain what will entertain not himself but his hearers? Shouldn't he try to appeal to their selfish interests? If, for example, he sells fire insurance, shouldn't he tell them how to prevent fires on their own property? If he is a banker, shouldn't he give them advice on finance or investments?

While preparing, study your audience. Think of their wants, their wishes. That is sometimes half the battle.

In preparing some topics, it is very advisable—if time permits—to do some reading, to discover what others have thought, what others have said on the same subject. But don't read until you have first thought yourself dry. That is important—very. Then go to the public library and lay your needs before the librarian. Tell her you are preparing a speech on such and such a topic. Ask her frankly for help. If you are not in the habit of doing research work, you will probably be surprised at the aids she can put at your disposal; perhaps a special volume on your very topic, outlines and briefs for debate, giving the principal arguments on both sides of the public questions of the day; the Reader's Guide to Periodical Literature listing the magazine articles that have appeared on various topics since the beginning of the century; the Century Book of Facts, the World Almanac, the Encyclopedias, and dozens of reference books. They are tools in your workshop. Use them.

## THE SECRET OF RESERVE POWER

LutherBurbank said, shortly before his death: "I have often produced a million plant specimens to find but one or two superlatively good ones, and have then destroyed all the inferior specimens." A speech ought to be prepared somewhat in that lavish and discriminating spirit. Assemble a hundred thoughts, and discard ninety.

Collect more material, more information, than there is any possibility of employing. Get it for the additional confidence it will give you, or the sureness of touch. Get it for the effect it will have on your mind and heart and whole manner of speaking. This is a basic, important factor of preparation; yet it is constantly ignored by speakers, both in public and private.

"I have drilled hundreds of salesmen, canvassers, and demonstrators," says Arthur Dunn, "and the principal weakness which I have discovered in most of them has been their failure to realize the importance of knowing everything possible about their products and getting such knowledge before they start to sell.

Many salesmen have come to my office and after getting a description of the article and a line of sales talk have been eager to get right out and try to sell. Many of these salesmen have not lasted a week and a large number have not lasted forty-eight hours. In educating and drilling canvassers and salesmen in the sale of a food specialy, I have endeavored to make food experts of them. I have compelled them to study food charts issued by the U. S. Department of Agriculture, which show in food the amount of water, the amount of protein, the amount of carbohydrates, the amount of fat, and ash. I have had them study the elements which make up the products which they are to sell. I have had them go to school for several days and then pass examinations. I have had them sell the product to other salesmen. I have offered prizes for the best sales talks.

I have often found salesmen who get impatient at the preliminary time required for the study of their articles. They have said, 'I will never have time to tell all of this to a retail grocer. He is too busy. If I talk protein and carbohydrates, he won't listen and, if he does listen, he won't know what I am talking about.' My reply has been, 'You don't get all of this knowledge for the benefit of your customer, but for the benefit of yourself. If you know your product from A to Z you will have a feeling about it that is difficult to describe. You will be so positively charged, so fortified, so strengthened in your own mental attitude that you will be both irresistible and unconquerable.'"

Miss Ida M. Tarbell, the well known historian of the Standard Oil Company, told the writer that years ago, when she was in Paris, Mr. S. S. McClure, the founder of Mcclure's Magazine, cabled her to write a short article about the Atlantic Cable. She went to London, interviewed the European manager of the principal cable, and obtained sufficient data for her assignment. But she did not stop there. She wanted a reserve supply of facts; so she studied all manner of cables on display in the British Museum; she read books on the history of the cable and even went to manufacturing concerns on the edge of London and saw cables in the process of construction.

Why did she collect ten times as much information as she could possibly use? She did it because she felt it would give her reserve power; because she realized that the things she knew and did not express would lend force and color to the little she did express.

Edwin James Cattell has spoken to approximately

thirty million people; yet he confided to me recently that if he did not, on the way home, kick himself for the good things he had left out of his talk, he felt that the performance must have been a failure. Why? Because he knew from long experience that the talks of distinct merit are those in which there abounds a reserve of material, a plethora, a profusion of it—far more than the speaker has time to use.

"What!" you object. "Does this author imagine that I can find time for all this? I would like him to know that I have a business to conduct and a wife and two children and a couple of Airedale dogs to support······ I can't be running to museums and looking at cables and reading books and sitting up in bed at daylight mumbling my speeches."

My dear sir, we know all about your case, and sympathetic allowance has been made for it. The assigned topics will be questions on which you have already done considerable thinking. Sometimes you will not be asked to plan any kind of a speech in advance; but you will be given an easy topic for impromptu speaking after you face your audience. This will afford you most useful practise in thinking on your feet—the sort of thing that you may be forced to do in business discussions.

Some of the men who join this course are only slightly interested in learning to prepare talks in advance. They want to be able to think on their feet and to join in discussions that come up at various business meetings. Such students sometimes prefer to come to the class, listen, and then take their cue from some of the preceding speakers. A limited amount of this may be advisable; but don't overdo it. Follow the suggestions given in this chapter. They will give you the ease and freedom you are seeking and also the ability to prepare talks effectively.

If you procrastinate until you have leisure to prepare and plan your talk, the leisure will probably never be found. However, it is easy to do the habitual, the accustomed thing, isn't it? So why not set aside one specific evening a week, from eight to ten o'clock, to be devoted to nothing but this task? That is the sure way, the systematic way. Why not try it?

## SUMMARY

1. When a speaker has a real message in his head and heart—an inner urge to spent, he is almost sure to do himself credit. A well-prepared speech

is already nine-tenths delivered.

2. What is preparation? The setting down of some mechanical sentences on paper? The memorizing of phrases? Not at all. Real preparation consists in digging something out of yourself, in assembling and arranging *your own* thoughts, in cherishing and nurturing *your own* convictions. (Illustrations: Mr. Jackson of New York failed when he attempted merely to reiterate another man's thoughts he had culled from an article in *Forbes' Magazine*. He succeeded when he used that article merely as a starting point for his own speech — when he thought out *his own* ideas, developed *his own* illustrations.

3. Do not sit down and try to manufacture a speech in thirty minutes. A speech can't be cooked to order like a steak. A speech must *grow*. Select your topic early in the week, think over it during odd moments, brood over it, sleep over it, dream over it. Discuss it with friends. Make it a topic of conversation. Ask yourself all possible questions concerning it. Put down on pieces of paper all thoughts and illustrations that come to you and keep reaching out for more. Ideas, suggestions, illustrations will come drifting to you at sundry

times—when you are bathing, when you are driving down town, when you are waiting for dinner to be served. That was Lincoln's method. It has been the method of almost all successful speakers.

4. After you have done a bit of independent thinking, go to the library and do some reading on your topic—if time permits. Tell the librarian your needs. She can render you great assistance.

5. Collect far more material than you intend to use. Imitate Luther Burbank. He often produced a million plant specimens to find one or two superlatively good ones. Assemble a hundred thoughts; discard ninety.

6. The way to develop reserve power is to know far more than you can use, to have a full reservoir of information. In preparing a speech, use the methods Arthur Dunn employed in training his salesmen to sell a breakfast food specialty, the methods that Ida Tarbell employed in preparing her article on the Atlantic cable.

# CHAPTER THREE

# HOW FAMOUS SPEAKERS PREPARED THEIR ADDRESSES

"There's a vast difference between having a carload of miscellaneous facts sloshing around loose in your head and getting all mixed up in transit, and carrying the same assortment properly boxed and crated for convenient handling and immediate delivery."
—Lorimer:Letters from a Self-Made Merchant to His Son at College.

"The power to grasp the essential features of problems is the great differentiation between the educated and the noneducated man. Undoubtedly the greatest advantage to be gained from a college education is the acquisition of a disciplined mind."
—John Grier Hibben, President of Princeton University.

"What is it that first strikes us, and strikes us at once, in a man of education and which, among educated men, so instantly distinguishes the man of superior mind?⋯⋯ The true cause of the impression made upon us is that his mind is methodical."
—S. T. Coleridge.

# CHAPTER 3

## HOW FAMOUS SPEAKERS PREPARED THEIR ADDRESSES

I was present once at a luncheon of the New York Rotary Club when the principal speaker was a prominent government official. The high position that he occupied gave him prestige, and we were looking forward with pleasure to hearing him. He had promised to tell us about the activities of his own department; and it was one in which almost every New York business man was interested.

He knew his subject thoroughly, knew far more about it than he could possibly use; but he had not planned his speech. He had not selected his material. He had not arranged it in orderly fashion. Nevertheless, with a courage born of inexperience, he plunged heedlessly, blindly, into his speech. He did not know where he was going, but he was on his way.

His mind was, in short, a mere hodgepodge, and so

was the mental feast he served us. He brought on the ice cream first, and then placed the soup before us. Fish and nuts came next. And, on top of that, there was something that seemed to be a mixture of soup and ice cream and good red herring. I have never, anywhere or at any time, seen a speaker more utterly confused.

He had been trying to talk impromptu; but, in desperation now, he drew a bundle of notes out of his pocket, confessing that his secretary had compiled them for him—and no one questioned the veracity of his assertion. The notes themselves evidently had no more order than a flat car full of scrap iron. He fumbled through them nervously, glancing from one page to another, trying to orient himself, trying to find a way out of the wilderness and he attempted to talk as he did so. It was impossible. He apologized and, calling for water, took a drink with a trembling hand, uttered a few more scattering sentences, repeated himself, dug into his notes again······Minute by minute he grew more helpless, more lost, more bewildered, more embarrassed. Nervous perspiration stood out on his forehead, and his handkerchief shook as he wiped it away. We in the audience sat watching the fiasco, our sympathies stirred, our feelings harrowed. We suffered positive and vicarious embarrassment. But with more doggedness than discretion, the speaker continued, floundering, studying his notes, apologizing and drinking. Every one except him felt that the spectacle was rapidly approaching total disaster, and it was a relief to us all when he sat down and ceased his death struggles. It was one of the most uncomfortable audiences I have ever been in; and he was the most ashamed and humiliated speaker I have ever seen. He had made his talk as Rousseau said a love letter should be written: he had begun without knowing what he was going to say, and he had finished without knowing what he had uttered.

The moral of the tale is just this: "When a man's knowledge is not in order," said Herbert Spencer, "the more of it he has, the greater will be his confusion of thought."

No sane man would start to build a house without some sort of plan; but why will he begin to deliver a speech without the vaguest kind of outline or program?

A speech is a voyage with a purpose, and it must be charted. The man who starts nowhere, generally gets there.

I wish that I could paint this saying of Napoleon's in

flaming letters of red a foot high over every doorway on the globe where students of public speaking foregather: "The art of war is a science in which nothing succeeds which has not been calculated and thought out."

That is just as true of speaking as of shooting. But do speakers realize it — or, if they do — do they always act on it? They do not. Most emphatically they do not. Many a talk has just a trifle more plan and arrangement than a bowl of Irish stew.

What is the best and most effective arrangement for a given set of ideas? No one can say until he has studied them. It is always a new problem, an eternal question that every speaker must ask and answer himself again and again. No infallible rules can be given; but we can, at any rate, illustrate briefly here, with a concrete case, just what we mean by orderly arrangements.

## HOW A PRIZE-WINNING SPEECH WAS CONSTRUCTED

Here is a speech that was delivered by a student of this course before the Thirteenth Annual Convention of the National Association of Real Estate Boards. It won first prize in competition with twenty-seven other speeches on various cities. This speech is well constructed, full of facts stated clearly, vividly, interestingly. It has spirit. It marches. It will merit reading and study.

Mr. Chairman and Friends:

Back 144 years ago, this great nation, the United States of America, was born in my City of Philadelphia, and so it is quite natural that a city having such an historical record should have that strong American spirit that has not only made it the greatest industrial center in this country, but also one of the largest and most beautiful cities in the whole world.

Philadelphia has a population close to two millions of people, and our city has an area that is equal to the combined size of Milwaukee and Boston, Paris and Berlin, and out of our 130 square miles of territory we have given up nearly 8,000 acres of our best land for beautiful parks, squares and boulevards, so that our people would have the proper places for recreation and pleasure, and the right kind of environment that belongs to every decent American.

Philadelphia, friends, is not only a large, clean and beautiful city, but it is also known everywhere as the great workshop of the world, and the reason it is called the workshop of the world is because we have a vast army of over 400,000 people employed in 9,200 industrial establishments that turn out one hundred thousand dollars' worth of useful commodities every ten minutes of the working day, and, according to a well-known statistician, there is no city in this country that equals Philadelphia in the production of woolen goods, leather goods, knit goods, textiles, felt hats, hardware, tools, storage batteries, steel ships and a great many other things. We build a railroad locomotive every two hours day and night, and more than one-half the people in this great country ride in street cars made in the City of Philadelphia. We manufacture a thousand cigars every minute, and last year, in our 115 hosiery mills, we made two pairs of stockings for every man, woman and child in this country. We make more carpets and rugs than all of Great Britain and Ireland combined, and, in fact, our total commercial and industrial business is so stupendous that our bank clearings last year, amounting to thirty-seven billions of dollars, would have paid for every Liberty Bond in the entire country.

But, friends, while we are very proud of our wonderful industrial progress, and while we are also very proud of being one of the largest medical, art and educational centers in this country, yet, we feel a still greater pride in the fact that we have more individual homes in the City of

Philadelphia than there are in any other city in the whole world. In Philadelphia we have 397,000 separate homes, and if these homes were placed on twenty-five-foot lots, side by side, in one single row, that row would reach all the way from Philadelphia clear through to this Convention Hall, at Kansas City, and then on to Denver, a distance of 1,881 miles.

But, what I want to call your special attention to, is the significance of the fact, that tens of thousands of these homes are owned and occupied by the working people of our city, and when a man owns the ground upon which he stands and the roof over his head, there is no I. W. W. argument ever presented that would infect that man with those imported diseases, known as Socialism and Bolshevism.

Philadelphia is not a fertile soil for European anarchy, because our homes, our educational institutions and our gigantic industry have been produced by that true American spirit that was born in our city, and is a heritage from our forefathers. Philadelphia is the mother city of this great country, and the very fountain head of American liberty. It is the city where the first American flag was made; it is the city where the first Congress of the United States met; it is the city where the Declaration of Independence was signed; it is the city where that best loved relic in America, the Liberty Bell, has inspired tens of thousands of our men, women and children, so that we believe, we have a sacred mission, which is not to worship the golden calf, but to spread the American spirit, and to keep the fires of freedom burning, so that with God's permission, the Government of Washington, Lincoln and Theodore Roosevelt may be an inspiration to all humanity.

Let us analyze that speech. Let us see how it is constructed, how it gets its effects. In the first place, it has a beginning and an ending. That is a rare virtue, my dear reader, more rare than you may be inclined to think. It starts somewhere. It goes there straight as wild geese on the wing. It doesn't dawdle. It loses no time.

It has freshness, individuality. The speaker opens by saying something about his city that the other speakers could not possibly say about theirs: he points out that his city is the birthplace of the entire nation.

He states that it is one of the largest and most beautiful cities in the world. But that claim is general, trite; standing by itself, it would not impress anyone very much. The speaker knew that; so he helped his audience visualize the magnitude of Philadelphia by stating it "has an area equal to the combined size of

Milwaukee, Boston, Paris and Berlin." That is definite, concrete. It is interesting. It is surprising. It makes a mark. It drives home the idea better than a whole page of statistics would have done.

Next he declares that Philadelphia is "known everywhere as the great workshop of the world." Sounds exaggerated, doesn't it? Like propaganda. Had he proceeded immediately to the next point no one would have been convinced. But he doesn't. He pauses to enumerate the products in which Philadelphia leads the world: "woolen goods, leather goods, knit goods, textiles, felt hats, hardware, tools, storage batteries, steel ships."

Doesn't sound so much like propaganda now, does it?

Philadelphia "builds a railroad locomotive every two hours day and night, and more than one-half the people in this great country ride in street cars made in the city of Philadelphia."

"Well, I never knew that," we muse, "Perhaps I rode down town yesterday in one of those street cars. I'll look tomorrow and see where my town buys its cars."

"A thousand cigars every minute ······ two pairs of stockings for every man, woman and child in this country."

We are still more impressed······ 'Maybe my

favorite cigar is made in Philadelphia ...... and these socks I have on......'

What does the speaker do next? Jump back to the subject of the size of Philadelphia that he covered first and give us some fact that he forgot then? No, not at all. He sticks to a point until he finishes it, has done with it, and need never return to it again. For that we are duly grateful, Mr. Speaker. For what is more confusing and muddling than to have a speaker darting from one thing to another and back again as erratic as a bat in the twilight? Yet many a speaker does just that. Instead of covering his points in order l, 2, 3, 4, 5, he covers them as a football captain calls out signals -27, 34, 19, 2. No, he is worse than that. He covers them like this-27, 34, 27, 19, 2, 34, 19.

But this speaker, however, steams straight ahead on schedule time, never idling, never turning back, swerving neither to the right nor left; like one of those locomotives he has been talking about.

But, he makes now the weakest point of his entire speech: Philadelphia, he declares, is "one of the largest medical, art and educational centers in this country." He merely announces that; then speeds on to something else—only twelve words to animate that fact, to make it vivid, to engrave it on the memory. Only twelve words lost, submerged, in a sentence containing a total of sixty-five. It doesn't work. Of course not. The human mind does not operate like a string of steel traps. He devotes so little time to this point, is so general, so vague, seems so unimpressed himself that the effect on the hearer is almost nil. What should he have done? He realized that he could establish this point with the selfsame technique that he just employed to establish the fact that Philadelphia is the workshop of the world. He knew that. He also knew that he would have a stop watch held on him during the contest, that he would have five minutes, not a second more; so he had to slur over this point or slight others.

There are "more individual homes in the city of Philadelphia than there are in any other city in the world." How does he make this phase of his topic impressive and convincing? First, he gives the number: 397,000. Second, he visualizes the number: "If these homes were placed on twenty-five foot lots, side by side, in one single row, that row would reach all the way from Philadelphia clear through this Convention Hall at Kansas City, and then on to Denver, a distance of 1,881 miles."

His audience probably forgot the number he gave before he had finished the sentence. But forget that picture? That would have been well nigh impossible.

So much for cold material facts. But they are not the stuff out of which eloquence is fashioned. This speaker aspired to build up to a climax, to touch the heart, to stir the feelings. So now on the home stretch, he deals with emotional material. He tells what the ownership of those homes means to the spirit of the city. He denounced "those imported diseases, known as Socialism and Bolshevism……European anarchy." He eulogizes Philadelphia as "the very fountain head of American liberty." Liberty! A magic word, a word full of feeling, a sentiment for which millions have laid down their lives. That phrase in itself is good, but it is a thousand times better when he backs it up with concrete references to historic events and documents, dear, sacred, to the hearts of his hearers. …… "It is the city where the first American Flag was made; it is the city where the first Congress of the United States met; it is the city where the Declaration of Independence was signed …… Liberty Bell …… a sacred mission ……, to spread the American spirit …… to keep the fires of freedom burning, so that with God's permission, the Government of Washington, Lincoln and Theodore Roosevelt may be an inspiration to all humanity." That is a real climax!

So much for the composition of this talk. But admirable as it is from the standpoint of construction, this speech could have come to grief, could easily have been brought to naught, had it been expressed in a calm manner devoid of all spirit and vitality. But the speaker delivered it as he composed it; with a feeling and enthusiasm born of the deepest sincerity. Small wonder that it won first prize, that it was awarded the Chicago cup.

## THE WAY DOCTOR CONWELL PLANNED HIS SPEECHES

There are not, as I have already said, any infallible rules that will solve the question of the best arrangement. There are no designs or schemes or charts that will fit all or even a majority of speeches; yet here are a few speech plans that will prove usable in some instances. The late Dr. Russell H. Conwell, the author of the famous "Acres of Diamonds"—see Appendix—once informed me that he had built many of his innumerable speeches on this outline:

1. State your facts.
2. Argue from them.

3. Appeal for action.

Many students of this course have found this plan very helpful and stimulating.

1. Show something that is wrong.
2. Show how to remedy it.
3. Ask for cooperation.

Or, to put it in another way:

1. Here is a situation that ought to be remedied.
2. We ought to do so and so about the matter.
3. You ought to help for these reasons.

Chapter XV of this course, entitled *How To Get Action*, outlines still another speech plan. Briefly it is this:
1. Secure interested attention.
2. Win confidence.
3. State your facts; educate people regarding the merits of your proposition.
4. Appeal to the motives that make men act.

If interested, turn now to Chapter XV and study this

plan in detail.

## SENATOR BEVERIDGE'S METHOD OF BUILDING A TALK

Senator Albert J. Beveridge wrote a very short and very practical book entitled "The Art of Public Speaking." "The speaker must be master of his subject," says this noted political campaigner. "That means that all the facts must be collected, arranged, studied, digested—not only data on one side, but material on the other side and on every side—all of it. And be sure that they are facts, not mere assumptions or unproved assertions. Take nothing for granted.

"Therefore check up and reverify every item. This means painstaking research, to be sure, but what of it?—are you not proposing to inform, instruct, and advise your fellow citizens? Are you not setting yourself up as an authority?

Having assembled and marshalled the facts of any problem, *think out for yourself the solution those facts compel*. Thus your speech will have originality and personal force—it will be vital and compelling. There will be *you* in it. Then write out your ideas as clearly and logically as you can."

In other words, present the facts on both sides, and then present the conclusion that those facts make clear and definite.

## WOODROW WILSON FITS THE BONES TOGETHER

"I begin," said Woodrow Wilson when asked to explain his methods, "with a list of the topics I want to cover, *arranging them in my mind in their natural relations*—that is, I fit the bones of the thing together; then I write it out in shorthand. I have always been accustomed to writing in shorthand, finding it a great saver of time. This done, I copy it on my own typewriter, changing phrases, correcting sentences, and adding material as I go along."

Roosevelt prepared his talks in the characteristic Rooseveltian manner: he dug up all the facts, reviewed them, appraised them, determined their findings, arrived at his conclusions, arrived with a feeling of certainty that was unshakable.

Then, with a pad of notes before him, he started dictating and he dictated his speech very rapidly so that it would have rush and spontaneity and the spirit of life. Then he went over this typewritten copy, revised it, inserted, deleted, filled it with pencil marks, and then dictated it all over again. "I never won anything," said he, "without hard labor and the exercise of my best judgment and careful planning and working long in advance."

Often he called in critics to listen to him as he dictated or read his speech to them. He refused to debate with them the wisdom of what he had said. His mind was already made up on that point, and made up irrevocably. He wanted to be told, not what to say, but how to say it. Again and again he went over his typewritten copies, cutting, correcting, improving. That was the speech that the newspapers printed. Of course, he did not memorize it. He spoke extemporaneously. So the talk he actually delivered often differed somewhat from the published and polished one. But the task of dictating and revising was excellent preparation. It made him familiar with his material, with the order of his points. It gave him a smoothness and sureness and polish that he could hardly have obtained in any other fashion.

Sir Oliver Lodge told me that dictating his talks—dictating them rapidly and with substance, dictating them just as if he were actually talking to an audience—he had discovered to be an excellent means of preparation and practise.

Many of the students of this course have found it illuminating to dictate their talks to the dictaphone, and then to listen to themselves. Illuminating? Yes, and sometimes disillusioning and chastening also, I fear. It is a most wholesome exercise. I recommend it.

This practise of actually writing out what you are going to say, will force you to think. It will clarify your ideas. It will hook them in your memory. It will reduce your mental wandering to a minimum. It will improve your diction.

## BENJAMIN FRANKLIN'S CLASSIC TALE

Benjamin Franklin tells in his *Autobiography* how he improved his diction, how he developed readiness in using words and how he taught himself method in arranging his thoughts. This story of his life is a literary classic, and, unlike most classics, it is easy to read and thoroughly enjoyable. It is almost a model of plain, straightforward English. Every business man can peruse it with pleasure and profit. I think you will like the selection I refer to; here it is:

"About this time I met with an odd volume of the

Spectator. It was the third. I had never before seen any of them. I bought it, read it over and over and was much delighted with it, I thought the writing excellent, and wished, if possible, to imitate it. With this view I took some of the papers, and, making short hints of the sentiment in each sentence laid them by a few days, and then, without looking at the book, try'd to compleat the papers again, by expressing each hinted sentiment at length, and as fully as it had been expressed before, in any suitable words that should come to hand. Then I compared my Spectator with the original, discovered some of my faults and corrected them. But I found a stock of words, and a readiness in recollecting and using them, which I thought I should have acquired before that time if I had gone on making verses; since the continual occasion for words of the same import, but of different length, to suit the measure, or of different sounds for the rhyme, would have laid me under a constant necessity of searching for variety, and also have tended to fix that variety in my mind, and make me master of it. Therefore I took some of the tales and turned them into verse; and, after a time, when I had pretty well forgotten the prose, turned them back again. I also sometimes jumbled my collections of hints into confusion, and after some weeks endeavored to reduce them into the best order, before I began to form the full sentences and compleat the paper. *This was to teach me method in the arrangement of thoughts.* By comparing my work afterwards with the original, I discovered many faults and amended them; but I sometimes had the pleasure of fancying that, in certain particulars of small import, I had been lucky enough to improve the method of the language, and this encouraged me to think I might possibly in time come to be a tolerable English writer, of which I was extremely ambitious."

## PLAY SOLITAIRE WITH YOUR NOTES

You were advised in the last lesson to make notes. Having gotten your various ideas and illustrations down on scraps of paper, play solitaire with them—toss them into series of related piles. These main piles ought to represent, approximately, the main points of your talk. Subdivide them into smaller lots. Throw out the chaff until there is nothing but number one wheat left—and even some of the wheat will probably have to be put aside and not used. No man, if he works right, is ever able to use but a percentage of the material he gathers.

One ought never to cease this process of revision until the speech has been made—even then he is very likely to think of points and improvements and refinements that ought to have been made.

A good speaker usually finds when he finishes that there have been four versions of his speech: the one that he prepared, the one that he delivered, the one that the newspapers said that he delivered, and the one that he wishes, on his way home, that he had delivered.

## "SHALL I USE NOTES WHILE SPEAKING?"

Although he was an excellent impromptu speaker, Lincoln, after he reached the White House, never made any address, not even an informal talk to his cabinet, until he had carefully put it all down in writing beforehand. Of course, he was obliged to read his inaugural addresses. The exact phraseology of historical state papers of that character is too important to be left to extemporizing. But, back in Illinois, Lincoln never used even notes in his speaking. "They always tend to tire and confuse the listener," he said.

And who of us, pray, would contradict him? Don't notes destroy about fifty per cent of your interest in a talk? Don't they prevent, or at least render difficult, a very precious contact and intimacy that ought to exist between the speaker and the audience? Don't they create an air of artificiality? Don't they restrain an audience from feeling that the speaker has the confidence and reserve power that he ought to have?

Make notes, I repeat, during the preparation — elaborate ones, profuse ones. You may wish to refer to them when you are practising your talk alone. You may possibly feel more comfortable if you have them stored away in your pocket when you are facing an audience; but, like the hammer and saw and axe in a Pullman coach, they should be emergency tools, only for use in the case of a smash-up, a total wreck, and threatening death and disaster.

If you must use notes, make them extremely brief and write them in large letters on an ample sheet of paper. Then arrive early at the place where you are to speak and hide your notes behind some books on a table. Glance at them when you must, but endeavor to screen your weakness from the audience. John Bright used to secrete his notes in his big hat tying on the table before him.

However in spite of all that has been said there may be times when it is the part of wisdom to use notes. For example, some men during their first few talks, are so nervous and self-conscious that they are utterly unable to remember their prepared speeches. The result? They shoot off at a tangent; they forget the material they had so carefully rehearsed; they drift off the high road and flounder about in a morass. Why should not such men hold a few very condensed notes in their hands during their maiden efforts? A child clutches the furniture when it is first attempting to walk; but it does not continue it very long.

## DO NOT MEMORIZE VERBATIM

Don't read, and don't attempt to memorize your talk word for word. That consumes time, and courts disaster. Yet, in spite of this warning, some of the men reading these lines will try it; if they do, when they stand up to speak they will be thinking of what? Of their messages? No, they will be attempting to recall their exact phraseology. They will be thinking backwards, not forwards, reversing the usual processes of the human mind. The whole exhibition will be stiff and cold and colorless and inhuman. Do not, I beg of you, waste hours and energy in such futility.

When you have an important business interview, do you sit down and memorize, verbatim, what you are going to say? Do you? Of course not. You reflect until you get your main ideas clearly in mind. You may make a few notes and consult some records. You say to yourself: "I shall bring out this point and that. I am going to say that a certain thing ought to be done for these reasons······" Then you enumerate the reasons to yourself and illustrate them with concrete cases. Isn't that the way you prepare for a business interview? Why not use the same common sense method in preparing a talk?

## GRANT AT APPOMATTOX

When Lee asked Grant to write down the terms of surrender, the leader of the Union forces turned to General Parker, asking for writing material. "When I put my pen to paper," Grant records in his *Memoirs*, "I did not know the first word I should make use of in writing the terms. I only knew what was in my mind, and I wished to express it clearly, so there could be no mistaking it."

General Grant, you did not need to know the first word. You had ideas. You had convictions. You had something that you very much wanted to say and to say clearly. The result was that your habitual phraseology came tumbling out without conscious effort. The same holds good for any man. If you doubt it, knock a street cleaner down; when he gets up, he will discover that he is hardly at a loss to find words to express himself.

Two thousand years ago, Horace wrote:

"Seek not for words, seek only fact and thought,
And crowding in will come the words unsought."

After you have your ideas firmly in mind, then rehearse your talk from beginning to end. Do it silently, mentally, as you walk the street, as you wait for cars and elevators. Get off in a room by yourself, and go over it aloud, gesturing, saying it with life and energy. Canon Knox Little, of Canterbury, used to say a preacher never got the real message out of a sermon until he had preached it half a dozen times. Can you hope, then, to get the real message out of your talk unless you have at least rehearsed it that many times? As you practise, imagine there is a real audience before you. Imagine it so strongly that when there is one, it will seem like an old experience. That is the reason why so many criminals are able to go to the scaffold with such bravado; they have already done it so many thousand times in their imagination that they have lost fear of it. When the actual execution does take place, it seems like something that they have gone through very often before.

## WHY THE FARMERS THOUGHT LINCOLN "AWFULLY LAZY"

If you practise your talks in this fashion, you will be faithfully following the examples of many famous speakers. Lloyd George, when he was a member of a debating society in his home town in Wales, often strolled along the country lanes, talking and gesturing to the trees and fence posts.

Lincoln, in his younger days, often walked a round trip of thirty or forty miles to hear a famous speaker like Breckenridge. He came home from these scenes so stirred, so determined to be a speaker that he gathered the other hired workers about him in the fields and, mounting a stump, he made speeches and told them stories. His employers grew angry, declaring that this country Cicero was "awfully lazy," that his jokes and his oratory were ruining the rest of the workers.

Asquith gained his first facility by becoming an active worker in the Union Debating Society in Oxford. Later he organized one of his own. Woodrow

Wilson learned to speak in a debating society. So did Henry Ward Beecher. So did the mighty Burke. Elihu Root practised before a literary society in the Twenty-Third Street Y.M.C.A. in New York.

Study the careers of famous speakers and you will find one fact that is true of them all: *they practised.* THEY PRACTISED. And the men who make the most rapid progress in this course are those who practise most.

No time for all this? Then do what Joseph Choate used to do. He bought a newspaper of a morning and buried his head in it as he rode to work so no one would bother him. Then, instead of reading the ephemeral scandal and gossip of the day, he thought out and planned his talks.

Chauncey M. Depew led a fairly active life as a railroad president and a United States Senator. Yet, during it all, he made speeches almost every night. "I did not let them interfere with my business," he says. "They were all prepared after I had arrived home from my office late in the afternoon."

We all have three hours a day that we can do with as we please. That was all Darwin had to work with, as he had poor health. Three hours out of twenty-four, wisely used, made him famous.

Roosevelt, when he was in the White House, often had an entire forenoon given over to a series of five minute interviews. Yet he kept a book by his side to utilize even the few spare seconds that came between his engagements.

If you are very busy and pushed for time, read Arnold Bennett's "How To Live On Twenty-Four Hours A Day." Rip out a hundred pages, put them in your hip pocket, read them during your spare seconds. I got through the book in two days in that fashion. It will show you how to save time, how to get more out of the day.

You must have relaxation and a change from your regular work. That is what the practising of your talks ought to be. If possible, arrange with the other men in this course to meet together an additional night each week for rehearsal. If you cannot do that, play the game of extemporaneous speaking in your own home with your own family.

## HOW DOUGLAS FAIRBANKS AND CHARLIE CHAPLIN ENTERTAINED THEMSELVES

It is common knowledge that Douglas Fairbanks and Charlie Chaplin have incomes permitting them to enjoy a little recreation; yet, with all their wealth and fame, they were able to find no greater entertainment, no more enjoyable way of spending their evenings, than by practising extemporaneous speaking.

Here is their story as Douglas Fairbanks told it in the *American Magazine* a few years ago:

"One evening we were fooling and I pretended to introduce Charlie Chaplin at a dinner. He had to rise and make a speech to fit the introduction. And out of that developed a game that we have been playing almost every night for two years. We three (Mary Pickford, Fairbanks, and Chaplin) each write a subject on a slip of paper and fold the slips and shake them up. Each of us draws. No matter what the word is, each of us has to rise and talk for sixty seconds on that word. We never use the same word again. That's what keeps the stunt new. And we use all kinds of words. I remember one evening when two of the words were 'Faith' and 'Lampshades.' 'Lampshades' fell to me, and I had one of the hardest times I ever had, talking for sixty seconds on 'Lampshades.' Just try if you think it is easy. You start out bravely: 'Lamrshades have two uses. They modify and soften the glare of light, and they are decorative.' Then you are through unless you know a lot more about lampshades than I do. I got through somehow.

But the point is how all three of us have sharpened up since we began that game. We know a lot more about a variety of miscellaneous subjects. But, far better than that, we are learning to assemble our knowledge and thoughts on any topic at a moment's notice and to give it out briefly. We are learning to think on our feet. I say 'we are learning' because we are still at this game. We haven't tired of it in almost two years, which means that it is still making us grow."

## SUMMARY

1. "The art of war," said Napoleon, "is a science in which nothing succeeds which has not been calculated and thought out." That is as true of speaking as of shooting. A talk is a voyage. It must be charted. The speaker who starts nowhere, usually gets there.
2. No infallible, iron-clad rules can be given for the arrangement of ideas and the construction of all talks. Each address presents its own particular problems.
3. The speaker should cover a point thoroughly while he is on it, and then not refer to it again. As

an illustration, see the prize-winning address on Philadelphia. There should be no darting from one thing to another and then back again as aimlessly as a bat in the twilight.

4. The late Dr. Conwell built many of his talks on this plan:

   a. State your facts.

   b. Argue from them.

   c. Appeal for action.

5. You will probably find this plan very helpful:

   a. Show something that is wrong.

   b. Show how to remedy it.

   c. Ask for cooperation.

6. Here is an excellent speech plan (for further details see Chapter XV):

   a. Secure interested attention.

   b. Win confidence.

   c. State your facts.

   d. Appeal to the motives that make men act.

7. "All the facts on both sides of your subject," advised Senator Albert J. Beveridge, "must be collected, arranged, studied, digested. Prove them; be sure they are facts; then think out for yourself the solution those facts compel."

8. Before speaking, Lincoln thought out his

conclusions with mathematical exactness. When he was forty years of age, and after he had been a member of Congress, he studied Euclid so that he could detect sophistry and demonstrate his conclusions.

9. When Roosevelt was preparing a speech, he dug up all the facts, appraised them, then dictated his speech very rapidly, corrected the typewritten copy, and finally dictated it all over again.

10. If possible, dictate your talk to a dictaphone and listen to it.

11. Notes destroy about fifty per cent of the interest in your talk. Avoid them. Above all, do not read your talk. An audience can hardly be brought to endure listening to a read speech.

12. After you have thought out and arranged your talk, then practise it silently as you walk along the street. Also get off somewhere by yourself and go over it from beginning to end, using gestures, letting yourself go. Imagine that you are addressing a real audience. The more of this you do, the more comfortable you will feel when the time comes for you to make your talk.

# CHAPTER FOUR

# THE IMPROVEMENT OF MEMORY

"One of the most irritating and costly things in business is forgetfulness.... No matter what walk of life one is in, a well developed memory is sure to prove of incalculable value."
—Saturday Evening Post.

"The man whose acquisitions stick is the man who is always achieving and advancing whilst his neighbors, spending most of their time in relearning what they once knew, but have forgotten, simply hold their own." —Professor William James.

"When I intend to speak on anything that seems to me important I consider what it is that I wish to impress upon my audience. I do not write my facts or my arguments, but make notes on two or three or four slips of note paper, giving the line of argument and the facts as they occur to my mind, and I leave the words to come at call while I am speaking. There are occasionally short passages which for accuracy, I may write down; as sometimes, also —almost invariably —the concluding words or sentences may be writtne." —John Bright.

## THE IMPROVEMENT OF MEMORY

"The average man," says the noted psychologist, Professor Carl Seashore, "does not use above ten percent of his actual inherited capacity for memory. He wastes the ninety percent by violating the natural laws of remembering."

Are you one of these average men? If so, you are struggling under a handicap both socially and commercially; consequently, you will be interested in, and profit by, reading and rereading this chapter. It describes and explains these natural laws of remembering and shows how to use them in business as well as in speaking.

These "natural laws of remembering" are very simple. There are only three. Every so-called "memory system" has been founded upon them. Briefly, they are *impression, repetition, and association*.

The first mandate of memory is: get a deep, vivid and lasting impression of the thing you wish to retain. And to do that, you must concentrate. Theodore Roosevelt's remarkable memory impressed everyone he met. And no little amount of his extraordinary facility was due to this: his impressions were scratched on steel, not written in water. He had, by persistence and practise, trained himself to concentrate under the most adverse conditions. In 1912, during the Bull Moose Convention in Chicago, his headquarters were in the Congress Hotel. Crowds surged through the street below, crying, waving banners, shouting "We want Teddy! We want Teddy!" The roar of the throng, the music of bands, the coming and going of politicians, the hurried conferences, the consultations—would have driven the ordinary individual to distraction; but Roosevelt sat in a rocking chair in his room, oblivious to it all, reading Herodotus, the Greek historian. On his trip through the Brazilian wilderness, as soon as he reached the camping ground in the evening, he found a dry spot under some huge tree, got out a camp stool and his copy of Gibbon's "Decline and Fall of the Roman Empire," and, at once, he was so immersed in the book that he was oblivious to the rain, to the noise and activity of the camp, to the sounds of the tropical forest. Small wonder that the man remembered what he read.

Five minutes of vivid, energetic concentration will produce greater results than days of mooning about in a mental haze. "One intense hour," wrote Henry Ward Beecher, "will do more than dreamy years." "If there is any one thing that I have learned which is more important than anything else," says Eugene Grace, who makes over a million a year as president of the Bethlehem Steel Company, "and which I practise every day under any and all circumstances, it is *concentration on the particular job I have in hand.*"

This is one of the secrets of power, especially memory power.

## THEY COULDN'T SEE A CHERRY TREE

Thomas Edison found that 27 of his assistants had used, every day for six months, a certain path which led from his lamp factory to the main works at Menlo Park, New Jersey. A cherry tree grew along that path, and yet not one of these 27 men had, when questioned, ever been conscious of that tree's existence.

"The average person's brain," observes Mr. Edison

with heat and energy, "does not observe a thousandth part of what the eye observes. It is almost incredible how poor our powers of observation—genuine observation—are."

Introduce the average man to two or three of your friends and, the chances are that two minutes afterwards he cannot recall the name of a single one of them. And why? Because he never paid sufficient attention to there in the first place, he never accurately observed them. He will likely tell you he has a poor memory. No, he has a poor observation. He would not condemn a camera because it failed to take pictures in a fog, but he expects his mind to retain impressions that are hazy and foggy to a degree. Of course, it can't be done.

The late Mr. Pulitzer, who made the *New York World*, had three words placed over the desk of every man in his editorial offices:

Accuracy
ACCURACY
ACCURACY

That is what we want. Hear the man's name precisely. Insist on it. Ask him to repeat it. Inquire how it is spelled. He will be flattered by your interest and you will be able to remember his name because you have concentrated on it. You have got a clear accurate impression.

## WHY LINCOLN READ ALOUD

Lincoln, in his youth, attended a country school where the floor was made out of split logs: grease pages, torn from the copybooks and pasted over the windows, served instead of glass to let in the light. Only one copy of the textbook existed, and the teacher read from it aloud. The pupils repealed the lesson after him, all of them talking at once. It made a constant uproar, and the neighbors called it the "blab school."

At the "blab school," Lincoln formed a habit that clung to him all his life: he forever after read aloud everything he wished to remember. Each morning, as soon as he reached his law office in Springfield, he spread himself out on the couch, hooked one long, ungainly leg over a neighboring chair, and read the newspaper audibly. "He annoyed me," said his partner, "almost beyond endurance. I once asked him why he read in this fashion. This was his explanation: 'When I read aloud, two senses catch the idea: first, I see what I read: second, I hear it, and therefore I can remember it better.'"

His memory was extraordinarily retentive. "My mind," he said, "is like a piece of steel—very hard to scratch anything on it, but almost impossible, after you get it there, to rub it out."

Appealing to two of the senses was the method he used to do the scratching. Go thou, and do likewise……

The ideal thing would be not only to see and hear the thing to be remembered, but to touch it, and smell it, and taste it.

But, above all else, see it. We are visual minded. Eye impressions stick. We can often remember a man's face, even though we cannot recall his name. The nerves that lead from the eye to the brain are twenty times as large as those leading from the ear to the brain. The Chinese have a proverb that says "one time seeing is worth a thousand times hearing."

Write down the name, the telephone number, the speech outline you want to remember. Look at it. Close your eyes. Visualize it in flaming letters of fire.

# HOW MARK TWAIN LEARNED TO SPEAK WITHOUT NOTES

The discovery of how to use his visual memory enabled Mark Twain to discard the notes that had hampered his speeches for years. Here is his story as he told it in *Harper's Magazine*:

"Dates are hard to remember because they consist of figures: figures are monotonously unstriking in appearance, and they don't take hold they form no pictures, and so they give the eye no chance to take hold. Pictures can make dates stick. They can make nearly anything stick — particularly if you make the picture yourself. Indeed, that is the great point—make the picture yourself. I know about this from experience. Thirty years ago I was delivering a memorized lecture every night, and every night I had to help myself with a page of notes to keep from getting myself mixed. The notes consisted of beginnings of sentences, and were eleven in number, and they ran something like this:

In that region the weather-
At that time it was a custom-
But in California one never heard-

Eleven of them. They initialed the brief of the lecture and protected me against skipping. But they all looked about alike on the page; they formed no picture; I had them by heart, but I could never with certainty remember the order of their succession; therefore, I always had to keep those notes by me and look at them every little while. Once I mislaid them; you will not be able to imagine the terrors of that evening. I now saw that I must invent some other protection. So I got ten of the initial letters by heart in their proper order—I, A, B, and so on—and I went on the platform the next night with these marked in ink on my ten finger nails. But it didn't answer. I kept track of the fingers for awhile; then I lost it, and after that I was never quite sure which finger I had used last. I couldn't lick off a letter after using it, for while that would have made success certain, it would also have provoked too much curiosity. There was curiosity enough without that. To the audience I seemed more interested in my finger nails than I was in my subject; one or two persons asked afterward what was the matter with my hands.

It was then that the idea of pictures occurred to me! Then my troubles passed away. In two minutes I made six pictures with my pen, and they did the work of the eleven catch-sentences and did it perfectly. I threw the pictures away as soon as they were made, for I was sure I could shut my eyes and see them any time. That was a quarter of a century ago; the lecture vanished out of my head more than twenty years ago, but I could rewrite it from the pictures—for they remain."

I recently had occasion to deliver a talk on memory. I wanted to use, very largely, the material in this chapter. I memorized the points by pictures. I visualized Roosevelt reading history while the crowds were yelling and bands playing outside his window. I saw Thomas Edison looking at a cherry tree. I pictured Lincoln reading a newspaper aloud. I imagined Mark Twain licking ink off his finger nails as he faced an audience.

How did I remember the order of the pictures? By one, two, three, and four? No, that would have been too difficult. I turned these numbers into pictures, and combined the pictures of the numbers with the pictures of the points. To illustrate. Number *one* sounds like *run*, so I made a race horse stand for *one*. I pictured Roosevelt in his room, reading astride a race horse. For *two*, I chose a word that sounds like two—*zoo*. I had the cherry tree that Thomas Edison was looking at standing in the bear cage at the zoo. For *three*, I pictured an object that sounds like *three*—tree. I had

Lincoln sprawled out in the top of a tree, reading aloud to his partner. For *four* I imagined a picture that sounds like four-*door*. Mark Twain stood in an open *door*, leaning against the jamb, licking the ink off his fingers as he talked to the audience.

I realize full well that many men who read this will think that such a method verges on the ridiculous. It does. That is one reason why it works. It is comparatively easy to remember the bizarre and ridiculous. Had I tried to remember the order of my points by numbers only, I might easily have forgotten; but by the system I have just described, it was almost impossible to forget. When I wished to recall my third point, I had but to ask myself what was in the top of the tree. Instantly I saw Lincoln.

I have, very largely for my own convenience, turned the numbers from one to twenty into pictures, choosing pictures that sound like the numbers. I have set them down here. If you will spend half an hour memorizing these picture-numerals you will then be able, after having a list of twenty objects called to you but once, to repeat them in their exact order and to skip about at random announcing which object was called to you eighth, which fourteenth, which third, and so on. Here are the picture numbers. Try the test.

You will find it decidedly amusing.

1. Run—visualize a race horse.
2. Zoo—see the bear cage in the zoo.
3. Tree—picture the third object called to you as lying in the top of a tree.
4. Door—or wild boar. Take any object or animal that sounds like four.
5. Bee hive.
6. Sick—see a Red Cross nurse.
7. Heaven—a street paved with gold, and angels playing on harps.
8. Gate.
9. Wine—the bottle has fallen over on the table, and the wine is streaming out and pouring down on something below. Put action into the pictures. It helps to make them stick.
10. Den of wild animals in a rocky cave in the deep woods.
11. A football eleven, rushing madly across the field. I picture them carrying aloft the object that I wish to recall as number eleven.
12. Shelve—see some one shoving something back on a shelf.
13. Hurting—see the blood spurting out of a wound and

reddening the thirteenth object.

14. Courting—a couple are sitting on something and making love.
15. Lifting—a strong man, a regular John L. Sullivan, is lifting something high above his head.
16. Licking—a fist fight.
17. Leavening—a housewife is kneading dough, and into the dough she kneads the seventeenth object.
18. Waiting—a woman is standing at a forked path in the deep woods waiting for some one.
19. Pining—a woman is weeping. See her tears falling on the nineteenth thing you wish to recall.
20. Horn of Plenty—a goat's horn overflowing with flowers and fruit and corn.

If you wish to try the test, spend a few minutes memorizing these picture-numbers. If you prefer, make pictures of your own. For ten, think of *wren* or fountain *pen* or *hen* or *sen-sen*—anything that sounds like ten. Suppose that the tenth object recalled to you a windmill. See the hen sitting on the windmill, or see it pumping ink to fill the fountain pen. Then, when you are asked what was the tenth object called, do not think of ten at all; but merely ask yourself where was the hen sitting. You may not think it will work, but try it. You can soon astound people with what they will consider to be an extraordinary capacity for remembering. You will find it entertaining if nothing else.

## MEMORIZING A BOOK AS LONG AS THE NEW TESTAMENT

One of the largest universities in the world is the El Hazar at Cairo. It is a Mohammedan institution with twenty-one thousand students. The entrance examination requires every applicant to repeat the Koran from memory. The Koran is about as long as the New Testament, and three days are required to recite it!

The Chinese students, or "study boys" as they are called, have to memorize some of the religious and classical books of China.

How are these Arab and Chinese students—many of them men of mediocre ability—able to perform these apparently prodigious feats of memory?

By *repetition*, the second "natural law of remembering."

You can memorize an almost endless amount of material if you will repeat it often enough. Go over the knowledge you want to remember. Use it. Apply it. Employ the new word in your conversation. Call the stranger by his name if you want to remember it. Talk over in conversation the points you want to make in your public address. The knowledge that is used tends to stick.

## THE KIND OF REPETITION THAT COUNTS

But the mere blind, mechanical going over a thing by rote is not enough. Intelligent repetition, repetition done in accordance with certain well-established traits of the mind—that is what we must have. For example, Professor Ebbinghaus gave his students a long list of nonsense syllables to memorize, such as "deyux," "qoli," and so on. He found that these students memorized as many of these syllables by thirty-eight repetitions, distributed over a period of three days, as they did by sixty-eight repetitions done at a single sitting…… Other psychological tests have repeatedly shown similar results.

That is a very significant discovery about the working of our memories. It means that we know now that the man who sits down and repeats a thing over and over until he finally fastens it in his memory, is using twice as much time and energy as is necessary to achieve the same results when the repeating process is done at judicious intervals.

This peculiarity of the mind—if we can call it such—can be explained by two factors:

First, during the intervals between repetitions, our subconscious minds are busy making the associations more secure. As Professor James sagely remarks: "We learn to swim during the winter and to skate during the summer."

Second, the mind, coming to the task at intervals, is not fatigued by the strain of an unbroken application. Sir Richard Burton, the translator of the "Arabian Nights," spoke twenty-seven languages like a native: yet he confessed that he never studied or practised any language for more than fifteen minutes at a time, "for, after that, the brain lost its freshness."

Surely, now, in the face of these facts, no man who prides himself on his common sense, will delay the preparation of a talk until the night before it is to be given. If he does, his memory will, of necessity, be working at only one-half its possible efficiency.

Here is a very helpful discovery about the way in which we forget. Psychological experiments have repeatedly shown that of the new material we have learned, we forget more during the first eight hours than during the next thirty days. An amazing ratio! So, immediately before you go into a business conference, immediately before you make a speech, look over your data, think over your facts, refresh your memory.

Lincoln knew the value of such a practise, and employed it. The scholarly Edward Everett preceded him on the program of speech-making at Gettysburg. When he saw that Everett was approaching the close of his long, formal oration, Lincoln "grew visibly nervous, as he always did when another man was speaking and he was to follow." Hastily adjusting his spectacles, he took his manuscript from his pocket and read it silently to himself to refresh his memory.

## PROFESSOR WILLIAM JAMES EXPLAINS THE SECRET OF A GOOD MEMORY

So much for the first two laws of remembering. The third one, *association*, however, is the indispensable element in recalling. In fact, it is the explanation of memory itself. "Our mind is," as Professor James has sagely observed, "essentially an associating machine······ Suppose I am silent for a moment, and then say in commanding accents: 'Remember!

Recollect!' Does your faculty of memory obey the order, and reproduce any definite image from your past? Certainly not. It stands staring into vacancy, and asking, 'What kind of thing do you wish me to remember?' It needs, in short, a cue. But, if I say, remember the date of your birth, or remember what you had for breakfast, or remember the succession of notes in the musical scale; then your faculty of memory immediately produces the required result: the *cue* determines its vast set of potentialities toward a particular point. And if you now look to see how this happens, you immediately perceive that the *cue* is something contiguously associated with the thing recalled. The words, 'date of my birth,' have an ingrained association with a particular number, month, and year; the words, 'breakfast this morning,' cut off all other lines of recall except those which lead to coffee and bacon and eggs; the words, 'musical scale,' are inveterate mental neighbors of do, re, mi, fa, sol, la, etc. The laws of association govern, in fact, all the trains of our thinking which are not interrupted by sensations breaking on us from without. Whatever appears in the mind must be *introduced*; and, when introduced, it is as the associate of something already there. This is as true of what you are recollecting as it is of everything else you think of······ An educated memory depends upon an organized system of associations; and its goodness depends on two of their peculiarities: first, on the persistency of the associations; and, second, on their number. ······ The 'secret of a good memory' is thus the secret of forming diverse and multiple associations with every fact we care to retain. But this forming of associations with a fact—what is it but thinking about the fact as much as possible? Briefly, then, of two men with the same outward experiences, *the one who thinks over his experiences most*, and weaves them into the most systematic relations with each other, will be the one with the best memory."

## HOW TO LINK YOUR FACTS TOGETHER

Very good, but how are we to set about weaving our facts into systematic relations with each other? The answer is: by finding their meaning, by thinking them over. For example, if you will ask and answer these questions about any new fact, that process will help to weave it into a systematic relation with other facts.

a. Why is this so?

b. How is this so?
   c. When is it so?
   d. Where is it so?
   e. Who said it is so?

If it is a stranger's name, for example, and it is a common one, we can perhaps tie it to some business friend who hears the same name. On the other hand, if it is unusual, we can take occasion to say so. This often leads the stranger to talk about his name. For example: while writing this chapter, I was introduced to a Mrs. Soter. I requested her to spell the name and remarked upon its unusualness. "Yes," she replied, "it is very uncommon. It is a Greek word meaning 'the Savior'." Then she told me about her husband's people who had come from Athens and of the high positions they had held in the government there. I have found it quite easy to get people to talk about their names, and it always helps me to remember them.

Observe the stranger's looks sharply. Note the color of his eyes and his hair, and look closely at his features. Note how he is dressed. Listen to his manner of talking. Get a clear, keen, vivid impression of his looks and personality, and associate these with his name. The next time these sharp impressions return to your mind, they will help bring the name with them.

Haven't you had the experience, when meeting a man for the second or third time, to discover that although you could remember his business or profession, you could not recall his name? The reason is this: a man's business is something definite and concrete. It has a meaning. It will adhere like a court plaster while his meaningless name will roll away like hail falling on a steep roof. Consequently, to make sure of your ability to recall a man's name, fashion a phrase about it that will tie it up to his business. There can be no doubt whatever about the efficacy of this method. For example, twenty men, strangers to one another, recently met in the Penn Athletic Club of Philadelphia to study this course. Each man was asked to rise, announce his name and business. A phrase was then manufactured to connect the two; and, within a few minutes, each person present could repeat the name of every other individual in the room. Even to the end of the course, neither the names nor businesses were forgotten, for they were linked together. They adhered.

Here are the first ten names, in alphabetical order, from that group; and here are the crude phrases that were used to tie the names to the businesses:

Mr. G. P. Albrecht (Sand business)—"Sand makes

all bright."

Mr. George A. Ansley (Real estate)—"To sell real estate, advertise in Ansley's Magazine."

Mr. S. W. Bayless (Asphalt)—"Use asphalt and pay less."

Mr. H. M. Biddle (Woolen cloth)—"Mr. Biddle piddles about the wool business."

Mr. Gideon Boericke (Mining)—"Boericke bores quickly for mines."

Mr. Thomas J. Devery (Printing)—"Every man needs Devery's printing."

Mr. O. W. Doolittle (Automobiles)—"Do little and you won't succeed in selling cars."

Mr. Thomas Fischer (Coal)—"He fishes for coal orders."

Mr. Frank H. Goldey (Lumber)—"There is gold in the lumber business."

Mr. J. H. Hancock (Saturday Evening Post)—"Sign your John Hancock to a subscription blank for the *Saturday Evening Post*."

## HOW TO REMEMBER DATES

Dates can best be retained by connecting them with important dates already firmly established in the mind.

Isn't it far more difficult, for example, for an American to remember that the Suez Canal was opened in 1869 than to remember that the first ship passed through it four years after the close of the Civil War? If an American tried to remember that the first settlement in Australia was made in 1788, the date is likely to drop out of his mind like a loose bolt out of a car; it is far more likely to stick if he thinks of it in connection with July 4, 1766, and remembers that it occurred twelve years after the Declaration of Independence. That is like screwing a nut on the loose bolt. It holds.

It is well to bear this principle in mind when you are selecting a telephone number. For example, the writer's phone number, during the war, was 1776. No one had difficulty in remembering it. If you can secure from the phone company some such number as 1492, 1861, 1865, 1914, 1918, your friends will not have to consult the directory. They might forget that your phone number was 1492, if you gave them the information in a colorless fashion; but would it slip their minds if you said, "You can easily remember my phone number; 1492, the year Columbus discovered America."

The Australians, New Zealanders, and Canadians

who are reading these lines would, of course, substitute for 1776, 1861, 1865 significant dates in their own history.

What is the best way to memorize the following dates?

a. 1564—Birth of Shakespeare.
b. 1607—The first English settlement in America was made in Jamestown.
c. 1819—The birth of Queen Victoria.
d. 1807—The birth of Robert E. Lee.
e. 1789—The Bastile was destroyed.

You would doubtlessly find it tiresome to memorize, by sheer mechanical repetition, the names of the thirteen original states in the order in which they entered the Union. But tie them together with a story and the memorizing can be done with a fraction of the time and trying. Read the following paragraph just once. Concentrate. When you have finished, see if you cannot name the thirteen states in their correct order:

One Saturday afternoon a young lady from Delaware bought a ticket over the Pennsylvania railroad for a little outing. She packed a New Jersey sweater in her suitcase and visited a friend, Georgia, in Connecticut, The next morning the hostess and her visiter attended Mass in a church on Mary's land. Then they took the South car line home, and dined on a new ham, which had been roasted by Virginia, the colored cook, from New York. After dinner they took the North car line and rode to the island.

## HOW TO REMEMBER THE POINTS OF YOUR TALK

There are only two ways by which we can possibly think of a thing: first, by means of an *outside stimulus*; second, by *association* with something already in the mind. Applied to speeches, that means just this: first, you can recall your points by the aid of some outside stimulus such as notes —but who likes to see a speaker use notes? Second, you can remember your points by associating them with something already in the mind. They should be arranged in such a logical order that the first one leads inevitably to the second, and the second to the third as naturally as the door of one room leads into another.

That sounds simple, but it may not prove so for the beginner whose thinking powers are rendered *hors de combat* with fear. There is, however, a method of tying your points together that is easy, rapid, and all but fool-proof. I refer to the use or a nonsense sentence.

To illustrate: suppose you wish to discuss a veritable jumble of ideas, unassociated and hence hard to remember, such as, for example, *cow, cigar, Napoleon, house, religion*. Let us see if we cannot weld those ideas like the links of a chain by means of this absurd sentence: "The cow smoked a cigar and hooked Napoleon, and the house burned down with religion."

Now, will you please cover the above sentence with your hand while you answer these questions? What is the third point in that talk; the fifth; fourth: second; first?

Does the method work? It does! And the members of this course are urged to use it.

Any group of ideas can be linked together in some such fashion, and the more ridiculous the sentence used for the linking, the easier it will be to recall.

## WHAT TO DO IN CASE OF A COMPLETE BREAKDOWN

Let us suppose that, in spite of all his preparation and precaution, a speaker, in the middle of his talk, suddenly finds his mind a blank—suddenly finds himself staring at his hearers completely balked, unable to go on—a terrifying situation. His pride rebels at sitting down in confusion and defeat. He feels that he might be able to think of his next point, of some point, if he had only ten, fifteen seconds of grace; but even fifteen seconds of frantic silence before an audience would be little less than disastrous. What is to be done? When a certain well known U. S. Senator recently found himself in this situation he asked his audience if he were speaking loudly enough, if he could be heard distinctly in the back of the room. He knew that he was. He was not seeking information. He was seeking time. And in that momentary pause, he grasped his thought and proceeded.

But perhaps the best life-saver in such a mental hurricane is this: use the last word, or phrase, or idea in your last sentence for the beginning of a new sentence. This will make an endless chain that, like Tennyson's brook and, I regret to say, with as little purpose as Tennyson's brook, will run on forever. Let us see how it works in practise. Let us imagine that a speaker, talking on Business Success, finds himself in a blind mental alley after having said: "The average employe does not get ahead because he takes so little real interest in his work, displays so little initiative."

"*Initiative.*" Start a sentence with "*initiative.*" You will probably have no idea of what you are going to say or how you are going to end the sentence, but, nevertheless, begin. Even a poor showing is more to be desired than utter defeat.

"Initiative means originality, doing a thing on your own, without eternally waiting to be told."

That is not a scintillating observation. It won't make speech history. But isn't it better than an agonizing silence? Our last phrase was what?—"waiting to be told." All right, let us start a new sentence with that idea.

"The constant telling and guiding and driving of employees who refuse to do any original thinking is one of the most exasperating things imaginable."

Well, we got through that one. Let us plunge again. This time we must say something about imagination:

"Imagination—that is what is needed. Vision. 'Where there is no vision,' Solomon said, 'the people perish.'"

We did two that time without a hitch. Let us take heart and continue:

"The number of employees who perish each year in the battle of business is really lamentable. I say lamentable, because with just a little more loyalty, a little more ambition, a little more enthusiasm, these same men and women might have lifted themselves over the line of demarcation between success and failure. Yet the failure in business never admits that this is the case."

And so on······While the speaker is saying these platitudes off the top of his mind, he should, at the same time, be thinking hard of the next point in his planned speech, of the thing he had originally intended to say.

This endless chain method of talking will, if continued very long, trap the speaker into discussing plum pudding or the price of canary birds. However, it is a splendid first aid to the injured mind broken down temporarily through forgetfulness: and, as such, it has been the means of resuscitating many a gasping and dying speech.

## WE CANNOT IMPROVE OUR MEMORIES FOR ALL CLASSES OF THINGS

I have pointed out in this chapter how we may

improve our *methods* of getting vivid impressions, of repeating and of tying our facts together. But memory is so essentially a matter of association that "there can be," as Professor James points out, "no improvement of the general or elementary faculty of memory; there can only be improvement of our memory for special systems of associated things,"

By memorizing, for instance, a quotation a day from Shakespeare, we may improve our memory for literary quotations to a surprising degree. Each additional quotation will find many friends in the mind to tie to. But the memorizing of everything from Hamlet to Romeo will not necessarily aid one in retaining facts about the cotton market or the Bessemer process for desiliconizing pig iron.

Let us repeat: if we apply and use the principles discussed in this chapter, we will improve our manner and *efficiency* for memorizing anything; but, if we do not apply these principles, then the memorizing of ten million facts about baseball will not help us in the slightest in memorizing facts about the stock market. Such unrelated data cannot be tied together. "Our mind is essentially an associating machine."

## SUMMARY

1. "The average man," says the noted psychologist, Professor Carl Seashore, "does not use above ten per cent of his actual inherited capacity for memory. He wastes the ninety per cent by violating the natural laws of remembering."
2. These "natural laws of remembering" are three: *impression, repetition, association*.
3. Get a deep, vivid impression of the thing you wish to remember. To do that you must—
   a. Concentrate. That was the secret of Roosevelt's memory.
   b. Observe closely. Get an accurate impression. A camera won't take pictures in a fog; neither will your mind retain foggy impressions.
   c. Get your impressions through as many of the senses as possible. Lincoln read aloud whatever he wished to remember so that he would get both a visual and an auditory impression.
   d. Above all else, be sure to get eye impressions. They stick. The nerves leading from the eye to the brain are twenty times as large as those leading from the ear to the brain. Mark Twain could not remember the outline of his speech

when he used notes; but when he threw away his notes and used pictures to recall his various headings, all his troubles vanished.

4. The second law of memory is repetition. Thousands of Mohammedan students memorize the Koran—a book about as long as the New Testament—and they do it very largely through the power of repetition. We can memorize anything within reason if we repeat it often enough. But bear these facts in mind as you repeat:

   a. Do not sit down and repeat a thing over and over until you have it engraved on your memory. Go over it once or twice, then drop it; come back later and go over it again. Repeating at intervals, in that manner, will enable you to memorize a thing in about one-half the time required to do it at one sitting.

   b. After we memorize a thing, we forget a much during the first eight hours as we do during the next thirty days; so go over your notes just a few minutes before you rise to make your talk

5. The third law of memory is association. The only way anything can possibly be remembered at all is by associating it with some other fact. "What ever

appears in the mind," says Professor James "must be introduced; and, when introduced, it is as the associate of something already there······ The one who thinks over his experiences most, and weaves them into the most systematic relation with each other, will be the one with the best memory."

6. When you wish to associate one fact with others already in the mind, think over the new fact from all angles. Ask about it such questions as these: "Why is this so? How is this so? When is it so? Where is it so? Who said it is so?"

7. To remember a stranger's name, ask questions about it—how is it spelled, etc.? Observe his looks sharply. Try to connect the name with his face. Find out his business and try to invent some nonsense phrase that will connect his name with his business, such as was done in the Penn Athletic Club group.

8. To remember dates, associate them with prominent dates already in the mind. For example, the three hundredth anniversary of Shakespeare's birth occurred during the Civil War.

9. To remember the points of your address, arrange them in such logical order that one leads naturally to the next. In addition, one can make a nonsense

sentence out of the main points—for example, "The cow smoked a cigar and hooked Napoleon, and the house burned down with religion."

10. If, in spite of all precautions, you suddenly forget what you intended to say, you may be able to save yourself from complete defeat by using the last words of your last sentence as the first words in a new one. This can be continued until you are able to think of your next point.

# CHAPTER FIVE

# KEEPING THE AUDIENCE AWAKE

"Genius is intensity. The man who gets anything worth having is the man who goes after his object as a bulldog goes after a cat—with every fiber in him tense with eagerness and determination."
—W. C. Holman, formerly Sales Manager for the National Cash Register Company.

"The man or woman of enthusiastic trend always exercises a magnetic influence over those with whom he or she comes in contact." —M. Addington Bruce.

"Be intensely in earnest. Enthusiasm invites enthusiasm." —Russell H. Conwell.

"I like the man who bubbles over with enthusiasm. Better be a geyser than a mud puddle."
—John G. Shedd, Former President of Marshall Field and Co.

"He did it with all his heart and prospered."
—Second Chronicles.

## KEEPING THE AUDIENCE AWAKE

Sherman Rogers and I once addressed the same meeting of the St. Louis Chamber of Commerce. I spoke first and, had I had a good excuse, I would have left immediately afterwards, for he was billed as "the lumberjack orator." I frankly expected to be bored for, like Mr. Dooley, I class the usual so-called "oratory" with wax flowers. This day, however, I was delightfully surprised; Mr. Rogers made easily one of the best talks I have ever heard.

And who is Sherman Rogers? A genuine lumberjack—he has spent most of his life in the big woods of the West. He knows nothing and cares less than nothing about the rules for public speaking that have been set down so elaborately in learned books on eloquence. His talk did not have polish: but it had punch. It lacked finesse; but it had fire. He made grammatical errors, and did half a dozen things that are not according to Hoyle; but it is not faults that kill a talk; it is a lack of virtues.

His speech was a huge, raw piece of palpitating experience torn right out of his own life as a laborer and a boss of laborers. It didn't smack of books. It was a live thing. It fairly crouched and sprang at you. Everything that he said leaped flaming hot from his heart. The effect on the audience was electrical.

The secret of his success? The secret of every phenomenal success: "Every great movement in the annals of history," said Emerson, "is the triumph of enthusiasm."

It is derived, that magic name, from two Greek words: *en*, meaning *in*; and *theos*, meaning *God*. Enthusiasm is literally *God in* us. The enthusiastic man is one who speaks as if he were possessed by God.

This quality is the most effective, the most important factor in advertising and selling goods and getting things done. The largest advertiser of any single product in the world came to Chicago thirty years ago with less than fifty dollars in his pocket. Wrigley now sells thirty million dollars worth of his chewing gum every year, and on the wall of his private office hang these framed words of Emerson: "Nothing great was ever achieved without enthusiasm."

There was a time when I put considerable reliance in the *rules* of public speaking; but with the passing of the years I have come to put more and more faith in the *spirit* of speaking.

"Eloquence," said the late Mr. Bryan, "may be defined as the speech of one who knows what he is talking about, and means what he says—it is thought on fire ······ Knowledge is of little use to the speaker without earnestness. Persuasive speech is from heart to heart, not from mind to mind. It is difficult for a speaker to deceive his audience as to his own feeling ······ Nearly two thousand years ago, one of the Latin poets expressed this thought when he said: 'If you would draw tears from others' eyes, yourself the signs of grief must show.'"

"If I wish to compose or write or pray or preach well," said Martin Luther, "I must be angry. Then all the blood in my veins is stirred, and my understanding is sharpened."

Perhaps we don't have to be exactly angry, you and I, but we must be aroused and sincere and intensely in earnest.

Even a horse is affected by spirited talk. Rainey, the famous animal trainer, said that he had known an angry word to raise the pulse of a horse ten beats per minute. Surely, an audience is as sensitive as a horse.

This is a most important fact to remember: every time we speak we determine the attitude of our hearers. We hold them in the hollow of our hands. If we are lackadaisical, they will be lackadaisical. If we are reserved, they will be reserved. If we are only mildly concerned, they will be only mildly concerned. But if we are deadly in earnest about what we say, and if we say it with feeling and spontaneity and force and contagious conviction, they cannot keep from catching our spirit to a degree.

"Much as we would like to think we are moved by reason," says Martin W. Littleton, a famous New York after-dinner speaker, "the whole world is, in fact, moved by emotion. The man who tries to be very serious or very witty may easily fail, but the speaker who appeals to you with real convictions never fails. No matter whether the greatest subject to him is the breeding of White Leghorns, the plight of Christians in Armenia, or the League of Nations—if he is really deeply convinced so that he has a message for *you*, his speech will go like a flame. It won't matter how his convictions are clothed, either, but only with what sincerity and emotional power they are launched at you."

Given heat and earnestness and enthusiasm, a speaker's influence expands like steam. He can have five hundred faults; but he can hardly fail. The great Rubinstein, it is said, played myriads of false notes; but nobody cared, for he could get the poetry of Chopin into souls that had never seen anything in a sunset before except a big red disk sinking behind a barn on the horizon.

History records that before Pericles, the mighty Athenian leader, spoke, he prayed to the gods that not a single unworthy word might escape his lips. He had his heart in his messages; and they went straight to the heart of a nation.

Willa Cather, one of America's most distinguished woman novelists, says: "Every artist's secret"—and every public speaker ought to be an artist—"is passion. It is an open secret and perfectly safe. Like heroism, it is inimitable in cheap materials."

Passion······ Feeling······ Spirit······ Emotional sincerity—get these qualities in your talk and your auditors will condone—yes, will hardly be conscious of—minor shortcomings. History bears this out: Lincoln spoke in an unpleasantly high tone. Demosthenes stammered. Hooker's voice was weak.

Curran stuttered notoriously. Sheil almost squealed. The younger Pitt's voice was neither clear nor pleasant. Yet all these men had an earnestness that triumphed over all handicaps—an emotional urge that blasted all handicaps to nothingness.

## HAVE SOMETHING THAT YOU VERY MUCH WANT TO SAY

"The essence of a good speech," said Professor Brander Matthews in an interesting article in the *New York Times*, "is that the speaker really has something which he really wants to say."

"This was brought home to me a few years ago when I was one of three judges called on to award the Curtis medal at Columbia University. There were half a dozen undergraduates, all of them elaborately trained, all of them anxious to acquit themselves well. But— with only a single exception—what they were striving for was to win the medal. They had little or no desire to persuade. They had chosen their topics because these topics permitted oratorical development. They had no deep personal interest in the arguments they were making. And their successive speeches were merely exercises in the art of delivery. The exception was a Zulu Prince. He had selected as his theme 'The Contribution of Africa to Modern Civilization.' He put intense feeling into every word he uttered. His speech was no mere exercise; it was a living thing, born of conviction and enthusiasm. He spoke as the representative of his people, of his continent; he had something to say that he wanted to say; and he said it with sympathetic sincerity. So we gave him the medal, although he was possibly no more accomplished in the art than two or three of his competitors. What we judges recognized was that his address had the true fire of the orator. In comparison with his fervid appeal, the other speeches were only gas-logs."

Right here is where many a speaker fails. His expression is motivated by no conviction; no desire, no impetus is stirring in his talk; there is no powder behind his shot.

"Ah, very good," you say, "but how am I to develop this earnestness and spirit and enthusiasm that you praise so highly?" This much is sure: you will never develop it by talking from the surface. Any discerning listener can detect whether a speaker is talking from skin-deep impressions or whether his expression is welling up from deep within him. So shake yourself out of your inertia. Put your heart in your work. Dig.

Seek for the hidden resources that lie buried away inside you. Get the facts and the causes behind the facts. Concentrate. Dwell on them, brood over them until they matter to you. In the last analysis, you see it is all conditioned back upon thorough preparation and the right kind of preparation. Heart preparation is as essential as head preparation. To illustrate:

I trained a number of men in the New York City Chapter of the American Institute of Banking to speak during a thrift campaign. One of the men in particular lacked force. He was talking merely because he wanted to speak, not because he was fired with zeal for thrift. The first step in training that man was to warm his mind and heart. I told him to go off by himself and to think over his subject until he became enthusiastic about it. I asked him to remember that the Probate Court Records in New York show that more than 85% of the people leave nothing at all at death; that only 3.3% leave $10,000 or over. He was to keep constantly in mind that he was not asking people to do him a favor or something that they could not afford to do. He was to say to himself: "I am preparing these people to have meat and bread and clothes and comfort in their old age, and to leave their wives and children protected." He must remember he was going to perform a great social service. He must be inspired by the crusader's faith that he was preaching the practical, applied gospel of Jesus Christ.

He thought over these facts. He burned them into his mind. He got a realizing sense of their importance. He aroused his *own* interest, stirred his *own* enthusiasm, and came to feel that his mission was almost holy. Then, when he went out to talk, there was a ring to his words that carried conviction. In fact, his talks on thrift attracted so much attention that he was invited to join the organization of the largest bank in America, and was later sent to one of its South American branches.

## THE SECRET OF A TRIUMPH

"I must live," cried a young man to Voltaire; and the philosopher replied: "I do not perceive the necessity."

That, in many instances, will be the attitude of the world towards what you have to say: it won't perceive the necessity of its being said. But *you*, if you would succeed, must *feel* the necessity—if there is one. The thing ought to grip you. It ought, for the time being, to seem to you like the most important thing on *terra firma*.

Dwight L. Moody became so stirred in the

preparation of his sermon on *Grace*, so wrought up in his search for truth, that he seized his hat, left his study, strode out into the street and accosted the first man he met with the abrupt inquiry: "Do you know what Grace is?" Is it any wonder that a man, fired with such emotional earnestness and intensity, exerted a magic power over audiences?

Some time ago a member of a course I was conducting in Paris spoke evening after evening in a colorless fashion. He was something of a student, and he had his facts all right, piles of them. But he had not welded them together with the heat of his own interest. He lacked spirit. He didn't talk as if what he had to say was very vital, so naturally the audience paid little heed. They took his speech at his own appraisement. Time and again, stopping him, I endeavored to drill force into him, to wake him up; but I often felt as if I were trying to coax steam out of a cold radiator. Finally, I did succeed in persuading him that his method of preparation was at fault. I convinced him that he ought to establish some kind of telegraphic communication between his head and his heart. I told him that he must give us not only the facts, but that he ought to reveal his attitude towards those facts.

The next week he appeared with ideas about which

he felt strongly enough to make the expression of them worth while. At last, he was passionately concerned about something. He had a message that he loved as Thackeray loved Becky Sharp. He was willing to sweat blood for it, and his talk won long and hearty applause. It was an abrupt triumph. He had generated a little heart-felt earnestness. That is a fundamental part of preparation. As we learned in Chapter II, the preparation of a speech, a real speech, does not consist in merely getting some mechanical words down on paper, nor of memorizing phrases. Neither does it consist in lifting a few thoughts second hand from some book or newspaper article. No, no. But it does consist in digging away down deep into your own mind and heart and life, and bringing forth some convictions and enthusiasms that are essentially yours. Yours! YOURS! Dig. Dig. Dig. It is there. Never doubt it. Mines of it, quantities of it, of whose existence you have never even dreamed. Do you, yourself, realize the strength of your own potentialities? I doubt it. The late Professor James said that the average man does not develop more than ten per cent of his possible mental powers. Worse than an eight-cylinder machine with only one cylinder sparking!

Yes, the great thing in a speech is not the cold phraseology, but the man, the spirit, the convictions behind that phraseology. Sheridan's renowned attack on Warren Hastings in the House of Commons was declared by the famous speakers who heard it—by Burke and Pitt, by Wilberforce and Fox—to be the most eloquent oration ever delivered on England's soil. Yet Sheridan felt that the superlative merit of it was too spiritual and evanescent a thing to be caught and enmeshed in cold type; so he refused an offer of five thousand dollars for its publication. No copy of it exists today. If we could read the address, no doubt it would be disappointing. The quality that made it great would be gone. Only the empty skin would remain, like some stuffed eagle with outspread wings in a taxidermist's shop.

Always remember that you are the most important factor in your talk. Hear these golden words from Emerson! They contain a world of wisdom: "*Use what language you will, you can never say anything but what you are.*" That is one of the most significant statements I ever heard about the art of self-expression; and, for the sake of emphasis, I am going to repeat it: "*Use what language yow will, you can never say anything but what you are.*"

# A LINCOLN SPEECH THAT WON A LAWSUIT

Lincoln may never have read that, but one thing is certain: he knew the truth of it. One day the widow of a Revolutionary War soldier, an old woman bent with age, hobbled into his office, telling him of a pension agent who had taken from her the exorbitant fee of two hundred dollars for collecting a sum of twice that amount that was due her. Lincoln was indignant, and he brought suit immediately.

How did he prepare for this case? He prepared by reading a biography of Washington and a history of the Revolutionary War, by quickening his enthusiasm, by kindling his feelings and emotions. When he spoke, he recounted the oppressions that had stirred the patriots to turn and fight for liberty. He pictured the untold hardships they had gone through, the suffering they had endured at Valley Forge, hungry, barefooted and with bleeding feet creeping over the ice and snow. Then, in wrath, he turned to the rascal who had fleeced a widow of one of those heroes out of half her pension. His eyes flashed as he poured out his bitterest denunciation, "skinning" the defendant, as he declared he would do.

"Time rolls by," he said in conclusion. "The heroes

of '76 have passed away, and are encamped on the other shore. The soldier has gone to rest and now, crippled, blinded, and broken, his widow comes to you and to me, gentlemen of the jury, to right her wrongs. She was not always thus. She was once a beautiful young woman. Her step was as elastic, her face as fair, and her voice as sweet as any that rang in the mountains of old Virginia. But now she is poor and defenseless. Out here on the prairies of Illinois, many hundreds of miles away from the scenes of her childhood, she appeals to us who enjoy the privileges achieved for us by the patriots of the Revolution, for our sympathetic aid and manly protection. All I ask is, shall we befriend her?"

As he finished, some of the jury were in tears, and they returned a verdict for every cent the old woman asked. Lincoln became her surety for costs, paid her hotel bill and her fare home, and charged her nothing for his legal services.

A few days later, Lincoln's partner picked up a little scrap of paper in the office, read Lincoln's outline for his speech, and burst into laughter:

"No contract.—Not professional services—Unreasonable charge.—Money retained by Def't not given to Pl'ff.—

Revolutionary war.—Describe Valley Forge privations.— Pl'ff's husband.—Soldier leaving for army.—Skin Def't.— Close."

I hope that I have made plain that the first requisite in generating your warmth and enthusiasm is to prepare until you have a real message you want to get across. The next step is—

## ACT IN EARNEST

As we noted in Chapter I, Professor James has pointed out "action and feeling go together; and, by regulating the action which is under the most direct control of the will, we can indirectly regulate the feeling which is not."

So, to feel earnest and enthusiastic, stand up and *act* in earnest and *be* enthusiastic. Stop leaning against the table. Stand tall. Stand still. Don't rock back and forth. Don't bob up and down. Don't shift your weight from one foot to the other and back again like a tired horse. In short, don't make a lot of nervous movements which will proclaim your lack of ease and self-possession to the housetops. Control yourself physically. It will convey a sense of poise and power.

Stand up and stand out "like a strong man rejoicing to run a race." I repeat: fill your lungs with oxygen. Fill them to the full. Look straight at your audience. Look at them as if you had something urgent to say and as if you knew it was urgent. Look at them with the confidence and courage of a teacher viewing his pupils, for you *are* a teacher, and they are there to hear you and to be taught. So speak out confidently and with energy. "Lift up your voice," said the Prophet Isaiah, "lift it up. Be not afraid."

And use emphatic gestures. Never mind, just now, whether they are beautiful or graceful. Think only of making them forceful and spontaneous. Make them now, not for the sense they will convey to others, but for what they will do for you. And they will do wonders. Even if you are speaking to a radio audience, gesture, gesture. Your gestures won't, of course, be visible to the unseen hearers, but the result of your gestures will be audible to them. They will give increased aliveness and energy to your tones and to your whole manner.

How often have I stopped a lifeless speaker in the midst of his talk and drilled him and compelled him to use emphatic gestures which he did not at the time feel like using. But the physical action of the forced gestures finally awakened and stimulated him until he gestured spontaneously. Even his face brightened and his whole bearing and attitude became more earnest, more emphatic.

*Acting in earnest makes one feel in earnest.* "Assume a virtue," Shakespeare advised, "if you have it not."

Above all else, open your mouth, and speak out. Attorney General Wickersham once remarked to me: "The average man who attempts to speak in public cannot be heard even thirty feet away."

Does that sound exaggerated? I recently listened to a public address by the head of a great university. I sat in the fourth row and could hardly hear more than half he said. The ambassador of an important European nation recently delivered the commencement address before Union College; his delivery was so flabby that his words were almost inaudible twenty feet from the platform.

If experienced speakers commit such errors, what is to be expected of the beginner? He is not used to having his voice enlarged so that it will carry over an audience; so, when he speaks with sufficient vitality, he will imagine that he is fairly shouting and that people are ready to laugh at him.

Use conversational tones; but enlarge them. Intensify them. We can read fine print a foot from the eye; but it takes bold headlines to be seen across a hall.

## THE FIRST THING TO DO WHEN THE AUDIENCE GOES TO SLEEP

A country preacher once asked Henry Ward Beecher how to keep an audience awake on a hot Sunday afternoon, and Beecher told him to have an usher take a sharp stick and prod the preacher.

I like that. It is superb. It is glorified common sense. It would do more for the average speaker than nine-tenths of all the erudite tomes that have ever been written on the art of eloquence.

One of the surest ways to get a student to limber up and abandon and really let himself go, would be to knock him down before he started. It would put fire and spirit and aliveness into his speech. Actors know the value of shaking themselves awake before they make their stage entrance. Houdini did it by leaping about the back stage, striking the air vigorously with his fists, sparring with an imaginary antagonist. Mansfield sometimes deliberately planned to work himself into a perfect rage over any pretext—perhaps it was because some stage hand was breathing too audibly—any excuse that would serve to give him the heightened energy, the surging of spirit that he courted. I have seen actors standing in the wings, waiting for their cues and beating their breasts savagely. I have sent students, just before they spoke, into an adjoining room to pummel their bodies, until their blood leaped and their faces and eyes glowed with life. I frequently force a student to preface his practise talks in this course, repeating the A.B.C.'s with violent gestures and all the vigor and anger that he can possibly command. Isn't it highly desirable to go before your hearers like a thoroughbred straining at the bit?

Immediately before you speak, get, if possible, a thorough rest. The ideal thing is to undress and go to bed for a few hours. If possible, follow that with a cold plunge and a vigorous rubdown. Better still, far better, take a swim.

Charles Frohman used to say that he hired actors because of their vitality. The kind of acting or speaking that counts consumes a lot of nerve force and Physical energy; and Frohman knew it. I have chopped down hickory trees and split logs; and I have talked to audiences for two hours at a time. I have found one of these tasks about as exhausting as the other. During the

War, Dudley Field Malone made a passionate appeal to a large audience assembled in the Century Theatre, New York. At the climax of it, after speaking for an hour and a half, he fainted from sheer exhaustion and was carried unconscious from the stage.

Sydney Smith described Daniel Webster as "a steam engine in trousers."

"The most successful speakers," declared Beecher, "are men of great vitality and recuperative force, men who have preeminently the explosive power by which they can thrust their materials out. They are catapults and men go down before them."

## "WEASEL WORDS" AND ONIONS

Put energy behind what you say, and say it positively. But don't be too positive. Only an ignoramus is positive about everything; but only a weakling prefaces every remark with an *it seems to me*, or *perhaps*, or *in my opinion*.

The almost universal trouble with beginning speakers is not that they are too positive, but that they vitiate their talks with these timid phrases. I remember listening to a New York business man describe a motor trip through Connecticut. "On the left side of the road," he said, "there *seemed* to be a field of onions." Now, there is no *seeming* about onions. They either are or are not. And it does not require extraordinary powers to recognize an onion field when one sees it. Yet this shows to what absurd lengths a speaker will sometimes go.

"Weasel words" is what Roosevelt called such expressions, for a weasel sucks the heart out of an egg, and leaves nothing but the empty shell. That is what these phrases do to your talk.

Shrinking, apologetic tones and egg-shell phrases will not beget much confidence and conviction. Imagine business houses using such slogans as these: "It seems to us the Underwood is the machine you will eventually buy." "In our opinion, the Prudential has the strength of Gibraltar." "We think you will use our flour eventually—why not now?"

In 1896, when Bryan first ran for the presidency, I, as a boy, wondered why he so emphatically and so often declared that he would be elected, that Mckinley would go down in defeat. The explanation is simple. Bryan knew that people in the mass cannot differentiate between emphasis and proof. He knew that if he said a thing often enough and vigorously enough, most of his hearers would end by believing it.

The world's great leaders have always thundered forth as if there were no possibility on top of the Seven Seas of anyone invalidating their assertions. When Buddha was dying he did not reason or whine or argue; he spoke as one having authority: "Walk as I have commanded you."

The Koran, which has been the dominant factor in millions of lives, immediately following the preliminary prayer, opens with these words: "There is no doubt in this book; it is a direction."

When the jailer at Philippi asked Paul, "What must I do to be saved?" the answer was not an argument, an equivocation, an it-seems-to-me or an I-should-think assertion. It came, a superior command: "Believe on the Lord Jesus Christ, and thou shalt be saved."

But do not, as I have said, be too positive on all occasions. There are times, there are places, there are subjects, there are audiences, where too much positiveness will hinder rather than help. In general, the higher the level of intelligence of one's hearers, the less successful mere forceful assertions will be. Thinking people want to be led, not driven. They want to have the facts presented and to draw their own conclusions. They like to be asked questions, not to have a ceaseless stream of direct statements poured at them.

# LOVE YOUR AUDIENCE

A few years ago I had to employ and train a number of public lecturers in England. After painful and costly trials, three of them had to be dismissed, and one had to be sent back three thousand miles to America. Their main trouble was that they were not genuinely interested in serving their audiences. They were chiefly concerned, not about others, but about themselves and their pay envelopes. Everyone could feel it. They were cold to their audiences; and their audiences, in return, were cold to them. Consequently, these speakers remained sounding brasses and tinkling cymbals.

The well known human race is very quick to detect whether a talk is coming from above the eyebrows or back of the breast bone. Even a dog can sense that.

I have made a special study of Lincoln as a public speaker. He is undoubtedly the most loved man America has ever produced; and unquestionably he has delivered some of America's best speeches. Although he was a genius in some ways, I am inclined to believe that his power with audiences was due, in no small measure, to his sympathy and honesty and goodness. He loved people. "His heart," said his wife, "is as large as his arms are long." He was Christlike. And two thousand years ago, one of the first books ever written on this art described the eloquent talker as "a good man skilled in speaking."

"The secret of my success," said Madam Schumann-Heink, the famous prima donna, "is absolute devotion to the audience. I love my audiences. They are all my friends. I feel a bond with them the moment I step before them." So that was the secret of her world-wide triumph ······ Let us try to cultivate the same spirit.

The finest thing in speaking is neither physical nor mental. It is spiritual. The Book that Daniel Webster had on his pillow while dying is a book that every speaker should have on his desk while living.

Jesus loved men and their hearts burned within them as He talked with them by the way. If you want a splendid text on public speaking, why not read your New Testament?

## SUMMARY

1. Every time you speak, you determine the attitude of your hearers toward what you say. If you are lackadaisical, they will be lackadaisical. If you are

only mildly concerned, they will be only mildly concerned. If you are enthusiastic, they will be sure to catch something of your spirit. Enthusiasm is one of the biggest—if not the biggest—factors in delivery.

2. "The man who tries to be very serious or very witty," says Martin W. Littleton, "may easily fail, but the speaker who appeals to you with real conviction never fails······ If he is really deeply convinced so that he has a message for you, his speech will go like a flame."

3. In spite of the tremendous importance of this quality of contagious conviction and enthusiasm, most men lack it.

4. "The essence of a good speech," says Professor Brander Matthews, "is that the speaker really has something which he really wants to say."

5. Think over your facts, burn their real importance into your mind. Try your own enthusiasm before you attempt to convince others.

6. Establish a telegraphic communication between your head and heart. We want you not only to give us the facts but to reveal your attitude towards those facts.

7. "Use what language you will, you can never say

anything but what you are." The big thing in a speech is not hiswords but the spirit of the man behind the words.

8. To develop earnestness, to feel enthusiastic, act enthusiastic. Stand tall, look straight at your audience. Use emphatic gestures.
9. Above all else, open your mouth and speak so you can be heard. Many speakers cannot be heard thirty feet away.
10. When a country minister asked Henry Ward Beecher what to do when an audience went to sleep on a hot Sunday afternoon, Beecher replied, "Have an usher get a sharp stick and prod the preacher." This is one of the best bits of advice ever given on the art of public speaking.
11. Don't weaken your speech with "weasel" words, such as "it seems to me," "in my humble opinion."
12. Love your audience.

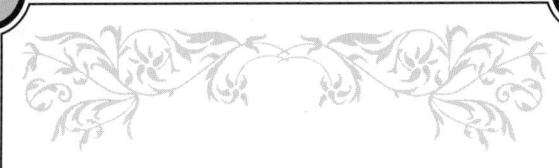

# CHAPTER SIX

# ESSENTIAL ELEMENTS IN SUCCESSFUL SPEAKING

"I never allow myself to become discouraged under any circumstances... The three great essentials to achieve anything worth while are, first, hard work; second, stick-to-itiveness, third, common sense."
—Thomas A. Edison.

"Much good work is lost for the lack of a little more."—E. H. Harriman.

"Never despair, but, if you do, work on in despair."—Edmund Burke.

"Patience is the best remedy for every trouble."
—Plautus, 225 B. C.

"Let patience have her perfect work."
—Favorite motto of Dr. Russell H. Conwell.

"They can conquer who believe they can.... He has not learned the first lesson of life who does not every day surmount a fear."—Emerson.

"Victory is will."—Napoleon.

# ESSENTIAL ELEMENTS IN SUCCESSFUL SPEAKING

The day these lines are written, January 5th, is the anniversary of the death of Sir Ernest Shackleton. He died while steaming southward on the good ship "Quest" to explore the Antarctic. The first thing that attracted one's eyes on going aboard the "Quest" were these lines engraved on a brass plate:

"If you can dream and not make dreams your master;
If you can think and not make thoughts your aim;
If you can meet with triumph and disaster;
And treat those two imposters just the same,

If you can force your heart, and nerve, and sinew
To serve your turn long after they are gone;
And so hold on when there is nothing in you
Except the will which says to them,'Hold on,'

If you can fill the unforgiving minute
with sixth seconds' worth of distance run,
Yours is the earth and everything that's in it,
And, what is more, you'll be a man, my son."

"The spirit of the Quest," Shackleton called those verses; and, truly, they are the proper spirit with which a man should start out to reach the South Pole or to gain confidence in public speaking.

But that is not the spirit, I regret to add, in which all men begin the study of public speaking. Years ago, when I first engaged in educational work, I was astounded to learn how large a percentage of students who enrolled in night schools of all sorts grew weary and fainted by the wayside before their goals were attained. The number is both lamentable and amazing. It is a sad commentary on human nature.

This is the sixth lesson of this course, and I know from experience that some of the men who are reading these lines are already growing disheartened because they have not, in six short weeks, conquered their fear of audiences and gained self-confidence. What a pity, for "how poor are they that have not patience. What wound did ever heal but by degrees?"

# THE NECESSITY OF PERSISTENCE

When we start to learn any new thing, like French, or golf, or public speaking, we never advance steadily. We do not improve gradually. We do it by sudden jerks, by abrupt starts. Then we remain stationary a time, or we may even slip back and lose some of the ground we have previously gained. These periods of stagnation, or retrogression, are well known by all psychologists; and they have been named "plateaus in the curve of learning." Students of public speaking will sometimes be stalled for weeks on one of these plateaus. Work as hard as they may, they cannot get off it. The weak ones give up in despair. Those with grit persist, and they find that suddenly, overnight, without their knowing how or why it has happened, they have made great progress. They have lifted from the plateau like an aeroplane. Abruptly they have gotten the knack of the thing. Abruptly they have acquired naturalness and force and confidence in their speaking.

You may always, as we have noted elsewhere in these pages, experience some fleeting fear, some shock, some nervous anxiety the first few moments you face an audience. John Bright felt it to the end of his busy career; so did Gladstone; so did Bishop

Wilberforce; so did a score of other eminent speakers. Even the greatest of the musicians have felt it in spite of their innumerable public appearances. Paderewski always fidgeted nervously with his cuffs immediately before he sat down at the piano. Nordica felt her heart racing. So did Sembrich. So did Emma Eames. But it vanished quickly, all of this audience fear, like a mist in the August sunshine.

Their experience will be yours. If you will but persevere, you will soon eradicate everything but this initial fear; and that will be initial fear, and nothing more. After the first few sentences, you will have control of yourself. You will be speaking with positive pleasure.

## KEEPING EVERLASTINGLY AT IT

One time a young man who aspired to study law, wrote to Lincoln for advice, and Lincoln replied: "If you are resolutely determined to make a lawyer of yourself, the thing is more than half done already······ Always bear in mind that your own resolution to succeed is more important than any other one thing."

Lincoln knew. He had gone through it all. He had never, in his entire life, had more than a total of one year's schooling. And books? Lincoln once said he had walked and borrowed every book within fifty miles of his home. A log fire was usually kept going all night in the cabin. Sometimes he read by the light of that fire. There were cracks between the logs, and Lincoln often kept a book sticking in a crack. As soon as it was light enough to read in the morning, he rolled over on his bed of leaves, rubbed his eyes, pulled out the book and began devouring it.

He walked twenty and thirty miles to hear a speaker and, returning home, he practised his talk everywhere—in the fields, in the woods, before the crowds gathered at Jones' grocery at Gentryville. He joined literary and debating societies in New Salem and Springfield, and practised speaking on the topics of the day much as you are doing now as a member of this course.

A sense of inferiority always troubled him. In the presence of women he was shy and dumb. When he courted Mary Todd he used to sit in the parlor bashful and silent, unable to find words, listening while she did the talking. Yet that was the man who, by practise and home study, made himself into the speaker who debated with the accomplished orator, Senator Douglas. That was the man who, at Gettysburg, and again in his second inaugural address, rose to heights of eloquence that have rarely been attained in all the annals of mankind.

Small wonder that, in view of his own terrific handicaps and pitiful struggle, he wrote: "If you are resolutely determined to make a lawyer out of yourself, the thing is more than half done already."

There is an excellent picture of Abraham Lincoln in the President's office. "Often when I had some matter to decide," said Theodore Roosevelt, "something involved and difficult to dispose of, something where there were conflicting rights and interests, I would look up at Lincoln, try to imagine him in my place, try to figure out what he would do in the same circumstances. It may sound odd to you, but, frankly, it seemed to make my troubles easier of solution."

Why not try Roosevelt's plan? Why not, if you are discouraged and feeling like giving up the fight to make a speaker of yourself, why not pull out of your pocket one of the five dollar bills that bear a likeness of Lincoln, and ask yourself what he would do under the circumstances. You know what he would do. You know what he did do. After he had been beaten by Stephen A. Douglas in the race for the U. S. Senate, he admonished his followers not to "give up after one nor one hundred defeats."

## THE CERTAINTY OF REWARD

How I wish I could get you to prop this book open on your breakfast table every morning for a week until you had memorized these words from Professor William James, the famous Harvard psychologist:

"Let no youth have any anxiety about the upshot of his education, whatever the line of it may be. If he keeps faithfully busy each hour of the working day, he may safely leave the final result to itself. He can, with perfect certainty, count on waking up some fine morning to find himself one of the competent ones of his generation, in whatever pursuit he may have singled out."

And now, with the renowned Professor James to fall back upon, I shall go so far as to say that if you pursue this course faithfully and with enthusiasm, and keep right on practising intelligently, you may confidently hope to wake up one fine morning and find yourself one of the competent speakers of your city or community.

Regardless of how fantastic that may sound to you

now, *it is true as a general principle*. Exceptions, of course, there are. A man with an inferior mentality and personality, and with nothing to talk about, is not going to develop into a local Daniel Webster; but, *within reason*, the assertion is correct.

Let me illustrate by a concrete example:

Former Governor Stokes of New Jersey attended the closing banquet of a public speaking class at Trenton. He remarked that the talks that he had heard the students make that evening were as good as the speeches that he had heard in the House of Representatives and Senate at Washington. Those Trenton speeches were made by business men who had been tongue-tied with audience-fear a few months previously. They were not incipient Ciceros, those New Jersey business men; they were typical of the business men one finds in any American city. Yet they woke up one fine morning to find themselves among the competent speakers of their city.

The entire question of your success as a speaker hinges upon only two things—your native ability, and the depth and strength of your desires.

"In almost any subject," said Professor James, "your passion for the subject will save you. If you only care enough for a result, you will most certainly attain it. If you wish to be rich, you will be rich; if you wish to be learned, you will be learned; if you wish to be good, you will be good. Only you must, then, *really* wish these things and wish them with exclusiveness, and not wish at the same time a hundred other incompatible things just as strongly."

And Professor James might have added, with equal truth, "If you want to be a confident public speaker, you will be a confident public speaker. But you must *really* wish it."

I have known and carefully watched literally thousands of men trying to gain self-confidence and the ability to talk in public. Those that succeeded were, in only a few instances, men of unusual brilliancy. For the most part, they were the ordinary run of business men that you will find in your own home town. But they kept on. Smarter men sometimes got discouraged or too deeply immersed in money making, and they did not get very far; but the ordinary individual with grit and singleness of purpose—at the end of the chapter, he was at the top.

That is only human and natural. Don't you see the same thing occurring all the time in commerce and the professions? Rockefeller said some time ago that the first essential for success in business was patience. It is likewise one of the first essentials for success in this course.

Marshal Foch led to victory by far the greatest army the world has ever seen, and he declared that he had only one virtue: never despairing.

When the French had retreated to the Marne in 1914, General Joffre instructed the generals under him in charge of two million men to stop retreating and begin an offensive. This new battle, one of the most decisive in the world's history, had raged for two days when General Foch, in command of Joffre's center, sent him one of the most impressive messages in military records: "My center gives way. My right recedes. The situation is excellent. I shall attack."

That attack saved Paris,

So, my dear speaker, when the fight seems hardest and most hopeless, when your center gives way and your right recedes, "the situation is excellent." Attack! Attack! Attack, and you will save the best part of your manhood—your courage and faith.

## CLIMBING THE "WILD KAISER"

A few summers ago, I started out to scale a peak in

the Austrian Alps called the *Wilder Kaiser*. Baedeker said that the ascent was difficult, and a guide was essential for amateur climbers. We, a friend and I, had none, and we were certainly amateurs; so a third party asked us if we thought we were going to succeed. "Of course," we replied.

"What makes you think so?" he inquired.

"Others have done it without guides," I said, "so I know it is within reason, and *I never undertake anything thinking defeat*."

As an Alpinist, I am the merest, bungling novice; but that is the proper psychology for anything from essaying public speaking to an assault on Mount Everest.

*Think success* in this course. See yourself in your imagination talking in public with perfect self-control.

*It is easily in your power to do this. Believe that you will succeed. Believe it firmly and you will then do what is necessary to bring success about.*

Admiral Dupont gave half a dozen excellent reasons why he had not taken his gunboats into Charleston harbor. Admiral Farragut listened intently to the recital. "But there was another reason that you have not mentioned," he replied.

"What is that?" questioned Admiral Dupont.

The answer came: "You did not believe you could do it."

The most valuable thing that most members acquire from a course in public speaking is an increased confidence in themselves, an additional faith in their ability to achieve. And than that, what is more important for one's success in almost any undertaking?

## THE WILL TO WIN

Here is a bit of sage advice from Elbert Hubbard that I cannot refrain from quoting. If the average man would only apply and live the wisdom contained in it, he would be happier, more prosperous:

"Whenever you go out of doors, draw the chin in, carry the crown of the head high and fill the lungs to the utmost; drink in the sunshine; greet your friends with a smile and put soul into every handclasp. Do not fear being misunderstood and do not waste a minute thinking about your enemies. Try to fix firmly in your mind what you would like to do, and then, without veering of direction, you will move straight to the goal. Keep your mind on the great and splendid things you would like to do, and then, as the days go gliding by, you will find yourself unconsciously seizing upon the opportunities that are required for the fulfillment of your desire, just as the coral insect takes from the running tide the elements it needs. Picture in your mind the able, earnest, useful person you desire to be, and the thought you hold is hourly transforming you into that particular individual……Thought is supreme. Preserve a right mental attitude—the attitude of courage, frankness and good cheer. To think rightly is to create. All things come through desire and every sincere prayer is answered. We become like that on which our hearts are fixed. Carry your chin in and the crown of your head high. We are gods in the chrysalis."

Napoleon, Wellington, Lee, Grant, Foch—all great military leaders have recognized that an army's will to win and its confidence in its ability to win, do more than any other one thing to determine its success.

"Ninety thousand conquered men," says Marshall Foch, "retire before ninety thousand conquering men only because they have had enough, because they no longer believe in victory, because they are demoralized—at the end of their moral resistance."

In other words, the ninety thousand retiring men are not really whipped physically; but they are conquered because they are whipped mentally, because they have lost their courage and confidence. There is no hope for an army like that. There is no hope for a man like that.

Chaplain Frazier, the ranking chaplain of the U.S, Navy, interviewed those who wished to enlist for the chaplaincy service during the World War. When asked what qualities were essential for the success of a navy chaplain, he replied with four *G's*: "Grace, gumption, grit, and *guts*."

Those are also the requisites for success in speaking. Take them as your motto. Take this Robert Service poem as your battle song:

"When you're lost in the wild, and you're scared as a child,
And death looks you bang in the eye.
And you're sore as a boil, it's according to Hoyle
To cock your revolver and ······ die.
But the code of a man, says: 'Fight all you can,'
And self-dissolution is barred.
In hunger and woe, oh, it's easy to blow ······
It's the hell-served-for-breakfast that's hard.

You're sick of the game! 'Well, now, that's a shame.'
You're young and you're brave and you're bright.
'You've had a raw deal!' I know —but don't squeal.

Buck up, do your damnedest, and fight.
It's the plugging away that will win you the day,
So don't be a piker, old pard!
Just draw on your grit; it's so easy to quit:
It's the keeping-your-chin-up that's hard.

It's easy to cry that you're beaten—and die.
It's easy to crawfish and crawl;
But to fight and to fight when hope's out of sight,
Why, that's the best game of them all!
And though you come out of each gruelling bout
All broken and beaten and scarred,
Just have one more try—it's dead easy to die,
It's the keeping-on-living that's hard."

## SUMMARY

1. We never learn anything—be it golf, French, or public speaking— by means of gradual improvement. We advance by sudden jerks and abrupt starts. Then we may remain stationary for a few weeks, or even lose some of the proficiency we have gained. Psychologists call these periods of stagnation "plateaus in the curve of learning."

We may strive hard for a long time and not be able to get off one of these "plateaus" and onto an upward ascent again. Some men, not realizing this curious fact about the way we progress, get discouraged on these plateaus and abandon all effort. That is extremely regrettable, for if they were to persist, if they were to keep on practising, they would suddenly find that they had lifted like an aeroplane and made tremendous progress again overnight.

2. You may never be able to speak without some nervous anxiety just before you begin. Bright, Gladstone, Bishop Wilberforce, to the end of their careers, experienced some initial nervousness. But, if you will persevere, you will soon eradicate everything but this initial fear; and, after you have spoken for a few seconds, that too will disappear.

3. Professor James has pointed out that one need have no anxiety about the upshot of his education, that if he keeps faithfully busy, "he can, with perfect certainty, count on waking up some fine morning to find himself one of the competent ones of his generation, in whatever pursuit he may have singled out." This psychological truth that the famous sage of Harvard has enunciated, applies to

you and your efforts in learning to speak. There can be no question about that. The men who have succeeded in this course have not been, as a general rule, men of extraordinary ability. But they were endowed with persistence and dogged determination. They kept on. They arrived.

4. Think success in your public speaking work. You will then do the things necessary to bring success about.
5. If you get discouraged, try Roosevelt's plan of looking at Lincoln's picture and asking yourself what he would have done under similar circumstances.
6. The ranking chaplain of the U. S. Navy during the world war said that the qualities essential for the success of a chaplain in the service could be enumerated with four words commencing with *G*. What are they?

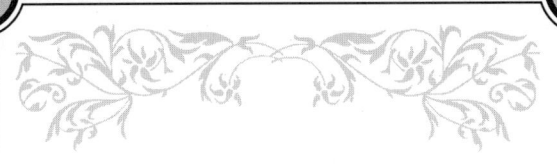

# CHAPTER SEVEN

# THE SECRET OF GOOD DELIVERY

"Know the fact—hug the fact. For the essential thing is heat, and heat comes from sincerity." —Emerson.

"It is necessary to have something more than knowledge of the subject. You must have earnestness in its presentation. You must feel that you have something to say that people ought to hear." —Bryan.

"Let the counsel of thine own heart stand, for no man is more faithful unto thee than it. It is sometimes wont to show thee more than seven watchmen who sit above in a high tower." —Kipling.

"Do one thing at a time, and do that one thing as if your life depended upon it."
—Motto of Eugene Grace, President Bethlehem Steel Company.

CHAPTER 7

## **THE SECRET OF GOOD DELIVERY**

Shortly after the close of the war, I met two brothers in London, Sir Ross and Sir Keith Smith. They had just made the first aeroplane flight from London to Australia, had won the fifty thousand dollar prize offered by the Australian government, had created a sensation throughout the British Empire, and had been knighted by the King.

Captain Hurler, a well-known scenic photographer, had flown with them over a part of their trip, taking motion pictures; so I helped them prepare an illustrated travel talk of their flight and trained them in the delivery of it. They gave it twice daily for four months in Philharmonic Hall, London, one speaking in the afternoon and the other at night.

They had had identically the same experience, had sat side by side as they flew half way around the world; and they delivered the same talk, almost word for word. Yet, somehow it didn't sound like the same talk at all.

There is something besides the mere words in a talk which counts. It is the flavor with which they are delivered. "It is not so much what you say as how you say it."

I once sat beside a young woman at a public concert who was reading, as Paderewski played them, the notes of a Mazurka by Chopin. She was mystified. She couldn't understand. His fingers were touching precisely the same notes that hers had touched when she had played it; yet her rendition had been commonplace, and his was inspired, a thing of surpassing beauty, a performance that held the audience enthralled. It was not the mere notes that he touched; it was the way he touched them, a feeling, an artistry, a personality that he put into the touching that made all the difference between mediocrity and genius.

Brullof, the great Russian painter, once corrected a pupil's study. The pupil looked in amazement at the altered drawing, exclaiming: "Why, you have touched it only a tiny bit, but it is quite another thing." Brullof replied: "Art begins where the tiny bit begins." That is as true of speaking as it is of painting and of Paderewski's playing.

The same thing holds true when one is touching words. There is an old saying in the English Parliament that everything depends upon the manner in which one speaks and not upon the matter, Quintilian said that long ago when England was one of the outlying colonies of Rome.

Like most old sayings, it needs to be taken *cum grano salis*; but good delivery will make very thin matter go a very long way. I have often noticed in college contests that it is not always the speaker with the best material who wins. Rather, it is the speaker who can talk so well that his material sounds best.

"Three things matter in a speech," Lord Morley once observed with gay cynicism, "who says it, how he says it, and what he says—and, of the three, the last matters the least." An exaggeration? Yes, but scratch the surface of it and you will find the truth shining through.

Edmund Burke wrote speeches so excellent in logic and reasoning and composition that they are today studied as classic models of oration in half the colleges of the land; yet Burke, as a speaker, was a notorious failure. He didn't have the ability to deliver his gems, to make them interesting and forceful; so he was called "the dinner bell" of the House of Commons. When he arose to talk, the other members coughed and shuffled and went out in droves.

You can throw a steel-jacketed bullet at a man with all your might, and you cannot make even a dent in his clothing. But put powder behind a tallow candle and you can shoot it through a pine board. Many a tallow-candle speech with powder makes, I regret to say, more of an impression than a steel-jacketed talk with no force behind it.

Look well, therefore, to your delivery.

## WHAT IS DELIVERY?

What does a department store do when it "delivers" the article you have bought? Does the driver just toss the package into the backyard and let it go at that? Is merely getting a thing out of one's own hands the same as getting it delivered? The messenger boy with a telegram delivers the "wire" into the direct possession of the person for whom it is intended. But do all speakers?

Let me give you an illustration that is typical of the fashion in which thousands of men talk. I happened on one occasion to be stopping in Mürren, a summer resort in the Swiss Alps. I was living at a hotel operated by a London company; and they usually sent out from England a couple of lecturers each week to talk to the guests. One of them was a well-known English novelist. Her topic was "The Future of the Novel." She admitted that she had not selected the subject herself; and, the long and short of it was that she had nothing to say about it that she really cared enough about saying to make it worth while expressing. She had hurriedly made some rambling notes; and she stood before the audience, ignoring her hearers, not even looking at them, staring sometimes over their heads, sometimes at her notes, sometimes at the floor. She called off her words into the primeval void with a far-away look in her eyes and a far-away ring in her voice.

That kind of performance isn't delivering a talk at all. It is a soliloquy. It has no sense of communication. And that is the first essential of good talking: *a sense of communication*. The audience must feel that there is a message being delivered straight from the mind and heart of the speaker to their minds and their hearts. The kind of talk I have just described might just as well have been spoken out in the sandy, waterless wastes of the Gobi desert. In fact, it sounded as if it were being delivered in some such spot rather than to a group of living human beings.

This matter of delivering a talk is, at the same time, a very simple and a very intricate process. It is also a very much misunderstood and abused one.

## THE SECRET OF GOOD DELIVERY

An enormous amount of nonsense and twaddle has been written about delivery. It has been shrouded in rules and rites and made mysterious. Old-fashioned "elocution," that abomination in the sight of God and man, has often made it ridiculous. The business man, going to the library or book shop, has found volumes on "oratory" that were utterly useless. In spite of progress in other directions, in almost every state in the Union today, schoolboys are still being forced to recite the ornate "oratory" of Webster and Ingersoll—a thing that is as much out of style and as far removed from the spirit of this age as the hats worn by Mrs. Ingersoll and Mrs. Webster would be if they were resurrected today.

An entirely new school of speaking has sprung up since the Civil War. In keeping with the spirit of the times, it is as modern as the *Saturday Evening Post*, direct as a telegram, businesslike as an auto-mobile advertisement. The verbal fireworks that were once the vogue would no longer be tolerated by an audience in this year of grace.

A modern audience, regardless of whether it is fifteen people at a business conference or a thousand people under a tent, wants the speaker to talk just as directly as he would in a chat, and in the same general manner that he would employ in speaking to one of them in conversation.

In the same *manner*, but not with the same amount of force. If he tries that, he will hardly be heard. In order to appear natural he has to use much more energy in talking to forty people than he does in talking to one; just as a statue on top of a building has to be of heroic size in order to make it appear of lifelike proportions to an observer on the ground.

At the close of Mark Twain's lecture in a Nevada mining camp, an old prospector approached him and inquired: "Be them your natural tones of eloquence?"

That is what the audience wants: "your natural tones of eloquence," enlarged a bit.

Speak to the Chamber of Commerce just as you would to John Henry Smith. What is a meeting of the

Chamber of Commerce, after all, but a mere collection of John Henry Smiths? Won't the same methods that are successful with those men individually be successful with them collectively?

I have just described the delivery of a certain novelist. In the same ballroom in which she had spoken, I had the pleasure, a few nights later, of hearing Sir Oliver Lodge. His subject was "Atoms and Worlds." He had devoted to it more than half a century of thought and study and experiment and investigation. He had something that was essentially a part of his heart and mind and life, something that he wanted very much to say. He forgot—and I, for one, thanked God that he did forget—that he was trying to make a speech. That was the least of his worries. He was concerned only with telling the audience about atoms, telling us accurately and lucidly and feelingly. He was earnestly trying to get us to see what he saw and to feel what he felt.

And what was the result? He delivered a remarkable talk. It had both charm and power. It made a deep impression. He is a speaker of unusual ability. Yet I am sure he doesn't regard himself in that light. I am sure that few people who hear him ever think of him as a public speaker at all.

If you, my dear reader, speak in public so that people hearing you will suspect that you have had training in public speaking, you will not be a credit to your instructor. He desires you to speak with such intensified and exalted naturalness that your auditors will never dream that you have been trained. A good window does not call attention to itself. It merely lets in the light. A good speaker is like that. He is so natural that his hearers never notice his manner of speaking; they are conscious only of his matter.

## HENRY FORD'S ADVICE

"All Fords are exactly alike," their maker used to say, "but no two men are just alike. Every new life is a new thing under the sun; there has never been anything just like it before, and never will be again. A young man ought to get that idea about himself; he should look for the single spark of individuality that makes him different from other folks, and develop that for all he is worth. Society and schools may try to iron it out of him; their tendency is to put us all in the same mould, but I say don't let that spark be lost it's your only real claim to importance."

All that is doubly true of public speaking. There is

no other human being in the world like you. Hundreds of millions of people have two eyes and a nose and a mouth; but none of them look precisely like you; and none of them have exactly your traits and methods and cast of mind. Few of them will talk and express themselves just as you do when you are speaking naturally. In other words, you have an individuality. As a speaker, it is your most precious possession. Cling to it. Cherish it. Develop it. It is the spark that will put force and sincerity into your speaking. "It is your only real claim to importance."

Sir Oliver Lodge speaks differently from other men, because he himself is different. The man's manner of speaking is as essentially a part of his own individuality as are his beard and bald head. If he had tried to imitate Lloyd George, he would have been false, he would have failed.

The most famous debates ever held in America took place in 1858 in the prairie towns of Illinois between Senator Stephen A. Douglas and Abraham Lincoln. Lincoln was tall and awkward. Douglas was short and graceful. These men were as unlike in their characters and mentality and personalities and dispositions as they were in their physiques.

Douglas was the cultured man of the world. Lincoln

was the rail splitter who went to the front door in his sock feet to receive company. Douglas' gestures were graceful. Lincoln's were ungainly. Douglas was utterly destitute of humor. Lincoln was one of the greatest story tellers who ever lived. Douglas seldom used a simile. Lincoln constantly argued by analogy and illustration. Douglas was haughty and overbearing. Lincoln was humble and forgiving. Douglas thought in quick flashes. Lincoln's mental processes were much slower. Douglas spoke with the impetuous rush of a whirlwind. Lincoln was quieter and deeper and more deliberate.

Both of these men, unlike as they were, were able speakers because they had the courage and good sense to be themselves. If either had tried to imitate the other, he would have failed miserably. But each one, by using to the utmost his own peculiar talents, made himself individual and powerful. *Go thou and do likewise*.

That is an easy direction to give. But is it an easy one to follow? Most emphatically it is not. As Marshal Foch said of the art of war: "It is simple enough in its conception, but unfortunately complicated in its execution."

It takes practise to be natural before an audience.

Actors know that. When you were a little boy, four years old, you probably could, had you but tried, have mounted a platform and "recited" naturally to an audience. But when you are twenty-and-four, or forty-and-four, what will happen if you mount a platform and start to speak? Will you retain that unconscious naturalness that you possessed at four? You may, but it is dollars to doughnuts that you will become stiff and stilted and mechanical, and draw back into your shell like a snapping turtle.

The problem of teaching or of training men in delivery is not one of superimposing additional characteristics; it is largely one of removing impediments, of freeing men, of getting them to speak with the same naturalness that they would display if some one were to knock them down.

Hundreds of times I have stopped speakers in the midst of their talks and implored them to "talk like a human being." Hundreds of nights I have come home mentally fatigued and nervously exhausted from trying to drill and force men to talk naturally. No, believe me, it is not so easy as it sounds.

And the only way under high Heaven by which you can get the knack of this enlarged naturalness is by practise. And, as you practise, if you find yourself talking in a stilted manner, pause and say sharply to yourself mentally: "Here! What is wrong? Wake up. Be human." Then pick out some man in the audience, some man in the back, the dullest looking chap you can find, and talk to him. Forget there is anyone else present at all. *Converse* with him. Imagine that he has asked you a question and that you are answering it. If he were to stand up and talk to you, and you were to talk back to him, that process would immediately and inevitably make your talking more conversational, more natural, more direct. So, imagine that that is precisely what is taking place.

You may go so far as actually to ask questions and answer them. For example, in the midst of your talk, you may say, "and you ask what proof have I for this assertion? I have adequate proof and here it is ……" Then proceed to answer the imaginary question. That sort of thing can be done very naturally. It will break up the monotony of one's delivery; it will make it direct and pleasant and conversational.

Sincerity and enthusiasm and high earnestness will help you, too. When a man is under the influence of his feelings, his real self comes to the surface. The bars are down. The heat of his emotions has burned all barriers away. He acts spontaneously. He talks spontaneously, He is natural.

So, in the end, even this matter of delivery comes back to the thing which has already been emphasized repeatedly in these pages: namely, put your heart in your talks.

"I shall never forget," said Dean Brown in his lectures on Preaching before the Yale Divinity School, "the description given by a friend of mine of a service which he once attended in the city of London. The preacher was George MacDonald. He read for the Scripture lesson that morning the eleventh Chapter of Hebrews. When the time came for the sermon, he said: 'You have all heard about these men of faith. I shall not try to tell you what faith is. There are theological professors who could do that much better than I could do it. I am here to help you believe.' Then followed such a simple, heartfelt and majestic manifestation of the man's own faith in those unseen realities which are eternal, as to beget faith in the minds and hearts of all his hearers. *His heart was in his work, and his delivery was effective because it rested back upon the genuine beauty of his own inner life.*"

"His heart was in his work." That is the secret. Yet I know that advice like this is not popular. It seems vague. It sounds indefinite. The average student wants foolproof rules. Something definite. Something he can put his hands on. Rules as precise as the directions for operating a Ford.

That is what he wants. That is what I would like to give him. It would be easy for him. It would be easy for me. There are such rules, and, there is only one little thing wrong with them: they don't work. They take all the naturalness and spontaneity and life and juice out of a man's speaking. I know. In my younger days I wasted a great deal of energy trying them. They won't appear in these pages for, as Josh Billings observed in one of his lighter moments: "There ain't no use in knowin' so many things that ain't so."

## DO YOU DO THESE THINGS WHEN YOU TALK IN PUBLIC?

We are going to discuss here some of the features of natural speaking in order to make them more clear, more vivid. I have hesitated about doing it, for someone is almost sure to say: "Ah, I see, just force myself to do these things and I'll be all right." No, you won't. *Force* yourself to do them and you will be all wooden and all mechanical.

You used most of these principles yesterday in your

conversation, used them as unconsciously as you digested your dinner last night. That is the way to use them. It is the *only* way. And it will come, as far as public speaking is concerned, as we have already said, only by practise.

## FIRST: STRESS IMPORTANT WORDS, SUBORDINATE UNIMPORTANT ONES

In conversation, we hit one syllable in a word, and hit it hard, and hurry over the others like a pay car passing a string of hoboes; e.g., MassaCHUsetts, afFLICtion, atTRACtiveness, enVIRonment. We do almost the same thing with a sentence. We make one or two important words tower up like the Woolworth skyscraper on lower Broadway.

This is not a strange or unusual process I am describing. Listen. You can hear it going on about you all the time. You yourself did it a hundred, maybe a thousand, times yesterday. You will doubtless do it a hundred times tomorrow.

Here is an example. Read the following quotation, striking the words in big type hard. Run over the others quickly. What is the effect?

"I have SUCCEEDED in whatever I have undertaken, because I have WILLED it. I have NEVER HESITATED which has given me an ADVANTAGE over the rest of mankind."—Napoleon.

This is not the only way to read these lines. Another speaker would do it differently perhaps. There are no ironclad rules for emphasis. It all depends.

Read these selections aloud in an earnest manner, trying to make the ideas clear and convincing. Don't you find yourself stressing the big, important words and hurrying over the others?

"If you think you are beaten, you are.
If you think you dare not, you don't.
If you'd like to win, but think you can't,
It's almost a cinch you won't.
Life's battles don't always go
To the stronger or faster man
But soon or late the man who wins
Is the one who thinks he can." —Anon.

"Perhaps there is no more important component of character than steadfast resolution. The boy who is going to make a great man, or is going to count in any way in afterlife, must make up his mind not merely to overcome a thousand obstacles, but to win in spite of a thousand repulse and defeats."—Theodore Roosevelt.

## SECOND: CHANGE YOUR PITCH

The pitch of our voices in conversation flows up and down the scale from high to low and back again, never resting, but always shifting like the face of the sea. Why? No one knows, and no one cares. The effect is pleasing, and it is the way of nature. We never had to learn to do this: it came to us as children, unsought and unaware, but let us stand up and face an audience, and the chances are our voices will become as dull and flat and monotonous as the alkali deserts of Nevada.

When you find yourself talking in a monotonous pitch—and usually it will be a high one—just pause for a second and say to yourself: "I am speaking like a wooden Indian. *Talk* to these people. Be human. Be natural."

Will that kind of lecture to yourself help you any? A little, perhaps. The pause itself will help you. You have to work out your own salvation by practice.

You can make any phrase or word that you choose stand out like a green hay tree in the front yard by either suddenly lowering or raising your pitch on it. Dr. Cadman, the famous Congregational minister of Brooklyn, often did it. So does Sir Oliver Lodge. So did Bryan. So did Roosevelt. So does almost every speaker of note.

In the following quotations, try saying the italicized words in a much lower pitch than you use for the rest of the sentence. What is the effect?

"I have but one merit, that of *never despairing*."
—Marshal Foch.

"The great aim of education is not knowledge, but action."—Herbert Spencer.

"I have lived eighty-six years. I have watched men climb up to success, hundreds of them, and of all the elements that are important for success, the most important is faith."—Cardinal Gibbons.

## THIRD: VARY YOUR RATE OF SPEAKING

When a little child talks, or when we talk in ordinary conversation, we *constantly change our rate of speaking*. It is pleasing. It is natural. It is unconscious. It is emphatic. It is, in fact, one of the very best of all possible ways to make an idea stand out prominently.

Walter B. Stevens, in his *Reporter's Lincoln*, issued by the Missouri Historical Society, tells us that this was one of Lincoln's favorite methods of driving a point home:

"He would speak several words with great rapidity, come to the word or phrase he wished to emphasize, and let his voice linger and bear hard on that, and then he would rush to the end of his sentence like lightning…… He would devote as much time to the word or two he wished to emphasize as he did to half a dozen less important words following it."

Such a method invariably arrests attention. To illustrate: I have often quoted in a public talk the following statement by Cardinal Gibbons. I wanted to emphasize the idea of courage; so I lingered on these italicized words, drew them out and spoke as if I, myself, were impressed with them—and I was. Will you please read the selection aloud, trying the same method and note the results.

"A short time before his death, Cardinal Gibbons said: 'I have lived *eighty-six* years. I have watched men *climb* up to *success*, *hundreds* of them, and of all the elements that are *important* for success, the *most important* is *faith. No great thing comes to any man unless he has courage.*'"

Try this: say "thirty million dollars" quickly and with an air of triviality so that it sounds like a very small sum. Now, say "thirty thousand dollars" say it slowly; say it feelingly; say it as if you were tremendously impressed with the hugeness of the amount. Haven't you now made the thirty thousand sound larger than the thirty million?

## FOURTH: PAUSE BEFORE AND AFTER IMPORTANT IDEAS

Lincoln often paused in his speaking. When he had come to a big idea that he wished to impress deeply on the minds of his hearers, he bent forward, looked directly into their eyes for a moment and said nothing at all. This sudden silence had the same effect as a sudden noise: it attracted notice. It made everyone attentive, alert, awake to what was coming next. For example, when his famous debates with Douglas were drawing to a close, when all the indications pointed to his defeat, he became depressed, his old habitual melancholy stealing over him at times, and imparting to his words a touching pathos. In one of his concluding speeches, he suddenly *"stopped and stood silent for a moment*, looking around upon the throng of half-indifferent, half-friendly faces before him, with those deep-sunken weary eyes that always seemed full of unshed tears. Folding his hands, as if they too were tired of the helpless fight, he said, in his peculiar monotone: 'My friends, it makes little difference, very little difference, whether Judge Douglas or myself is elected to the United States Senate; but the great issue which we have submitted to you today is far above and beyond any personal interests or the political fortunes of any man. And my friends,' here he paused again, and the audience were intent on every word, 'that issue will live and breathe and burn when the poor, feeble, stammering tongues of Judge Douglas and myself are silent in the grave.'"

"These simple words," relates one of his biographers, "and the manner in which they were spoken, touched every heart to the core."

Lincoln also paused after the phrase he wanted to emphasize. He added to their force by keeping silent while the meaning sank in and effected its mission.

Sir Oliver Lodge pauses frequently in his speaking, both before and after important ideas pauses as often as three or four times in one sentence, but he does it naturally and unconsciously. No man, unless he were analyzing Sir Oliver's methods, would notice it.

"By your silence," says Kipling, "ye shall speak," Nowhere is silence more golden than when it is judiciously used in talking. It is a powerful tool, too important to be ignored, yet it is usually neglected by the beginning speaker.

In the following excerpt from Holman's *Ginger Talks*, I have marked the places where a speaker might profitably pause. I do not say that these are the *only* places where one ought to pause, or even the best places. I say only that it is one way of doing it. Where to pause is not a matter of hard and fast rules. It is a matter of meaning and temperament and feeling. You might pause one place in a speech today, and in another place in the same speech tomorrow.

Read this selection aloud without pausing then read it again, making the pauses I have indicated. What is the effect of the pauses?

"Selling goods is a battle" (pause and let the idea of *battle* soak in) "and only fighters can win in it." (Pause and let that point soak in.) "We may not like these conditions, but we didn't have the making of them and we can't alter them." (Pause.) "Take your courage with you when you enter the selling game." (Pause.) "If you don't," (pause and lengthen out suspense for a second) "you'll strike out every time you come to bat, and score nothing higher than a string of goose eggs." (Pause.) "No man ever made a three-base hit who was afraid of the pitcher" (pause and let your point soak in)—"remember that." (Pause and let it soak in some more.) "The fellow who knocks the cover off the ball or lifts it over the fence for a home run is always the chap who steps up to the plate" (pause and increase the suspense as to what you are going to say about this extraordinary player) "with grim determination in his heart."

Read the following quotations aloud and with force and meaning. Observe where you naturally pause.

"The great American desert is not located in Idaho, New Mexico or Arizona. It is located under the hat of the average man. The great American desert is a mental desert rather than a physical desert."—J. S. Knox.

"There is no panacea for human ills; the nearest approach to it is publicity."—Professor Foxwell.

"There are two people I must please—God and Garfield. I must live with Garfield here, with God hereafter."—James A. Garfield.

A speaker may follow the directions I have set down in this lesson and still have a hundred faults. He may talk in public just as he does in conversation and consequently, he may speak with an unpleasant voice and make grammatical errors and be awkward and offensive and do a score of unpleasant things. A man's natural method of everyday talking may need a vast number of improvements. Perfect your natural method of talking in conversation, and then carry that method to the platform.

## SUMMARY

1. There is something besides the mere words in a talk which counts. It is the flavor with which they are delivered. "It is not so much what you say as how you say it."
2. Many speakers ignore their hearers, stare over their heads or at the floor. They seem to be delivering a soliloquy. There is no sense of communication, no give and take between the audience and the speaker. That kind of attitude would kill a conversation; it also kills a speech.
3. Good delivery is conversational tone and

directness enlarged. Talk to the Chamber of Commerce just as you would to John Smith. What is the Chamber of Commerce, after all, but a collection of John Smiths?

4. Every man has the ability to deliver a talk. If you question this statement, try it out for yourself; knock down the most ignorant man you know; when he gets on his feet, he will probably say some things, and his manner of saying them will be almost flawless. We want you to take that same naturalness with you when you speak in public. To develop it, you must practise. Don't imitate others. If you speak spontaneously you will speak differently from anyone else in the world. Put your own individuality, your own characteristic manner into your delivery.

5. Talk to your hearers just as if you expected them to stand up in a moment and talk back to you. If they were to rise and ask you questions, your delivery would almost be sure to improve emphatically and at once. So *imagine* that someone has asked you a question, and that you are repeating it. Say aloud, "You ask how do I know this? I'll tell you," ······ That sort of thing will seem perfectly natural; it will break up the

formality of your phraseology; it will warm and humanize your manner of talking.

6. Put your heart into your talking. Real emotional sincerity will help more than all the rules in Christendom.

7. Here are four things that all of us do unconsciously in earnest conversation. But do you do them when you are talking in public? Most people do not.

   a. Do you stress the important words in a sentence and subordinate the unimportant ones? Do you give almost every word including *the, and, but,* approximately the same amount of attention, or do you speak a sentence in much the same way that you say MassaCHUsetts?

   b. Does the pitch of your voice flow up and down the scale from high to low and back again—as the pitch of a little child does when speaking?

   c. Do you vary your rate of speaking, running rapidly over the unimportant words, spending more time on the ones you wish to make stand out?

   d. Do you pause before and after your important ideas?

# CHAPTER EIGHT

# PLATFORM PRESENCE AND PERSONALITY

"Action is eloquence, and the eyes of the ignorant are more learned than their ears."—Shakespeare.

"Too little gesture is as unnatural as too much. It is strange that the happy medium is so rarely observed, considering that every child is an illustration of its proper use, and that we may see examples of it in almost every man that talks to his neighbor on the street."—Matthews, Oratory and Orators.

"When you speak, forget action entirely. Concentrate your attention on what you have to say and why you want to say it. Put all the fire and spirit of your being into the expression of your thought. Be enthusiastic, sincere, deadly earnest. Some action is bound to result. Your restraints will be broken down if you make the inner thought-urge strong enough. Your body will respond with some kind of expressive action. In all your actual speaking, think only of what you want to say. Do not plan your gestures in advance. Let the natural urge determine the action."
—George Rowland Collins, Platform Speaking.

# CHAPTER 8

# PLATFORM PRESENCE AND PERSONALITY

The Carnegie Institute of Technology at one time gave intelligence tests to one hundred prominent business men. The tests were similar to those used in the army during the war; and the results led the Institute to declare that personality contributes more to business success than does superior intelligence.

That is a very significant pronouncement: very significant for the business man, very significant for the educator, very significant for the professional man, very significant for the speaker.

Personality—with the exception of preparation—is probably the most important factor in public address. "In eloquent speaking," declared Elbert Hubbard, "it is manner that wins, not words." Rather it is manner plus ideas. But personality is a vague and elusive thing, defying analysis like the perfume of the violet. It is the whole combination of the man, the physical, the spiritual, the mental; his traits, his predilections, his tendencies, his temperament, his cast of mind, his vigor, his experience, his training, his life. It is as complex as Einstein's theory of relativity, almost as little understood.

A man's personality is very largely the result of his inheritances. It is largely determined before birth. True, his later environment has something to do with it. But, all in all, it is an extremely difficult factor to alter or improve. Yet we can, by taking thought, strengthen it to some extent and make it more forceful, more attractive. At any rate, we can strive to get the utmost possible out of this strange thing that nature has given us. The subject is of vast importance to every one of us. The possibilities for improvement, limited as they are, are still large enough to warrant a discussion and investigation.

If you wish to make the most of your individuality, go before your audience rested. A tired man is not magnetic nor attractive. Don't make the all-too-common error of putting off your preparation and your planning until the very last moment, and then working at a furious pace, trying to make up for lost time. If you do, you are bound to store up bodily poisons and brain fatigues that will prove terrific drags, holding you down, sapping your vitality, weakening both your brain and your nerves.

If you must make an important talk to a committee meeting at four, do not, if you can well avoid it, come back to the office after lunch. Go home, if possible, have a light lunch and the refreshment of a siesta. Rest—that is what you need, physical and mental and nervous.

Geraldine Farrar used to shock her newly made friends by saying good night and retiring early, leaving them to talk the remainder of the evening with her husband. She knew the demands of her art.

Madame Nordica said that being a prima donna meant giving up everything one liked: social affairs, friends, tempting meals.

When you have to make an important talk, beware of your hunger. Eat as sparingly as a saint. On Sunday afternoons, Henry Ward Beecher used to have crackers and milk at five, and nothing after that.

"When I am singing in the evening," said Madame Melba, "I do not dine but have a very light repast at five o'clock, consisting of either fish, chicken, or sweetbread, with a baked apple and a glass of water. I always find myself very hungry for supper when I get home from the opera or concert."

How wisely Melba and Beecher acted, I never realized until after I became a professional speaker myself and tried to deliver a two-hour talk each evening after having consumed a hearty meal. Experience taught me that I couldn't enjoy a *filet de sole aux pommes nature* and follow that by a beefsteak and French fried potatoes and salad and vegetables and a dessert, and then stand up an hour afterwards and do either myself or my subject or my body justice. The blood that ought to have been in my brain was down in my stomach wrestling with that steak and potatoes. Paderewski was right: he said when he ate what he wanted to eat before a concert, the animal in him got uppermost, that it even got into his finger tips and clogged and dulled his playing.

## WHY ONE SPEAKER DRAWS BETTER THAN ANOTHER

Do nothing to dull your energy. It is magnetic. Vitality, aliveness, enthusiasm: they are among the first qualities I have always sought for in employing speakers and instructors of speaking. People cluster around the energetic speaker, the human dynamo of energy, like wild geese around a field of autumn wheat.

I have often seen this illustrated by the open air speakers in Hyde Park, London. A spot near Marble Arch entrance is a rendezvous for speakers of every creed and color. On a Sunday afternoon, one can take his choice and listen to a Catholic explaining the doctrine of the infallibility of the Pope, to a Socialist propounding the economic gospel of Karl Marx, to an Indian explaining why it is right and proper for a Mohammedan to have four wives, and so on. Hundreds crowd about one speaker, while his neighbor has only a handful. Why? Is the topic always an adequate explanation of the disparity between the drawing powers of different speakers? No. More often the explanation is to be found in the speaker himself: he is more interested and, consequently, interesting. He talks with more life and spirit. He radiates vitality and animation; they always challenge attention.

## HOW ARE YOU AFFECTED BY CLOTHES?

An inquiry was sent to a large group of people by a psychologist and university president, asking them the impression clothes made on them. All but unanimously, they testified that when they were well groomed and faultlessly and immaculately attired, the knowledge of it, the feeling of it, had an effect which, while it was difficult to explain, was still very definite, very real. It gave them more confidence; brought them increased faith in themselves; heightened their self-respect. They declared that when they had the look of success they found it easier to think success, to achieve success. Such is the effect of clothes on the wearer himself.

What effect do they have on an audience? I have noticed time and again that if a speaker has baggy trousers, shapeless coat and footwear, fountain pen and pencils peeping out of his breast pocket, a newspaper or a pipe and can of tobacco bulging out the sides of his garment—I have noticed that an audience has as little respect for that man as he has for his own appearance. Aren't they very likely to assume that his mind is as sloppy as his unkempt hair and unpolished shoes?

## ONE OF THE REGRETS OF GRANT'S LIFE

When General Lee came to Appomattox Court House to surrender his army, he was immaculately attired in a new uniform and, at his side, hung a sword of extraordinary value. Grant was coatless, swordless, and was wearing the shirt and trousers of a private. "I must have contrasted very strangely," he wrote in his Memoirs, "with a man so handsomely dressed, six feet high, and of faultless form." The fact that he had not been appropriately attired for this historic occasion came to be one of the real regrets of Grant's life.

The Department of Agriculture in Washington has several hundred stands of bees on its experimental farm. Each hive has a large magnifying glass built into it, and the interior can be flooded with electric light by pressing a button; so, any moment, night or day, these bees are liable to be subject to the minutest scrutiny. A speaker is like that: he is under the magnifying glass, he is in the spotlight, all eyes are upon him. The smallest disharmony in his personal appearance now looms up like Pike's Peak from the plains.

## "EVEN BEFORE WE SPEAK, WE ARE CONDEMNED OR APPROVED"

A number of years ago I was writing for the *American Magazine* the life story of a certain New York banker. I asked one of his friends to explain the reason for his success. No small amount of it, he said, was due to the man's winning smile. At first thought, that may sound like exaggeration but I believe it is really true. Other men, scores of them, hundreds of them, may have had more experience and as good financial judgment, but he had an additional asset they didn't possess—he had a most agreeable personality. And a warm, welcoming smile was one of the striking features of it. It gained one's confidence immediately. It secured one's good will instantly. We all want to see a man like that succeed; and it is a real pleasure to give him our patronage.

"He who cannot smile," says a Chinese proverb, "ought not to keep a shop." And isn't a smile just as welcome before an audience as behind a counter? I am thinking now of a particular student who attended a course in public speaking conducted by the Brooklyn Chamber of Commerce. He always came out before the audience with an air that said he liked to be there, that he loved the job that was before him. He always smiled and acted as if he were glad to see us; and so immediately and inevitably his hearers warmed towards him and welcomed him.

But I have seen speakers—students of this course, I regret to admit—who walked out before the other members in a cold, perfunctory manner as if they had a disagreeable task to perform, and that, when it was over, they would thank God. We in the audience were soon feeling the same way. These attitudes are contagious.

"Like begets like," observes Professor Overstreet in *Influencing Human Behavior*. "If we are interested in our audience, there is a likelihood that our audience will be interested in us. If we scowl at our audience, there is every likelihood that inwardly or outwardly they will scowl at us. If we are timid and rather flustered, they likewise will lack confidence in us. If we are brazen and boastful, they will react with their own self-protective egotism. Even before we speak, very often, we are condemned or approved. There is every reason, therefore, that we should make certain that our attitude is such as to elicit warm response."

## CROWD YOUR AUDIENCE TOGETHER

As a public lecturer, I have frequently spoken to a small audience scattered through a large hall in the afternoon, and to a large audience packed into the same hall at night. The evening audience has laughed heartily at the same things that brought only a smile to the faces of the afternoon *group* the evening crowd has applauded generously at the very places where the afternoon gathering was utterly unresponsive. Why?

For one thing, the elderly women and the children that are likely to come in the afternoon cannot be expected to be as demonstrative as the more vigorous and discriminating evening crowd; but that is only a partial explanation.

The fact is that no audience will be easily moved when it is scattered. Nothing so dampens enthusiasm as wide, open spaces and empty chairs between the listeners.

Henry Ward Beecher said in his Yale Lectures on Preaching:

"People often say, 'Do you not think it is much more inspiring to speak to a large audience than a small one?' No, I say; I can speak just as well to twelve persons as to a thousand, provided those twelve are crowded around me and close together, so that they can touch each other. But even a thousand people with four feet of space between every two of them, would be just the same as an empty room⋯⋯ Crowd your audience together and you will set them off with half the effort."

A man in a large audience tends to lose his individuality. He becomes a member of the crowd and is swayed far more easily than he would be as a single individual. He will laugh at and applaud things that would leave him unmoved if he were only one of half a dozen people listening to you.

It is far easier to get people to act as a body than to act singly. Men going into battle, for example, invariably want to do the most dangerous and reckless thing in the world—they want to huddle together. During the late war, German soldiers were known to go into battle at times with their arms locked about one another.

Crowds! Crowds! Crowds! They are a curious phenomenon. All great popular movements and reforms have been carried forward by the aid of the crowd mentality. An interesting book on this subject is Everett Dean Martin's *The Behavior of Crowds*.

If we are going to talk to a small group, we should choose a small room. Better to pack the aisles of a small place than to have people scattered through the lonely, deadening spaces of a large hall.

If your hearers are scattered, ask them to move down front and be seated near you. Insist on this, before you start speaking.

Unless the audience is a fairly large one, and there is a real reason, a necessity, for the speaker standing on a platform, don't do so. Get down on the same level with them. Stand near them. Break up all formality. Get an intimate contact. Make the thing conversational.

## MAJOR POND SMASHED THE WINDOWS

Keep the air fresh. In the well known process of public speaking, oxygen is just as essential as the larynx, pharynx and human epiglottis. All the eloquence of Cicero, and all the feminine pulchritude in Ziegfeld's Follies, could hardly keep an audience awake in a room poisoned with bad air. So, when I am one of a number of speakers, before beginning, I almost always ask the audience to stand up and rest for two minutes while the windows are thrown open.

For fourteen years Major James B. Pond traveled all over the United States and Canada as manager for Henry Ward Beecher when that famous Brooklyn preacher was at his flood tide as a popular lecturer. Before the audience assembled, Pond always visited the hall or church or theater where Beecher was to appear, and rigorously inspected the lighting, seating, temperature and ventilation. Pond had been a blustering, roaring old army officer; he loved to exercise authority; so if the place was too warm or the air was dead and he could not get the windows open, he hurled books through them, smashing and shattering the glass. He believed with Spurge on that "the next best thing to the Grace of God for a preacher is oxygen."

## LET THERE BE LIGHT—ON YOUR FACE

Unless you are demonstrating Spiritualism before a group of people, flood the room, if possible, with lights. It is as easy to domesticate a quail as to develop enthusiasm in a half-lighted room gloomy as the inside of a thermos bottle.

Read David Belasco's articles on stage production, and you will discover that the average speaker does not have the foggiest shadow of the ghost of an idea of the tremendous importance of proper lighting.

Let the light strike your face. People want to see you. The subtle changes that ought to play across your features are a part, and a very real part, of the process of self-expression. Sometimes they mean more than your words. If you stand directly under a light, your face may be dimmed by a shadow; if you stand directly in front of a light, it is sure to be. Would it not, then, be the part of wisdom to select, before you arise to speak, the spot that will give you the most advantageous illumination?

## NO TRUMPERY ON THE PLATFORM

And do not hide behind a table. People want to look at the whole man. They will even lean out in the aisles to see all of him.

Some well meaning soul is pretty sure to give you a table and a water pitcher and a glass; but if your throat becomes dry, a pinch of salt or a taste of lemon will start the saliva again better than Niagara.

You do not want the water nor the pitcher. Neither do you want all the other useless and ugly impedimenta that clutter up the average platform.

The Broadway sales rooms of the various auto mobile makers are beautiful, orderly, pleasing to the eye. The Paris offices of the large perfumers and jewelers are artistically and luxuriously appointed. Why? It is good business. One has more respect, more confidence, more admiration for a concern housed like that.

For the same reason, a speaker ought to have a

pleasing background. The ideal arrangement, to my way of thinking, would be no furniture at all. Nothing behind the speaker to attract attention or at either side of him—nothing but a curtain of dark blue velvet.

But what does he usually have behind him? Maps and signs and tables, perhaps a lot of dusty chairs, some piled on top of the others. And what is the result? A cheap, slovenly, disorderly atmosphere. So clear all the trumpery away.

"The most important thing in public speaking," said Henry Ward Beecher, "is the man."

So let the man stand out like the snow clad top of the Jungfrau towering against the blue skies of Switzerland.

## NO GUESTS ON THE PLATFORM

I was once in London, Ontario, when the Prime Minister of Canada was speaking. Presently the janitor, armed with a long pole, started to ventilate the room, moving about from window to window. What happened? The audience, almost to a man, ignored the speaker for a little while and stared at the janitor as intently as if he had been performing some miracle.

An audience cannot resist—or, what comes to the

same thing, it *will not* resist—the temptation to look at moving objects. If a speaker will only remember that truth, he can save himself some trouble and needless annoyance.

First, he can refrain from twiddling his thumbs, playing with his clothes and making little nervous movements that detract from him. I remember seeing a New York audience watch a well-known speaker's hands for half an hour while he spoke and played with the covering of a pulpit at the same time.

Second, the speaker should arrange, if possible, to have the audience seated so they won't have their attention distracted by seeing the late comers enter.

Third, he should have no guests on the platform. A few fears ago Raymond Robins delivered a series of talks in Brooklyn. I, along with a number of others, was invited to sit on the platform with him. I declined on the ground that it was unfair to the speaker. I noted the first night how many of these guests shifted about and put one leg over the other and back again, and so on; and every time one of them moved, the audience looked away from the speaker to the guest. I called Mr. Robins' attention to this the next day; and during the remainder of his evenings with us, he very wisely occupied the platform alone.

David Belasco did not permit the use of red flowers on the stage because they attract too much attention. Then why should a speaker permit a restless human being to sit facing the audience while he talks? He shouldn't. And, if he is wise, he won't.

## THE ART OF SITTING DOWN

Isn't it well for the speaker himself not to sit facing the audience before he begins? Isn't it better to arrive as a fresh exhibit than an old one?

But, if we *must* sit, let us be careful of *how* we sit. You have seen men look around to find a chair with the modified movements of a foxhound lying down for the night. They turned around and when they did locate a chair, they doubled up and flopped down into it with all the self-control of a sack of sand.

A man who knows how to sit feels the chair strike the back of his legs, and, with his body easily erect from head to hips, he *sinks* into it with his body under perfect control.

## POISE

We just said, a few pages previously, not to play

with your clothes because it attracted attention. There is another reason also. It gives an impression of weakness, a lack of self-control. Every movement that does not add to your presence detracts from it. There are no neutral movements. None. So stand still and control yourself physically and that will give you an impression of mental control, of poise.

After you have risen to address your audience, do not be in a hurry to begin. That is the hallmark of the amateur. Take a deep breath. Look over your audience for a moment; and, if there is a noise or disturbance, pause until it quiets down.

Hold your chest high. But why wait until you get before an audience to do this? Why not do it daily in private? Then you will do it unconsciously in public.

"Not one man in ten," says Luther H. Gulick in his book, *The Efficient Life* "carries himself so as to look his best ······Keep the neck pressed against the collar." Here is a daily exercise he recommends: "Inhale slowly and as strongly as possible. At the same time press the neck back firmly against the collar. Now hold it there hard. There is no harm in doing this in an exaggerated way. The object is to straighten out that part of the back which is directly between the shoulders. This deepens the chest."

And what shall you do with your hands? Forget them. If they fall naturally to your sides, that is ideal. If they feel like a bunch of bananas to you, do not be deluded into imagining that anyone else is paying the slightest attention to them or has the slightest interest in them.

They will look best hanging relaxed at your sides. They will attract the minimum of attention there. Not even the hypercritical can criticize that position. Besides, they will be unhampered and free to flow naturally into gestures when the urge makes itself felt.

But suppose that you are very nervous and that you find putting them behind your back or shoving them into your pockets helps to relieve your self-consciousness—what should you do? Use your common sense. I have heard a number of the celebrated speakers of this generation. Many, if not most, put their hands into their pockets occasionally while speaking. Bryan did it. Chauncey M. Depew did it. Teddy Roosevelt did it. Even so fastidious a dandy as Disraeli sometimes succumbed to this temptation. But the sky did not fall and, according to the weather reports, if my memory serves me right, the sun came up on time as usual the next morning. If a man has something to say worth while, and says it with contagious conviction, surely it will matter little what he does with his hands and feet. If his head is full and heart stirred, these secondary details will very largely take care of themselves. After all, the stupendously important thing in making a talk is the psychological aspect of it, not the position of the hands and feet.

## ABSURD ANTICS TAUGHT IN THE NAME OF GESTURE

And this brings us very naturally to the much-abused question of gesture. My first lesson in public speaking was given by the president of a college in the middle west. This lesson, as I remember it, was chiefly concerned with gesturing; it was not only useless but misleading and positively harmful. I was taught to let my arm hang loosely at my side palm facing the rear, fingers half closed and thumb touching my leg. I was drilled to bring the arm up in a graceful curve, to make a classical swing with the wrist and then to unfold the forefinger first, the second finger next, and the little finger last. When the whole aesthetic and ornamental movement had been executed, the arm was then to retrace the same graceful and unnatural curve and rest again by the side of the leg. The whole performance was wooden and affected. There was nothing sensible or honest about it. I was drilled to act as no man, in his right mind, ever acted anywhere.

There was no attempt whatever to get me to put my own individuality into my movements; no attempt to spur me on to feeling like gesturing; no endeavor to get the flow and blood of life in the process, and make it natural and unconscious and inevitable; no urging me to let go, to be spontaneous, to break through my shell of reserve, to talk and act like a human being. No, the whole regrettable performance was as mechanical as a typewriter, as lifeless as a last year's bird nest, as ridiculous as a Punch and Judy show.

That was in 1902. It seems incredible that such absurd antics could have been taught in the twentieth century; but they are still going on. Only a few years ago a whole book about gesturing was published by a professor teaching in one of the large colleges of the East—a whole book trying to make automatons out of men, telling them which gesture to make on this sentence, which to make on that, which to make with one hand, which with both, which to make high, which to make medium, which to make low, how to hold this finger and how to hold that. I have seen twenty men at a time standing before a class, all reading the same ornate oratorical selections from such a book, all making precisely the same gestures on precisely the same words, and all making themselves precisely ridiculous. Artificial, time-killing, mechanical, injurious—it has brought this whole subject into disrepute with many men. The dean of a large college in Massachusetts recently said that his institution had no course in public speaking because he had never seen one that was practical, one that taught men to speak sensibly. My sympathy was all with the dean.

Nine-tenths of the stuff that has been written on gestures has been a waste and worse than a waste of good white paper and good black ink. Any gesture that is gotten out of a book is very likely to look like it. The place to get it is out of yourself, out of your heart, out of your mind, out of your own interest in the subject, out of your own desire to make some one else see as you see, out of your own impulses. The only gestures that are worth one, two, three, are those that are born on the spur of the instant. An ounce of spontaneity is worth a ton of rules.

Gesture is not a thing to be put on at will like a dinner jacket. It is merely an outward expression of inward condition just as are kisses and colic and laughter and sea sickness.

And a man's gestures, like his tooth brush, should be very personal things. And, as all men are different, their gestures will be individual if they will only act natural.

No two men should be drilled to gesture in precisely the same fashion. In the last chapter, I discussed the difference between Lincoln and Douglas as speakers. Imagine trying to make the long, awkward, slow-thinking Lincoln gesture in the same fashion as did the rapidly-talking, impetuous and polished Douglas. It would be ridiculous.

"Lincoln," according to his biographer and law partner, Herndon, "did not gesticulate as much with his hands as with his head. He used the latter frequently, throwing it with vim this way and that. This movement was a significant one when he sought to enforce his statement. It sometimes came with a quick jerk, as if throwing off electric sparks into combustible material. He never sawed the air or rent space into tatters and rags as some orators do. He never acted for stage effect······ As he moved along in his speech he became freer and less uneasy in his movements; to that extent he was graceful. He had a perfect naturalness, a strong individuality; and to that extent he was dignified. He despised glitter, show, set forms and shams ...... There was a world of meaning and emphasis in the long, bony finger of his right hand as he dotted the ideas on the minds of his hearers. Sometimes, to express joy or pleasure, he would raise both hands at an angle of about fifty degrees, the palms upward, as if desirous of embracing the spirit of that which he loved. If the sentiment was one of detestation—denunciation of slavery, for example— both arms, thrown upward and fists clenched, swept through the air, and he expressed an execration that was truly sublime. This was one of his most effective gestures, and signified most vividly a fixed determination to drag down the object of his hatred and trample it in the dust. He always stood squarely on his feet, toe even with toe; that is, he never put one foot before the other. He neither touched nor leaned on anything for support. He made but few changes in his positions and attitudes. He never ranted, never walked backward and forward on the platform. To ease his arms, he frequently caught hold, with his left hand, of the lapel of his coat, keeping his thumb upright and leaving his right hand free to gesticulate." St. Gaudens caught him in just that attitude in the statue which stands in Lincoln Park, Chicago.

Such was Lincoln's method. Theodore Roosevelt

was more vigorous, fiery, active, his whole face alive with feeling, his fist clenched, his entire body an instrument of expression. Bryan often used the outstretched hand with open palm. Gladstone often struck a table or his open palm with his fist, or stamped his foot with a resounding thud on the floor. Lord Rosebery used to raise his right arm and bring it down with a bold sweep that had tremendous force. Ah, but there was force first in the speaker's thoughts and convictions; that was what made the gesture strong and spontaneous.

Spontaneity ...... life ...... they are the *summum bonum* of action. Burke was angular and exceedingly awkward in his gestures. Pitt sawed the air with his arms "like a clumsy clown." Sir Henry Irving was handicapped by a lame leg and decidedly odd movements. Lord Macaulay's actions on the platform were ungainly. So were Grattan's. So were Parnell's. "The answer then appears to be," said the late Lord Curzon at Cambridge University, in an address on Parliamentary Eloquence, "that great public speakers make their own gestures; and that while a great orator is doubtless aided by a handsome exterior and graceful action, it does not matter very much if he happens to be ugly and awkward."

Some years ago, I heard the famous Gypsy Smith preach. I was enthralled by the eloquence of this man who has led so many thousands to Christ. He used gestured—lots of them—and was no more conscious of them than of the air he breathed. Such is the ideal way.

And such is the way you, my dear reader, will find yourself making gestures if you will but practise and apply the principles already enunciated in this course. I can't give you any rules for gesturing, for everything depends upon the temperament of the speaker, upon his preparation, his enthusiasm, his personality, the subject, the audience, the occasion.

## SUGGESTIONS THAT MAY PROVE HELPFUL

Here are, however, a few limited suggestions that may prove useful, Do not repeat one gesture until it becomes monotonous. Do not make short, jerky movements from the elbow. The movements from the shoulder look better on the platform. Do not end your gestures too quickly. If you are using the index finger to drive home your thought, do not be afraid to hold that gesture through an entire sentence. The failure to do this is a very common error and a serious one. It distorts your emphasis, making small things unimportant, and truly important points seem trivial by comparison.

When you are doing real speaking before a real audience, make only the gestures that come natural. But while you are practising before the members of this course, *force* yourself, if necessary, to use gestures. Force yourself to do it and, as I pointed out in Chapter V, the doing of it will so awaken and stimulate you that your gestures will soon be coming unsought.

Shut your book. You can't learn gestures from a printed page. Your own impulses, as you are speaking, are more to be trusted, more valuable than anything any instructor can possibly tell you.

If you forget all else we have said about gesture and delivery, remember this: if a man is so wrapped up in what he has to say, if he is so eager to get his message across that he forgets himself and talks and acts spontaneously, then his gestures and his delivery, unstudied though they may be, are very likely to be almost above criticism. If you doubt this, walk up to a man and knock him down. You will probably discover that, when he regains his feet, the talk he delivers will be well nigh flawless as a gem of eloquence.

Here are the best eleven words I have ever read on the subject of delivery:

Fill up the barrel.
Knock out the bung.
Let nature caper.

## SUMMARY

1. According to experiments conducted by the Carnegie Institute of Technology, personality has more to do with business success than has superior knowledge. This pronouncement is as true of speaking as of business. Personality, however, is such an intangible, elusive, mysterious thing that it is almost impossible to give directions for developing it, but some of the suggestions given in this chapter will help a speaker to appear at his best.
2. Don't speak when you are tired. Rest, recuperate, store up a reserve of energy.
3. Eat sparingly before you speak.
4. Do nothing to dull your energy. It is magnetic. People cluster around the energetic speaker like wild geese around a field of autumn wheat.
5. Dress neatly, attractively. The consciousness of being well dressed heightens one's self-respect,

increases his self-confidence. If a speaker has baggy trousers, unkempt shoes, ungroomed hair, fountain pen and pencils peeping out of his coat pocket, the audience is liable to feel as little respect for him as he seems to feel for himself.

6. Smile. Come before your hearers with an attitude that seems to say you are glad to be there. "Like begets like," says Professor Overstreet. "If we are interested in our audience there is every likelihood that our audience will be interested in us. Even before we speak, very often, we are condemned or approved. There is every reason, therefore, that we should make certain that our attitude is such as to elicit warm response."

7. Crowd your audience together. No group is easily influenced when it is scattered. An individual, as a member of a compact audience, will laugh at, applaud and approve things that he might question and oppose if he were addressed singly or if he were one of a group scattered through a large room.

8. If you are speaking to a small group, pack them in a small room. Don't stand on a platform. Get down on the same level with them. Make your talk intimate, informal, conversational.

9. Keep the air fresh.
10. Flood the place with lights. Stand so that the light will fall directly in your face, so all your features can be seen.
11. Don't stand behind furniture. Push the tables and chairs to one side. Clear away all the unsightly signs and trumpery that often clutter up a platform.
12. If you have guests on the platform, they are sure to move occasionally and, each time they make the slightest movement, they are certain to seize the attention of your hearers. An audience cannot resist the temptation to look at any moving object or animal or person; so why store up trouble and create competition for yourself?
13. Do not flop down in your chair. Feel it strike the back of your legs, and, with your body easily erect, sink into it.
14. Stand still. Do not make a lot of nervous movements. They give an impression of weakness. Every movement that does not add to your presence, detracts from it.
15. Let your hands fall easily at your sides. That is the ideal position. However, if it makes you feel more comfortable to hold them behind your

back, or even to put them in your pockets—it won't matter much. If your head and your heart are full of what you are saying, these secondary details will largely take care of themselves.

16. Don't try to get your gestures out of a book. Get them out of your impulses. Let yourself go. Spontaneity and life and abandon are the indispensable requisites of gesture, not studied grace and an obedience to rules.

17. In gesturing, do not repeat one movement until it becomes monotonous, do not make short jerky movements from the elbow. Above all else, hold your gestures, continue them until the climax of your movements coincides with the climax of your thought.

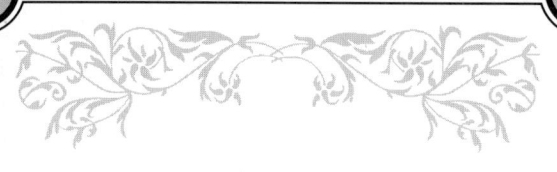

# CHAPTER
# NINE

## HOW TO OPEN A TALK

"If you happen to be one of a circle of public speakers who are relating their experiences, you will often hear some one remark apropos of the proper construction of an address: 'Get a good beginning and a good ending; stuff it with whatever you please.'" —Victor Murdock.

"In public address, it is all-important to make a good start. In the whole hard process of speech-making, there is nothing quite so hard as to make easy and skilful contact with an audience…… Much depends upon first impressions and opening words. Often an audience is either won or lost by the first half dozen sentences of a speech."
—Public Speaking Today, by Lockwood-Thorpe.

"Compared with what we ought to be, we are only half awake. We are making use of only a small part of our physical and mental resources. Stating the thing broadly, the human individual thus lives far within his limits. He possesses powers of various sorts which he habitually fails to use."
—Professor William James.

**CHAPTER 9**

# HOW TO OPEN A TALK

I once asked Dr. Lynn Harold Hough, formerly president of Northwestern University, what was the most important fact that his long experience as a speaker had taught him. After pondering for a minute, he replied "To get an arresting opening, something that will seize the attention immediately." He plans in advance almost the precise words of both his opening and closing. John Bright did the same thing. Gladstone did it. Webster did it. Lincoln did it. Practically every speaker with common sense and experience does it.

But does the beginner? Seldom. Planning takes time, requires thought, demands will-power. Cerebration is a painful process. Thomas Edison has this quotation from Sir Joshua Reynolds nailed on the walls of his plants:

"There is no expedient to which a man will not resort to

avoid the real labor of thinking."

The tyro usually trusts to the inspiration of the moment with the consequence that he finds:

"Beset with pitfall and with gin,
The road he is to wander in."

The late Lord Northcliffe, who fought his way up from a meager weekly salary to being the richest and most influential newspaper owner in the British Empire, said that these five words from Pascal had done more to help him succeed than anything else he had ever read:

"To foresee is to rule."

That is also a most excellent motto to have on your desk when you are planning your talk. Foresee how you are going to begin when the mind is fresh to grasp every word you utter. Foresee what impression you are going to leave last—when nothing else follows to obliterate it.

Ever since the days of Aristotle, books on this subject have divided the speech into three sections: the introduction, the body, the conclusion. Until comparatively recently, the introduction often was, and could really afford to be, as leisurely as a buggy ride. The speaker then was both a bringer of news and an entertainer. A hundred years ago he often filled the niche in the community that is usurped today by the newspaper, the radio, the telephone, the movie theater.

But conditions have altered amazingly. The world has been made over. Inventions have speeded up life more in the last hundred years than they had formerly in all the ages since Belshazzar and Nebuchadnezzar. Automobiles, aeroplanes, radio; we are moving with increasing speed. And the speaker must fall in line with the impatient tempo of the times. If you are going to use an introduction, believe me, it ought to be short as a billboard advertisement. This is about the temper of the average modern audience: "Got anything to say? All right, let's have it quickly and with very little trimmings. No oratory! Give us the facts quickly and sit down."

When Woodrow Wilson addressed Congress on such a momentous question as an ultimatum on submarine warfare, he announced his topic and centered the audience's attention on the subject with just twenty-three words:

"A situation has arisen in the foreign relations of the country of which it is my plain duty to inform you very frankly."

When Charles Schwab addressed the Pennsylvania Society of New York, he strode right into the heart of his talk with his second sentence:

"Uppermost in the minds of American citizens today is the question: What is the meaning of the existing slump in business and what of the future? Personally, I am an optimist……"

The salesmanager for the National Cash Register Company opened one of his talks to his men in this fashion. Only three sentences in this introduction; and they are all easy to listen to, they all have vigor and drive:

"You men who get the orders are the chaps who are supposed to keep the smoke coming out of the factory chimney. The volume of smoke emitted from our chimney during the past two summer months hasn't been large enough to darken the landscape to any great extent. Now that the dog days are over and the business-revival season has begun, we are addressing to you a short, short request on this subject: We want more smoke."

But do inexperienced speakers usually achieve such commendable swiftness and succinctness in their openings? Strict veracity compels us to record that they do not. The majority of untrained and unskilled speakers will begin in one of two ways—both of which are bad. Let us discuss them forthwith.

## BEWARE OF OPENING WITH A SO-CALLED HUMOROUS STORY

For some lamentable reason, the novice often feels that he ought to be funny as a speaker. He may, by nature, mind you, be as solemn as the encyclopedia, utterly devoid of the lighter touch; yet the moment he stands up to talk he imagines he feels, or ought to feel, the spirit of Mark Twain descending upon him. So he is inclined to open with a humorous story, especially if the occasion is an after-dinner affair. What happens? The chances are twenty to one that the narration, the manner of this hardware merchant newly-turned raconteur, is as heavy as the dictionary. The chances are his stories don't "click." In the immortal language of the immortal Hamlet, they prove "weary, stale, flat and unprofitable,"

If an entertainer were to misfire a few times like that before a vaudeville audience that had paid for their seats, they would "boo" and shout "give him the hook." But the average group listening to a speaker is very sympathetic; so, out of sheer charity, they will do their best to manufacture a few chuckles; while, deep in their hearts, they pity the would-be humorous speaker for his failure! They themselves feel uncomfortable. Haven't you, my dear reader, witnessed this kind of fiasco time after time? The writer has.

In all the difficult realm of speech-making, what is more difficult, more rare, than the ability to make an audience laugh? Humor is a hair trigger affair; it is so much a matter of individuality, of personality. You are either born with the predilection for being humorous or you are not—much as you are born with or without brown eyes. Not much can be done about either.

Remember, it is seldom the story that is funny of, by, and in itself. It is the way it is told that makes it a success. Ninety-nine men out of a hundred will fail woefully with the identical stories that made Mark Twain famous. Read the stories that Lincoln repeated in the taverns of the Eighth Judicial District of Illinois, stories that men drove miles to hear, stories that men sat up all night to hear, stories that, according to an eye witness, sometimes caused the natives to "whoop and roll off their chairs." Read those stories aloud to your family and see if you conjure up a smile. Here is one Lincoln used to tell with roaring success. Why not try it? Privately, please—not before an audience. A late traveler, trying to reach home over the muddy roads of the Illinois prairies, was overtaken by a storm. The night was black as ink; the rain descended as if some dam in the heavens had broken; thunder rent the angry clouds like the explosion of dynamite. Chain lightning showed trees falling around. The roar of it was very nearly deafening. Finally, a crash more terrific, more terrible, than any the helpless man had ever heard in his life, brought him to his knees. He was not given to praying, usually, but "Oh, Lord," he gasped, "if it is all the same to you, please give us a little more light and a little less noise,"

You may be one of those fortunately endowed individuals who has the rare gift of humor. If so, by all means, cultivate it. You will be thrice welcome wherever you speak. But if your talent lies in other directions, it is folly—and it ought to be high treason—for you to attempt to wear the mantle of Chauncey M. Depew.

Were you to study his speeches, and Lincoln's, and Job Hedges', you would probably be surprised at the few stories they told, especially in their openings. Edwin James Cattell confided to me that he had never told a funny story for the mere sake of humor. It had to be relevant, had to illustrate a point. Humor ought to be merely the frosting on the cake, merely the chocolate between the layers, not the cake itself. Strickland Gillilan, the best humorous lecturer in these United States makes it a rule never to tell a story during the first three minutes of his talk. If he finds that practise advisable, I wonder if you and I would not also.

Must the opening, then, be heavy-footed, elephantine and excessively solemn? Not at all. Tickle our risibilities, if you can, by some local reference, something anent the occasion or the remarks of some other speaker. Observe some incongruity. Exaggerate it. That brand of humor is forty times more likely to succeed than stale jokes about Pat and Mike, or a mother-in-law, or a goat.

Perhaps the easiest way to create merriment is to tell a joke on yourself. Depict yourself in some ridiculous and embarrassing situation. That gets down to the very essence of much humor. The Eskimos laugh even at a chap who has broken his leg. The Chinese chuckle over the dog that has fallen out of a second story window and killed himself. We are a bit more sympathetic than that, but don't we smile at the fellow chasing his hat, or slipping on a banana skin?

Most any one can make an audience laugh by grouping incongruous ideas or qualities as, for example, the statement of a newspaper writer that he "hated children, tripe, and Democrats."

Note how cleverly Rudyard Kipling raised laughs in this opening to one of his political talks in England. He is retailing here, not manufactured anecdotes, but some of his own experiences and playfully stressing their incongruities:

"My Lords, Ladies and Gentlemen: When I was a young man in India I used to report criminal cases for the newspaper that employed me. It was interesting work because it introduced me to forgers and embezzlers and murderers and enterprising sportsmen of that kind. (Laughter.) Sometimes, after I had reported their trials, I used to visit my friends in jail when they were doing their sentences. (Laughter.) I remember one man who got off with a life sentence for murder. He was a clever, smooth-speaking chap, and he told me what he called the story of his life. He said: 'Take it from me that when a man gets crooked, one thing leads to another until he finds himself in such a position that he has to put somebody out of the way to get straight again.' (Laughter.) Well, that exactly describes the present position of the cabinet. (Laughter and cheers.)"

This is the way William Howard Taft managed a bit of humor at the annual banquet of the Superintendents of the Metropolitan Life Insurance Company. The beautiful part of it is this: he is humorous and pays his audience a gracious compliment at the same time:

*"Mr. President and Gentlemen of the Metropolitan Life Insurance Company:*

I was out in my old home about nine months ago, and I heard an after-dinner speech there by a gentleman who had some trepidation in making it; and he said he had consulted a friend of his, who had had a great deal of experience in making after-dinner speeches, which friend advised him that the best kind of audience to address, as an after-dinner speaker, was an audience intelligent and well-educated but half-tight. (Laughter and applause.) Now, all I can say is that this audience is one of the best audiences I ever saw for an after-dinner speaker. Something has made up for the absence of that element that the remark implied (applause), and I must think it is the spirit of the Metropolitan Life Insurance Company. (Prolonged applause.)"

## DO NOT BEGIN WITH AN APOLOGY

The second egregious blunder that the beginner is wont to make in his opening, is this: He apologizes. "I am no speaker······ I am not prepared to talk······ I have nothing to say······

Don't! Don't! The opening words of a poem by Kipling are: "There's no use in going further." That is precisely the way an audience feels when a speaker opens in that fashion.

Anyway, if you are not prepared, some of us will discover it without your assistance. Others will not. Why call their attention to it? Why insult your audience by suggesting that you did not think them worth preparing for, that just any old thing you happened to have on the fire would be good enough to serve them? No. No. We don't want to hear your apologies. We are there to be informed and interested, to be *interested*, remember that.

The moment you come before the audience, you have our attention naturally, inevitably. It is not difficult to get it for the first five seconds, but it is difficult to hold it for the next five minutes. If you once lose it, it will be doubly difficult to win it back. So begin with something interesting in your very first sentence. Not the second. Not the third. The first! F-I-R-S-T. First!

"How?" you ask. Rather a large order, I admit. And in attempting to harvest the material to fill it, we must tread our way down devious and dubious paths, for so much depends upon you, upon your audience, your subject, your material, the occasion, and so on. However, we hope that the tentative suggestions discussed and illustrated in the remainder of this chapter will yield something usable and of value.

AROUSE CURIOSITY

Here is an opening used by Mr. Howell Healy in a talk given before a session of this course in the Penn Athletic Club, Philadelphia. Do you like it? Does it get your interest immediately?

"Eighty-two years ago, and just about this time of year, there was published in London a little volume, a story, which was destined to become immortal. Many people have called it 'the greatest little book in the world.' When it first appeared, friends meeting one another on the Strand or Pall Mall, asked the question, 'Have you read it? The answer invariably was: 'Yes, God bless him, I have.

The day it was published a thousand copies were sold. Within a fortnight, the demand had consumed fifteen thousand. Since then it has run into countless editions, and has been translated into every language under heaven. A few years ago, J. P. Morgan purchased the original manuscript for a fabulous sum; it now reposes among his other priceless treasures in that magnificent art gallery in New York City which he calls his library.

What is this world-famous book? Dickens' 'Christmas Carol.' ……"

Do you consider that a successful opening? Did it hold your attention, heighten your interest as it progressed? Why? Was it not because it aroused your curiosity, held you in suspense?

Curiosity! Who is not susceptible to it?

I have seen birds in the woods fly about by the hour watching me out of sheer curiosity. 1 know a hunter in the high Alps who lures chamois by throwing a bed sheet around him and crawling about and arousing their curiosity. Dogs have curiosity, and so have kittens, and all manner of animals including the well-known *genus homo*.

So arouse your audience's curiosity with your first sentence, and you have their interested attention.

The writer used to begin his lecture on Colonel Thomas Lawrence's adventures in Arabia in this fashion:

"Lloyd George says that he regards Colonel Lawrence as one of the most romantic and picturesque characters of modern times."

That opening had two advantages. In the first place, a quotation from an eminent man always has a lot of attention value. Second, it aroused curiosity: "Why romantic?" was the natural question, and "why picturesque?" "I never heard about him before······ What did he do?"

Lowell Thomas began his lecture on Colonel Thomas Lawrence with this statement:

"I was going down Christian Street in Jerusalem one day when I met a man clad in the gorgeous robes of an oriental potentate; and, at his side, hung the curved gold sword worn only by the descendants of the prophet Mohammed. But this man had none of the appearances of an Arab, He had blue eyes; and the Arabs' eyes are always black or brown."

That piques your curiosity, doesn't it? You want to hear more. Who was he? Why was he posing as an Arab? What did he do? What became of him?

The student who opened his talk with this question:

"Do you know that slavery exists in seventeen nations the world today?"

not only aroused curiosity, but in addition, he shocked his auditors. "Slavery? today? Seventeen countries? Seems incredible. What nations? Where are they?"

One can often arouse curiosity by beginning with an effect, and making people anxious to hear the cause. For example, one student began with this striking statement:

"A member of one of our legislatures recently stood up in his legislative assembly and proposed the passage of a law prohibiting tadpoles from becoming frogs within two miles of any school house."

You smile. Is the speaker joking? How absurd. Was that actually done?······ Yes. The speaker went on to explain.

An article in *The Saturday Evening Post*, entitled "With The Gangsters," began:

"Are gangsters really organized? As a rule they are. How? ······"

With ten words, you see, the writer of that article announced his subject, told you something about it, and aroused your curiosity as to how gangsters are organized. Very creditable. Every man who aspires to speak in public ought to study the technique that magazine writers employ to hook the reader's interest immediately. You can learn far more from them about how to open a speech than you can by studying collections of printed speeches.

## WHY NOT BEGIN WITH A STORY?

Harold Bell Wright has admitted in an interview that his novels have brought him more than a hundred thousand dollars a year. Booth Tarkington and Robert W. Chambers have earned similar amounts. For seventeen years Doubleday Page and Company had one large press which did nothing in all that time but turn out a ceaseless flood of the novels by the late Gene Stratton Porter. Over seventeen million copies of her books were sold; and they brought her more than three million dollars in royalties. Do people like to hear stories? Those figures sound like it, don't they?

We especially like to hear a man relate narratives from his own experience. The late Russell E. Conwell delivered his lecture, "Acres of Diamonds," over six thousand times, and received millions for it.

And how does this marvelously popular lecture begin? Read it yourself. It is printed in the Appendix to this course. Here is the way it opens:

"In 1870 we went down the Tigris River. We hired a guide at Bagdad to show us Persepolis, Nineveh, and Babylon······"

And he is off—with *a story*. That is what hooks the attention. That kind of opening is almost foolproof. It can hardly fail. It moves. It marches. We follow. We want to know what is going to happen.

The story-opening was used to launch Chapter III of

this book. Here are opening sentences taken from two stories that appeared in a single issue of *The Saturday Evening Post:*

1. "The sharp crack of a revolver punctuated the silence."
2. "An incident, trivial in itself but not at all trivial in its possible consequences, occurred at the Montview Hotel, Denver, during the first week of July. It so aroused the curiosity of Goebel, the resident manager, that he referred it to Steve Faraday, owner of the Montview and half a dozen other Faraday hotels, when Steve made his regular visit a few days later on his midsummer swing of inspection."

Note that those openings have action. They start something. They arouse your curiosity. You want to read on; you want to know more; you want to find out what it is all about.

Even the unpracticed beginner can usually manage a successful opening if he employs the story technique and arouses our curiosity.

## BEGIN WITH A SPECIFIC ILLUSTRATION

It is difficult, it is arduous, for the average audience

to follow abstract statements very long. Illustrations are easier to listen to, far easier. Then, why not start with one? It is hard to get men to do that. I know. I have tried. They feel somehow that they must first make a few general statements. Not at all. Open with your illustration, arouse the interest; then follow with your general remarks. If you wish an example of this technique, please turn to the opening of Chapter V of this book, or Chapter VII.

What technique was employed to open this chapter you are now reading?

USE AN EXHIBIT

Perhaps the easiest way in the world to gain attention is to hold up something for people to look at. Even savages and half-wits, and babes in the cradle and monkeys in a store window and dogs on the street will give heed to that kind of stimulus. It can be used sometimes with effectiveness before the most dignified audience. For example, Mr. S. S. Ellis, of Philadelphia, opened one of his talks by holding a coin between his thumb and forefinger, and high above his shoulder. Naturally every one looked. Then he inquired: "Has any one here ever found a coin like this on the sidewalk? It announces that the fortunate finder will be given a lot free in such and such a real estate development. He has but to call and present this coin······" Mr. Ellis then proceeded to reveal the colored man in the cordwood and to condemn the misleading and unethical practises involved.

## ASK A QUESTION

Mr. Ellis' opening has another commendable feature. It begins by asking a question, by getting the audience thinking with the speaker, cooperating with him. Note that *the Saturday Evening Post* article on Gangsters opens with two questions in the first three sentences: "Are gangsters really organized? ······ How?" The use of this question-key is really one of the simplest, surest ways to unlock the minds of your audience and let yourself in. When other tools prove useless, you can always fall back on it.

## WHY NOT OPEN WITH A QUESTION FROM SOME FAMOUS MAN?

The words of a prominent man always have attention power; so a suitable quotation is one of the very best ways of launching a harangue. Do you like the following opening of a discussion on Business Success?

"The world bestows its big prizes both in money and honors for but one thing," says Elbert Hubbard. "And that is initiative. And what is initiative? I'll tell you: it is doing the right thing without being told."

As a starter, that has several commendable features. The initial sentence arouses curiosity; it carries us forward, we want to hear more. If the speaker pauses skillfully after the words, "Elbert Hubbard," it arouses suspense. "What does the world bestow its big prizes for?" we ask. Quick. Tell us. We may not agree with you, but give us your opinion anyway······ The second sentence leads us right into the heart of the subject. The third sentence, a question, invites the audience to get in on the discussion, to think, to do a little something. And how audiences like to do things. They love it! The fourth sentence defines initiative······ After this opening the speaker led off with a human interest story illustrating that quality As far as construction is concerned, Moody might have rated the stock of that talk *Aaa*.

# TIE YOUR TOPIC UP TO THE VITAL INTERESTS Of YOUR HEARERS

Begin on some note that goes straight to the selfish interests of the audience. That is one of the best of all possible ways to start. It is sure to get attention. We are mightily interested in the things that touch us significantly, momentously.

That is only common sense, isn't it? Yet the use of it is very uncommon. For example, recently I heard a speaker begin a talk on the necessity or periodic health examinations. How did he open? By telling the history of the Life Extension Institute, how it was organized and the service it was rendering. Absurd! Our hearers have not the foggiest, not the remotest, interest in how some company somewhere was formed; but they are stupendously and eternally interested in themselves.

Why not recognize that fundamental fact? Why not show how that company is of vital concern to them? Why not begin something like this? "Do you know how long you are expected to live according to life insurance tables? Your expectancy of life, as insurance statisticians phrase it, is two-thirds of the time between your present age and eighty. For example, if you are thirty-five now, the difference between your present age and eighty is forty-five; you can expect to live two-thirds of that amount, or another thirty years······ Is that enough? No, no, we are all passionately eager for more. Yet those tables are based upon millions of records. May you and I, then, hope to beat them? Yes, with proper precaution, we may; but the very first step is to have a thorough physical examination······"

Then, if we explain in detail why the periodic health examination is necessary, the hearer might be interested in some company formed to render that service. But to begin talking about the company in an impersonal way. It is disastrous! Deadly!

Take another example: During the last season, I heard a student begin a talk on the prime urgency of conserving our forests. He opened like this: "We, as Americans, ought to be proud of our national resources······" From that sentence, he went on to show that we were wasting our timber at a shameless and indefensible pace. But the opening was bad, too general, too vague. He did not make his subject seem vital to us. There was a printer in that audience. The destruction of our forests will mean something very real to his business. There was a banker; it is going to affect him for it will affect our general prosperity······ and so on. Why not begin, then, by saying: "The subject I am going to speak about affects your business, Mr. Appleby; and yours, Mr. Saul. In fact, it will, in some measure, affect the price of the food we eat and the rent that we pay. It touches the welfare and prosperity of us all."

Is that exaggerating the importance of conserving our forests? No, I think not. It is only obeying Elbert Hubbard's injunction to "paint the picture large and put the matter in a way that compels attention."

## THE ATTENTION POWER OF SHOCKING FACTS

"A good magazine article," said S. S. McClure, the founder of the periodical bearing his name, "is a series of shocks."

They jar us out of our day dreams; they seize, they demand attention. Here are some illustrations: Mr. N. D. Ballantine, of Baltimore, began his address on *The Marvels of Radio* with this statement:

"Do you realize that the sound of a fly walking across a pane of glass in New York can be broadcasted by radio and made to roar away off in Central Africa like the falls of Niagara?"

Mr. Harry G. Jones, president of Harry G. Jones Company, of New York City, began his talk on the *Criminal Situation* with these words;

"The administration of our criminal law," declared William Howard Taft, then chief justice of the supreme court of the United States, "is a disgrace to civilization."

That has the double advantage of being not only a shocking opening, but the shocking statement is quoted from an authority on jurisprudence.

Mr. Paul Gibbons, former President of the Optimist Club of Philadelphia, opened an address on *Crime* with these arresting statements:

"The American people are the worst criminals in the world. Astounding as that assertion is, it is true. Cleveland, Ohio, has six times as many murders as all London. It has one hundred and seventy times as many robberies, according to its population, as has London. More people are robbed every year, or assaulted with intent to rob, in Cleveland than in all England, Scotland and Wales combined. More people are murdered every year in St. Louis than in all England and Wales. There are more murders in New York City than in all France or Germany or Italy or the British Isles. The sad truth of the matter is that the criminal is not punished. If you commit a murder, there is less than one chance in a hundred that you will ever be executed for it. You, as a peaceful citizen are ten times as liable to die from cancer as you would be to be hanged if you shot a man."

That opening was successful, for Mr. Gibbons put the requisite power and earnestness behind his words. They lived. They breathed. However, I have heard other students begin their talks on the crime situation with somewhat similar illustrations; yet their openings were mediocre. Why? Words. Words. Words. Their technique of construction was flawless, but their spirit was nil. Their manner vitiated and emaciated all they said.

## THE VALUE OF THE SEEMINGLY CASUAL OPENING

How do you like the following opening, and why? Mary E. Richmond is addressing the annual meeting of the New York League of Women Voters in the days before legislation against child marriages:

"Yesterday, as the train passed through a city not far away from here, 1 was reminded of a marriage that took place there a few years ago. Because many other marriages in this state have been just as hasty and disastrous as this one, I am going to begin what I have to say today with some of the details of this individual instance.

It was on December 12th that a high school girl of fifteen in that city met for the first time a junior in a nearby college who had just attained his majority. On December 15th, only three days later, they procured a marriage license by swearing that the girl was eighteen and was therefore free from the necessity of procuring parental consent. Leaving the city clerk's office with their license, they applied at once to a priest (the girl was a Catholic), but very properly he refused to marry them. In some way, perhaps through this priest, the child's mother received news of the attempted marriage. Before she could find her daughter, however, a justice of the peace had united the pair. The bridegroom then took his bride to a hotel where they spent two days and two nights, at the end of which time he abandoned her and never lived with her again."

Personally, I like that opening very much. The very first sentence is good. It forecasts an interesting reminiscence. We want to hear the details. We settle down to listen to a human interest story. In addition to that, it seems very natural. It does not smack of the study, it is not formal, it does not smell of the lamp······ "Yesterday, as the train passed through a city not far from here, I was reminded of a marriage that took place there a few years ago." Sounds natural, spontaneous, human. Sounds like one person relating an interesting story to another. An audience likes that. But it is very liable to shy at something too elaborate, something that reeks of preparation with malice aforethought. We want the art that conceals art.

## SUMMARY

1. The opening of a talk is difficult. It is also highly important, for the minds of our hearers are fresh then and comparatively easy to impress. It is of too much consequence to be left to chance; it ought to be carefully worked out in advance.
2. The introduction ought to be short, only a sentence or two. Often it can be dispensed with altogether. Wade right into the heart of your subject with the smallest possible number of words. No one objects to that.

3. Novices are prone to begin either with attempting to tell a humorous story or by making an apology. Both of these are usually bad. Very few men — very, very, very few — can relate a humorous anecdote successfully. The attempt usually embarrasses the audience instead of entertaining them. Stories should be relevant, not dragged in just for the sake of the story. Humor should be the icing on the cake, not the cake itself······ Never apologize. It is usually an insult to your audience; it bores them. Drive right into what you have to say, say it quickly and sit down.

4. A speaker may be able to win the immediate attention of his audience by:

   a. Arousing curiosity. (Illustration: Story of Dickens' "Christmas Carol.")
   b. Relating a human interest story. (Illustration: "Acres of Diamonds" lecture.)
   c. Beginning with a specific illustration. (See the openings of Chapters V and VII of this book.)
   d. Using an exhibit. (Illustration: The coin that entitled the finder to a free lot.)
   e. Asking a question. (Illustration: "Has any one here ever found a coin like this, on the sidewalk?")

    f. Opening with a striking quotation. (Illustration: Elbert Hubbard on the Value of Initiative.)

    g. Showing how the topic affects the vital interest of the audience. (Illustration: "Your expectancy of life is two-thirds of amount of time between your present age and eighty. You may be able to increase that by having periodic health examinations," etc.)

    h. Starting with shocking facts. (Illustration: "The American people are the worst criminals in the civilized world.")

5. Don't make your opening too formal. Don't let the bones show. Make it appear free, casual, inevitable. This can be done by referring to something that has just happened, or something that has just been said. (Illustration: "Yesterday, as the train passed through a city not far from here, I was reminded ······")

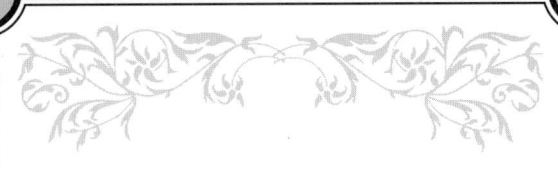

# CHAPTER
# TEN

# CAPTURING YOUR AUDIENCE AT ONCE

"You must please the audience. You must lull their fears, dissipate their suspicions, get them to lay down their arms and say, 'Come let us reason together.' This you will do by finding some common grounds and mutual interest. There are things which bind us that are stronger than the forces that sever. What are they? On your discovery of that will depend the success of your speech. If you really cannot please the audience, then show a splendid courage and extort their admiration and respect. As an illustration of the first, if I were addressing an audience of Orangemen in Belfast I should pay a tribute to loyalty to conscience. I should speak of our common admiration for our great ancestors, that is, of the things which we had in common. If I were addressing employees I should not start with raging rebukes, but seek to remind them of happier occasions, of loyal cooperation in the past, of the worries and troubles that press upon all engaged in industry. I should let them see that I was sincerely and without bitterness seeking a way out. In every case appeal to the best instincts in the audience; it is amazing how a group of people will respond to such an appeal." —Sidney F. Wicks, "Public Speaking for Business Men."

## CAPTURING YOUR AUDIENCE
## AT ONCE

Several years ago the Colorado Fuel and Iron Company was suffering from labor troubles. Shooting had taken place; there had been bloodshed. The air was electric with bitter hatreds. The very name of Rockefeller was anathema. Yet John D. Rockefeller, Jr., wanted to talk to the employes of that concern. He wanted to explain, to persuade them to his way of thinking, to get them to accept his beliefs. He realized that, in the very opening of his speech, he must eradicate all ill feeling, all antagonism. At the very outset, he did it beautifully and sincerely. Most public speakers can study his method with profit:

"This is a red-letter day in my life. It is the first time I have ever had the good fortune to meet the representatives of the employees of this great company, its officers and superintendents, together, and I can assure you that I am proud to be here, and that I shall remember this gathering as long as I live. Had this meeting been held two weeks ago, I should have stood here a stranger to most of you, recognizing few faces. Having had the opportunity last week of visiting all the camps in the southern coal fields and of talking individually with practically all of the representatives, except those who were away; having visited in your homes, met many of your wives and children, we meet here not as strangers but as friends, and it is in that spirit of mutual friendship that I am glad to have this opportunity to discuss with you our common interests.

Since this is a meeting of the officers of the company and the representatives of the employees, it is only by your courtesy that I am here, for I am not so fortunate as to be either one or the other; and yet I feel that I am intimately associated with you men, for, in a sense, I represent both the stockholders and the directors."

That is tact—supreme tact. And the speech, in spite of the bitter hatred that had existed, was successful. The men who had been striking and fighting for higher wages never said anything more about it after Rockefeller had explained all the facts in the situation.

# A DROP OF HONEY AND TWO-GUN MEN

"It is an old and true maxim 'That a drop of honey catches more flies than a gallon of gall.' So with men. If you would win a man to your cause, first convince him that you are his sincere friend. Therein is a drop of honey that catches his heart; which, say what he will, is the great high road to his reason, and when once gained, you will find but little trouble in convincing his judgment of the justice of your cause, if, indeed, that cause really be a just one."

That was Lincoln's plan. In 1858, during his campaign for the United States Senate, he was announced to speak in what was, at that time, the semi-barbarous part of Southern Illinois called "Egypt." They were a rough lot, the men in that section, and they carried ugly looking knives and pistols strapped to their belts even on public occasions. Their hatred of all anti-slavery men was equalled only by their love of fighting and corn whiskey. Southern men, some of them slave owners from Kentucky and Missouri, had crossed over the Mississippi and the Ohio to be on hand for the excitement and trouble. Plenty of it was in prospect, for the rougher elements had sworn that, if Lincoln tried to talk, they would "run the damned Abolitionist out of town," and "shoot him to fiddle strings."

Lincoln had heard these threats, and he knew the intense feeling that existed, the positive danger. "But if only they will give me a fair chance to say a few opening words," he declared, "I'll fix them all right." So, before beginning to talk, he had himself introduced to the ringleaders, and shook their hands cordially. He made one of the most tactful openings I have ever read:

"Fellow citizens of Southern Illinois, fellow citizens of the State of Kentucky, fellow citizens of Missouri —I am told there are some of you here present who would like to make trouble for me. I don't understand why they should. I am a plain, common man, like the rest of you; and why should I not have as good a right to speak my sentiments as the rest of you? Why, good friends, I am one of you. I am not an interloper here. I was born in Kentucky, and raised in Illinois, just like the most of you, and worked my way along by hard scratching. I know the people of Kentucky, and I know the people of Southern Illinois, and I think I know the Missourians. I am one of them, and therefore ought to know them; and they ought to know me better, and, if they did know me better, they would know that I am not disposed to make them trouble. Then, why should they, or any one of them, want to make trouble for me? Don't do any such foolish thing, fellow citizens. Let us be friends, and treat each other like friends. I am one of the humblest and most peaceful men in the world—would wrong no man, would interfere with no man's rights. And all I ask is that, having something to say, you give me a decent hearing. And, being Illinoisans, Kentuckians, and Missourians—brave and gallant people—I feel sure that you will do that. And now let us reason together like the honest fellows we are."

As he spoke these words, his face was the very picture of good nature, and his voice vibrated with sympathetic earnestness. That tactful opening calmed the on-coming storm, silenced his enemies. In fact, it transformed many of them into friends. They cheered his speech, and, later, those rough and rude "Egyptians" were among his most ardent supporters for the Presidency.

"Interesting," you remark, "but what has all this got to do with me? I am no Rockefeller; I am not going to address hungry strikers longing to strangle and batter the life out of me. I am no Lincoln; I am not going to talk to two-gun desperadoes full of corn whiskey and hatred."

True, true, but aren't you, almost every day of your life, talking to people who differ from you on some subject under discussion? Aren't you constantly trying to win people to your way of thinking—at home, in the office, in the market place? Is there room for improvement in your methods? How do you begin? By showing Lincoln's tact? And Rockefeller's? If so, you are a person of rare finesse and extraordinary discretion. Most men begin, not by thinking about the other fellow's views and desires, not by trying to find a common ground of agreement, but by unloading their own opinions.

For example, I have heard hundreds of speeches on the hotly contested subject of prohibition. In almost every instance, the speaker, with all the tact of a bull in a china shop, opened with some positive and perhaps belligerent statement. He showed once and for all which direction he faced and under which flag he fought. He showed that his mind was made up so firmly that there was not the slightest chance of it being changed; yet he was expecting others to abandon their cherished beliefs and to accept his. The effect? About the same that results from all arguments: no one was convinced. Instantly, he lost by his blunt, aggressive opening the sympathetic attention of all who differed with him; instantly, they discounted all he said and would say; instantly, they challenged his statements; instantly, they held his opinions in contempt. His talk served but to entrench them more strongly behind the bulwark of their own beliefs.

You see, he made, at the very outset, the fatal mistake of prodding his listeners, of getting them bending backwards and saying through their shut teeth: "No! No! No!"

Is not that a very serious situation if one wishes to win converts to his way of thinking? A most illuminating statement on this point is the following quotation from Professor Overstreet's lectures before the New School for Social Research in New York City.

"A 'No' response is a most difficult handicap to overcome. When a person has said 'No,' all his pride of personality demands that he remain consistent with himself. He may later feel that the 'No' was ill advised; nevertheless, there is his precious pride to consider! Once having said a thing, he must stick to it. Hence it is of the very greatest importance that we start a person in the affirmative direction······ The skillful speaker gets at the outset a number of 'yes-responses.' He has thereby set the psychological processes of his listeners moving in the affirmative direction. It is like the movement of a billiard ball. Propel it in one direction, and it takes some force to deflect it; far more force to send it back in the opposite direction.

The psychological patterns here are quite clear. When a person says 'No' and really means it, he is doing far more than saying a word of two letters. His entire organism—glandular, nervous, muscular—gathers itself together into a condition of rejection. There is, usually in minute but sometimes in observable degree, a physical withdrawal, or readiness for withdrawal. The whole neuro-muscular system, in short, sets itself on guard against acceptance. Where, on the contrary, a person says 'Yes,' none of the withdrawing activities take place. The organism is in a forward-moving, accepting, open attitude. Hence the more 'Yesses' we can, at the very outset, induce, the more likely we are to succeed in capturing the attention for our ultimate proposal.

It is a very simple technique—this Yes-Response. And yet how much neglected! It often seems as if people get a sense of their own importance by antagonizing at the outset. The radical comes into a conference with his conservative brethren; and immediately he must make them furious! What, as a matter of fact, is the good of it? If he simply does it in order to get some pleasure out of it for himself, he may be pardoned. But if he expects to achieve something, he is only psychologically stupid.

Get a student to say 'No' at the beginning, or a customer, child, husband, or wife, and it takes the wisdom and the patience of angels to transform that bristling negative into an affirmative."

How is one going to get these desirable "yes responses" at the very outset? Fairly simple. "My way of opening and winning an argument," confided Lincoln, "is to first find a common ground of agreement." Lincoln found it even when he was discussing the highly inflammable subject of slavery. "For the first half hour," declared *The Mirror*, a neutral paper reporting one of his talks, "his opponents would agree with every word he uttered. From that point he began to lead them off, little by little, until it seemed as if he had got them all into his fold."

## SENATOR LODGE'S WAY OF DOING IT

Shortly after the close of the World War, the late Senator Lodge and President Lowell of Harvard were scheduled to debate the League of Nations question before a Boston audience. Senator Lodge felt that most of the audience were hostile to his view; yet he must win them to his way of thinking. How? By a direct, frontal, aggressive attack on their convictions? Ah, no. The Senator was far too shrewd a psychologist to bungle his plea with such crude tactics. He began with supreme tact, with admirable finesse. The opening of his speech is quoted in a following paragraph. Note that even his most bitter opponents could not have differed with the sentiments expressed in his first dozen sentences. Note how he appeals to their emotion of patriotism in his salutation: "My Fellow Americans." Observe how he minimizes the differences in the views they are to defend, how he deftly stresses the things they cherish in common.

See how he praises his opponent, how he insists upon the fact that they differ only on minor details of method, and not at all upon the vital question of the welfare of America and the peace of the world. He even goes further and admits that he is in favor of a League of Nations of some kind. So, in the last analysis, he differed from his opponent only in this: he felt that we ought to have a more ideal and efficacious League.

"Your Excellency, Ladies and Gentlemen, My Fellow Americans:

I am largely indebted to President Lowell for this opportunity to address this great audience. He and I are friends of many years, both Republicans. He is the president of our great university, one of the most important and influential places in the United States. He is also an eminent student and historian of politics and government. He and I may differ as to methods in this great question now before the people, but I am sure that in regard to the security of the peace of the world and the welfare of the United States we do not differ in purposes.

I am going to say a single word, if you will permit me, as to my own position. I have tried to state it over and over again. I thought I had stated it in plain English. But there are those who find in misrepresentation a convenient weapon for controversy, and there are others, most excellent people, who perhaps have not seen what I have said and who possibly have misunderstood me. It has been said that I am against any League of Nations. I am not; far from it. I am anxious to have the nations, the free nations of the world, united in a league, as we call it, a society, as the French call it, but united, to do all that can be done to secure the future peace of the world and to bring about a general disarmament."

No matter how determined you were beforehand to differ with a speaker, an opening like that would make you soften and relent a bit, wouldn't it? Wouldn't it make you willing to listen to more? Wouldn't it tend to convince you of the speaker's fairmindedness?

What would have been the result had Senator Lodge set out immediately to show those who believed in the League of Nations that they were hopelessly in error, cherishing a delusion? The result would have been futile; the following quotation from Professor James Harvey Robinson's enlightening and popular book, *The Mind in the Making*, shows the psychological reason why such an attack would have been futile:

"We sometimes find ourselves changing our minds without any resistance or heavy emotion, but if we are told we are wrong we resent the imputation and harden our hearts. We are incredibly heedless in the formation of our beliefs, but find ourselves filled with an illicit passion for them when anyone proposes to rob us of their companionship. It is obviously not the ideas themselves that are dear to us, but our self-esteem which is threatened······ The little word *my* is the most important one in human affairs, and properly to reckon with it is the beginning of wisdom. It has the same force whether it is *my* dinner, *my* dog and *my* house, or *my* faith, *my* country and *my* God. We not only resent the imputation that our watch is wrong, or our car shabby, but that our conception of the canals of Mars, of the pronunciation of 'Epictetus,' of the medicinal value of salicine, or of the date of Sargon I, are subject to revision······ We like to continue to believe what we have been accustomed to accept as true, and the resentment aroused when doubt is cast upon any of our assumptions leads us to seek every manner of excuse for clinging to it. The result is that most of our so-called reasoning consists in finding arguments for going on believing as we already do."

## THE BEST ARGUMENT IS AN EXPLANATION

Is it not quite evident that the speaker who argues with his audience is merely arousing their stubbornness, putting them on the defensive, making it well nigh impossible for them to change their minds? Is it wise to start by saying, "I am going to prove so and so?" Aren't your hearers liable to accept that as a challenge and remark silently, "Let's see you do it."

Is it not much more advantageous to begin by stressing something that you and all of your hearers believe, and then to raise some pertinent question that everyone would like to have answered? Then take your audience with you in an earnest search for the answer. While on that search, present the facts as you see them so clearly that they will unconsciously be led to accept your conclusions as their own. They will have much more faith in some truth that they believe they have discovered for themselves. "The best argument is that which seems merely an explanation."

In every controversy, no matter how wide and bitter the differences, there is always some common ground of agreement on which the speaker can invite everyone to assemble for the search after facts that he is going to conduct. To illustrate: even if the head of the Communist Party were addressing a convention of the American Bankers' Association, he could find some mutual beliefs, some analogous desires to share with his hearers. Couldn't he? Let us see:

"Poverty has always been one of the cruel problems of human society. As Americans we have always felt it our duty to alleviate, whenever and wherever possible, the sufferings of the poor. We are a generous nation. No other people in all history have poured out their wealth so prodigally, so unselfishly to help the unfortunate. Now, with this same mental generosity and spiritual unselfishness that has characterized our givings in the past, let us examine together the facts of our industrial life and see if we can find some means, fair and just and acceptable to all, that will tend to prevent as well as to mitigate, the evils of poverty."

Who could object to that? Could Father Coughlin, or Norman Thomas, or Doctor Townsend, or J. Pierpont Morgan? Hardly.

Do we seem to be contradicting here the gospel of force and energy and enthusiasm so fervently praised in Chapter V? Hardly. There is a time for everything. But the time for force is seldom in the beginning of a talk. Tact is more likely to be needed then.

## HOW PATRICK HENRY LAUNCHED HIS STORMY ADDRESS

Every school boy in the land is familiar with the fiery close of Patrick Henry's famous speech before the Virginia Convention of 1775: "Give me liberty or give me death." But few of them realize the comparative calm, the tactful manner in which Henry launched that stormy and emotional and history-making address. Should the American colonies separate from and go to war with England? The question was being debated with intense passion. Feelings flamed at white heat; yet Patrick Henry began by complimenting the abilities and praising the patriotism of those who opposed him. Note, in the second paragraph, how he gets his audience thinking with him by asking questions, by letting them draw their own conclusions:

"Mr. President: No man thinks more highly than I do of the patriotism, as well as abilities, of the very worthy gentlemen who have just addressed the house. But different men often see the same subject in different lights; and, therefore, I hope it will not be thought disrespectful to those gentlemen, if, entertaining as I do opinions of a character very opposite to theirs, I shall speak forth my sentiments freely, and without reserve. This is no time for ceremony. The question before the house is one of awful moment to the country. For my own part, I consider it as nothing less than a question of freedom or slavery. And in proportion to the magnitude of the subject ought to be the freedom of the debate. It is only in this way that we can hope to arrive at truth, and fulfill the great responsibility which we hold to God and our country. Should I keep back my opinions at such a time, through fear of giving offense,

I should consider myself as guilty of treason towards my country, and of an act of disloyalty toward the Majesty of Heaven, which I revere above all earthly things.

"Mr. President, it is natural to man to indulge in the illusions of hope. We are apt to shut our eyes against a painful truth, and listen to the song of that Siren till she transforms us into beasts. Is this the part of wise men, engaged in a great and arduous struggle for liberty? Are we disposed to be of the number of those who, having eyes see not, and having ears hear not, the things which so nearly concern their temporal salvation? For my part, whatever anguish of spirit it may cost, I am willing to know the whole truth; to know the worst and to provide for it."

## THE BEST SPEECH SHAKESPEARE WROTE

The most famous speech that Shakespeare put into the mouth of any of his characters—Mark Antony's funeral oration over the body of Julius Caesar—is a classic example of supreme tact.

This was the situation. Caesar had become dictator. Naturally, inevitably, a score of his political enemies were envious, were eager to tear him down, to destroy him, to make his power their own. Twenty-three of them banded together under the leadership of Brutus and Cassius and thrust their daggers into his body ······ Mark Antony had been Caesar's Secretary of State. He was a handsome chap, this Antony, a ready writer, a powerful speaker. He could represent the government well at public affairs. Small wonder Caesar had chosen him as his right hand man. Now, with Caesar out of the way, what should the conspirators do with Antony? Remove him? Kill him? There had been enough blood shed already; there was enough to justify as it was. Why not win this Antony to their side, why not use his undeniable influence, his moving eloquence, to shield them and further their own ends? Sounded safe and reasonable; so they tried it. They saw him and went so far as to permit him to "say a few words" over the corpse of the man who had all but ruled the world ······

Antony mounts the rostrum in the Roman Forum. Before him lies the murdered Caesar. A mob surges noisily and threateningly about Antony, a rabble friendly to Brutus, Cassius and the other assassins. Antony's purpose is to turn this popular enthusiasm into intense hatred, to stir the plebeians to rise in mutiny and slay those that had struck Caesar down. He raises his hands, the tumult ceases, he starts to speak. Note how ingeniously, how adroitly he begins, praising Brutus and the other conspirators:

"For Brutus is an honorable man;
So are they all, all honorable men."

Observe that he does not argue. Gradually, unobtrusively, he presents certain facts about Caesar; tells how the ransom from his captives filled the general coffers, how he wept when the poor cried, how he refused a crown, how he willed his estates to the public. He presents the facts; asks the mob questions; lets them draw their own conclusions. The evidence is presented, not as something new, but as something they had for the moment forgotten:

"I tell you that which you yourselves do know."

And with a magic tongue through it all, he whipped up their feelings, stirred their emotions, aroused their pity, heated their anger. Antony's masterpiece of tact and eloquence is given here in its entirety. Search where you will, range through all the broad fields of literature and oratory, and I doubt if you will find half a dozen speeches to equal this. It merits the serious study of every man who aspires to excel in the fine art of influencing human nature. But there is another reason, entirely aside from the one we are considering now, why Shakespeare ought to be read and reread by business men; he possessed a larger vocabulary than did any other writer who ever lived; he used words more magically, more beautifully. No one can study Macbeth and Hamlet and Julius Caesar without unconsciously brightening and widening and refining his own diction.

*Ant.* Friends, Romans, countrymen, lend me your ears:
I come to bury Caesar, not to praise him.
The evil that men do lives after them;
The good is oft interred with their bones:
So let it be with Caesar. The noble Brutus
Hath told you Caesar wag ambitious:
If it were so, it was a grievous fault;
And grievously hath Caesar answer'd it.
Here, under leave of Brutus and the rest, —
For Brutus is an honorable man;
So are they all, all honorable men, —
Come I to speak in Caesar's funeral.
He was my friend, faithful and just to me:
But Brutus says he was ambitious;
And Brutus is an honorable man.
He hath brought many captives home to Rome,
Whose ransoms did the general coffers fill:

Did this in Caesar seem ambitious?
When that the poor have cried, Caesar hath wept:
Ambition should be made of sterner stuff:
Yet Brutus says he was ambitious;
And Brutus is an honorable man.
You all did see that on the Lupercal
I thrice presented him a kingly crown,
Which he did thrice refuse. Was this ambition?
Yet Brutus says he was ambitious;
And, sure, he is an honorable man.
I speak not to disprove what Brutus spoke,
But here I am, to speak what I do know.
You all did love him once, not without cause;
What cause withholds you, then, to mourn for him?
O judgment, thou art fled to brutish beasts,
And men have lost their reason! Bear with me;
My heart is in the coffin there with Caesar,
And I must pause till it come back to me.

*1 Cit.* Methinks there is much reason in his sayings.

*2 Cit.* If thou consider rightly of the matter, Caesar has had great wrong.

*3 Cit.* Has he not, masters?
I fear there will a worse come in his place.

*4 Cit.* Mark'd ye his words? He would not take the crown;

Therefore 'tis certain he was not ambitious.

*1 Cit.* If it be found so, some will dear abide it,

*2 Cit.* Poor soul! his eyes are red as fire with weeping.

*3 Cit.* There's not a nobler man in Rome than Antony.

*4 Cit.* Now mark him; he begins again to speak.

*Ant.* But yesterday the word of Caesar might
Have stood against the world: now lies he there,
And none so poor to do him reverence.
O masters, if I were dispos'd to stir
Your hearts and minds to mutiny and rage,
I should do Brutus wrong, and Cassius wrong,
Who, you all know, are honorable men.
I will not do them wrong: I rather choose
To wrong the dead, to wrong myself, and you,
Than I will wrong such honorable men.
But here's a parchment with the seal of Caesar,—
I found it in his closet,—'tis his will:
Let but the commons hear this testament
(Which, pardon me, I do not mean to read),
And they would go and kiss dead Caesar's wounds,
And dip their napkins in his sacred blood;
Yea, beg a hair of him for memory,
And, dying, mention it within their wills,
Bequeathing it as a rich legacy
Unto their issue.

*4 Cit.* We'll hear the will; read it, Mark Antony.

*Citizens.* The will, the will! We will hear Caesar's will.

*Ant.* Have patience, gentle friends; I must not read it:
It is not meet you know how Caesar lov'd you.
You are not wood, you are not stones, but men;
And, being men, hearing the will of Caesar,
It will inflame you, it will make you mad.
'Tis good you know not that you are his heirs;
For, if you should, O what would come of it!

*4 Cit.* Read the will! We'll hear it, Antony;
You shall read us the will—Caesar's will!

*Ant.* Will you be patient? Will you stay awhile?
I have o'ershot myself, to tell you of it.
I fear I wrong the honorable men
Whose daggers have stabb'd Caesar; I do fear it.

*4 Cit.* They were traitors: honorable men!

*Citizens.* The will! the testament!

*2 Cit.* They were villains, murderers. The will! read the will!

*Ant.* You will compel me, then, to read the will?
Then make a ring about the corpse of Caesar,
And let me show you him that made the will.
Shall I descend? and will you give me leave?

*Citizens.* Come down. [*He comes down.*]

*2 Cit.* Descend.

*3 Cit.* You shall have leave.

*4 Cit.* A ring! stand round.

*1 Cit.* Stand from the hearse; stand from the body.

*2 Cit.* Room for Antony!—most noble Antony!

*Ant.* Nay, press not so upon me; stand far off.

*Citizens.* Stand back; room! bear back.

*Ant.* If you have tears, prepare to shed them now.
You all do know this mantle: I remember
The first time ever Caesar put it on;
'Twas on a summer's evening, in his tent,
That day he overcame the Nervii.
Look, in this place ran Cassius' dagger through:
See what a rent the envious Casca made:
Through this the well-beloved Brutus stabb'd;
And, as he pluck'd his cursed steel away,
Mark how the blood of Caesar follow'd it,—
As rushing out of doors, to be resolv'd
If Brutus so unkindly knock'd, or no;
For Brutus, as you know, was Caesar's angel:
Judge, O you gods, how dearly Caesar lov'd him!
This was the most unkindest cut of all;
For, when the noble Caesar saw him stab,
Ingratitude, more strong than traitors' arms,
Quite vanquish'd him: then burst his mighty heart;
And, in his mantle muffling up his face,

Even at the base of Pompey's statua,
Which all the while ran blood, great Caesar fell.
O, what a fall was there, my countrymen!
Then I, and you, and all of us fell down,
Whilst bloody treason flourish'd over us.
O, now you weep; and, I perceive, you feel
The dint of pity: these are gracious drops.
Kind souls, what, weep you, when you but behold
Our Caesar's vesture wounded? Look you here,
Here is himself, marr'd, as you see, with traitors.

*1 Cit.* O piteous spectacle!

*2 Cit.* O noble Caesar!

*3 Cit.* O woful day!

*4 Cit.* O traitors, villains!

*1 Cit.* O most bloody sight!

*2 Cit.* We will be reveng'd.

*Citizens.* Revenge, —about, —seek, —burn, —fire, —kill, —slay, —let not a traitor live!

*Ant.* Stay, countrymen.

*1 Cit.* Peace there! hear the noble Antony.

*2 Cit.* We'll hear him, we'll follow him, we'll die with him.

*Ant.* Good friends, sweet friends, let me not stir you up
To such a sudden flood of mutiny.
They that have done this deed are honorable:

What private griefs they have, alas, I know not,
That made them do 't; they're wise and honorable,
And will, no doubt, with reasons answer you.
I come not, friends, to steal away your hearts:
I am no orator, as Brutus is;
But, as you know me all, a plain blunt man,
That love my friend; and that they know full well
That gave me public leave to speak of him.
For I have neither wit, nor words, nor worth,
Action, nor utterance, nor the power of speech,
To stir men's blood: I only speak right on;
I tell you that which you yourselves do know;
Show you sweet Caesar's wounds, poor, poor dumb mouths,
And bid them speak for me: but were I Brutus,
And Brutus Antony, there were an Antony
Would ruffle up your spirit, and put a tongue
In every wound of Caesar, that should move
The stones of Rome to rise and mutiny.

*Citizens.* We'll mutiny.

*1 Cit.* We'll burn the house of Brutus.

*3 Cit.* Away, then! come, seek the conspirators.

*Ant.* Yet hear me, countrymen; yet hear me speak.

*Citizens.* Peace, ho! hear Antony; most noble Antony.

*Ant.* Why, friends, you go to do you know not what.

Wherein hath Caesar thus deserv'd your loves?

Alas, you know not; I must tell you, then:

You have forgot the will I told you of.

*Citizens.* Most true; the will!—let's stay, and hear the will.

*Ant.* Here is the will, and under Caesar's seal.

To every Roman citizen he gives.

To every several man, seventy-five drachmas.

*2 Cit.* Most noble Caesar!—we'll revenge his death.

*3 Cit.* O, royal Caesar!

*Ant.* Hear me with patience.

*Citizens.* Peace, ho!

*Ant.* Moreover, he hath left you all his walks,

His private arbors, and new-planted orchards,

On this side Tiber; he hath left them you,

And to your heirs for ever; common pleasures,

To walk abroad, and recreate yourselves.

Here was a Caesar! when comes such another?

*1 Cit.* Never, never.—Come, away, away!

We'll burn his body in the holy place,

And with the brands fire the traitors' houses.

Take up the body.

*2 Cit.* Go, fetch fire.

*3 Cit.* Pluck down benches.

*4 Cit.* Pluck down forms, windows, any thing.

[*Exeunt Citizens with the body*]

*Ant.* Now let it work:—Mischief, thou art afoot,
Take thou what course thou wilt!

## SUMMARY

1. Begin on common ground. Get everyone agreeing with you at the outset.
2. Don't state your case so that people will be saying "no, no" at the start. When a person once says "no" his pride demands that he stick to it. "The more 'yesses' we can, at the very outset, induce, the more likely we are to succeed in capturing the attention for the ultimate proposal."
3. Do not begin by saying that you are going to prove so and so. That is liable to arouse opposition. Your hearers may say "let's see you do it." Raise some pertinent question, and let them go with you in a hunt for the answer······ "The best argument is that which seems merely an explanation."
4. The most famous speech that Shakespeare ever wrote is Mark Antony's funeral oration over Caesar. It is a classic example of supreme tact.

The Roman populace is friendly to the conspirators. Note how adroitly Antony turns this friendliness into a fury of hate. Note that he does it without arguing. He presents the facts, and lets them form their own opinions.

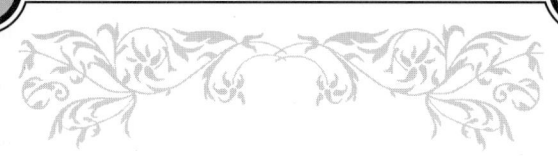

# CHAPTER ELEVEN

## HOW TO CLOSE A TALK

"The conclusion, too, has definite work to perform. It rounds out the talk; it holds the audience's earnest attention for a brief moment on the speech as a whole. It draws the thread of thought together; it binds and finishes the fabric of the speech ⋯⋯ Definitely plan and word your conclusion. Never break off your speech awkwardly and hurriedly with a mumbled: 'I guess that's all I have to say.' Complete your task and let the audience know it is complete."

—Platform Speaking by George Rowland Collins.

"The clock has nothing to do with the length of a sermon. Nothing whatever!⋯⋯ A long sermon is a sermon that seems long⋯⋯ And the short sermon is the one that ends while people are still wishing for more. It may have lasted only twenty minutes or it may have lasted for an hour and a half. If it leaves the people wishing for more, they do not know nor care what the clock said about the length of it. You cannot tell, therefore, how long a sermon is by watching the hands of a clock —watch the people."

—The Art of Preaching, by Charles R. Brown, Dean of the Divinity School, Yale University.

# CHAPTER 11

# HOW TO CLOSE A TALK

Would you like to know in what parts of your speech you are most likely to reveal your inexperience or your expertness, your inaptitude or your finesse? I'll tell you: in the opening and the closing. There is an old saying in the theater, referring, of course, to actors, that goes like this: "By their entrances and their exits shall ye know them."

The beginning and the ending! They are the hardest things in almost any activity to manage adroitly. For example, at a social function aren't the most trying feats the graceful entrance and the graceful leave-taking? In a business interview, aren't the most difficult tasks the winning approach and the successful close?

The close is really the most strategic point in a speech; what one says last, the final words left ringing in the ears when one ceases—these are likely to be remembered longest. Beginners, however, seldom appreciate the importance of this coign of vantage. Their endings often leave much to be desired.

What are their most common errors? Let us discuss a few and search for remedies.

First, there is the man who finishes with: "That is about all I have to say on the matter; so I guess I shall stop." That is not an ending. That is a mistake. That reeks of the amateur. That is almost unpardonable. If that is all you have to say, why not round off your talk, and promptly take your seat and stop without talking about stopping. Do that, and the inference that that is all you have to say may, with safety and good taste, be left to the discernment of the audience.

Then there is the speaker who says all he has to say, but he does not know how to stop. I believe it was Josh Billings who advised people to take your bull by the tail instead of the horns, since it would be easier to let go. This speaker has the bull by the frontal extremities, and wants to part company with him, but try as hard as he will, he can't get near a friendly fence or tree. So he finally thrashes about in a circle, covering the same ground, repeating himself, leaving a bad impression······

The remedy? An ending has to be planned some

time, doesn't it? Is it the part of wisdom to try to do it after you are facing an audience, while you are under the strain and stress of talking, while your mind must be intent on what you are saying? Or does common sense suggest the advisability of doing it quietly, calmly, beforehand?

Even such accomplished speakers as Webster, Bright, Gladstone, with their admirable command of the English language, felt it necessary to write down and all but memorize the exact words of their closings.

The beginner, if he follows in their footsteps, will seldom have cause to regret it. He ought to know very definitely with what ideas he is going to close. He ought to rehearse the ending several times, using not necessarily the same phraseology during each repetition, but putting the thoughts definitely into words.

An extemporaneous talk, during the process of delivery, sometimes has to be altered very materially, has to be cut and slashed to meet unforeseen developments, to harmonize with the reactions of one's hearers; so it is really wise to have two or three closings planned. If one does not fit, another may.

Some speakers never get to the end at all. Along in the middle of their journey, they begin to sputter and misfire like an engine when the gasoline supply is about exhausted; after a few desperate lunges, they come to a complete standstill, a breakdown. They need, of course, better preparation, more practise — more gasoline in the tank.

Many novices stop too abruptly. Their method of closing lacks smoothness, lacks finish. Properly speaking, they have no close; they merely cease suddenly, jerkily. The effect is unpleasant, amateurish. It is as if a friend in a social conversation were to break off brusquely and dart out of the room without a graceful leave-taking.

No less a speaker than Lincoln made that mistake in the original draft of his First Inaugural. That speech was delivered at a tense time. The black storm clouds of dissension and hatred were already milling overhead. A few weeks later, the cyclone of blood and destruction burst upon the nation. Lincoln, addressing his closing words to the people of the South, had intended to end in this fashion:

"In your hands, my dissatisfied fellow-countrymen, and not in mine, is the momentous issue of the civil war. The government will not assail you. You can have no conflict without being yourselves the aggressors. You have no oath registered in heaven to destroy the government, while I have a most solemn one to preserve, protect and defend it. You can forbear the assault upon it. I cannot shrink from the defense of it, With you and not with me is the solemn question of 'Shall it be peace or a sword?'"

He submitted his speech to Secretary Seward. Seward quite appropriately pointed out that the ending was too blunt, too abrupt, too provocative. So Seward himself tried his hand at a closing; in fact, he wrote two. Lincoln accepted one of them and used it, with slight modifications, in place of the last three sentences of the close he had originally prepared. The result was that his First Inaugural Address now lost its provocative abruptness and rose to a climax of friendliness, of sheer beauty and poetical eloquence:

"I am loth to close. We are not enemies but friends. We must not be enemies. Though passion may have strained, it must not break our bonds of affection. The mystic chords of memory, stretching from every battlefield and patriot's grave to every living heart and hearthstone all over this broad land, will swell the chorus of the Union when again touched, as surely they will be, by the better angel of our nature."

How can a beginner develop the proper *feeling* for the close of an address? By mechanical rules?

No. Like culture, it is too delicate for that. It must be a matter of sensing, almost of intuition. Unless a speaker can *feel* when it is done harmoniously, adroitly, how can he himself hope to do it?

However, this *feeling* can be cultivated; this expertness can be developed somewhat, by studying the ways in which accomplished speakers have achieved it. Here is an illustration, the close of an address by the then Prince of Wales before the Empire Club of Toronto:

"I am afraid, gentlemen, that I have departed from my reserve, and talked about myself a good deal too much. But I wanted to tell you, as the largest audience that I have been privileged to address in Canada, what I feel about my position and the responsibility which it entails. I can only assure you that I shall always endeavor to live up to that great responsibility and to be worthy of your trust."

A blind man listening to that talk would *feel* that it was ended. It isn't left dangling in the air like a loose rope. It isn't left ragged and jagged. It is rounded off, it is finished.

The famous Dr. Harry Emerson Fosdick spoke in the Geneva Cathedral of St. Pierre the Sunday after the opening of the sixth assembly of the League of Nations. He chose for his text: "All they that take the sword shall perish with the sword." Note the beautiful and lofty and powerful way in which he brought his sermon to a close:

"We cannot reconcile Jesus Christ and war—that is the essence of the matter. That is the challenge which today should stir the conscience of Christendom. War is the most colossal and ruinous social sin that afflicts mankind; it is utterly and irremediably unchristian; in its total method and effect it means everything that Jesus did not mean and it means nothing that he did mean; it is a more blatant denial of every Christian doctrine about God and man than all the theoretical atheists on earth ever could devise. It would be worth while, would it not, to see the Christian Church claim as her own this greatest moral issue of our time, to see her lift once more as in our fathers' days, a clear standard against the paganism of this present world and, refusing to hold her conscience at the beck and call of belligerent states, put the kingdom of God above nationalism and call the world to peace? That would not be the denial of patriotism but its apotheosis.

Here today, as an American, under this high and hospitable roof, I cannot speak for my government, but both as an American and as a Christian I do speak for millions of my fellow citizens in wishing your great work, in which we believe, for which we pray, our absence from which we painfully regret, the eminent success which it deserves. We work in many ways for the same end—a world organized for peace. Never was an end better worth working for. The alternative is the most appalling catastrophe mankind has ever faced. Like gravitation in the physical realm, the law of the Lord in the moral realm bends for no man and no nation: 'All they that take the sword shall perish with the sword.'"

But this collection of speech endings would not be complete without the majestic tones, the organ-like melody of the close of Lincoln's Second Inaugural. The late Earl Curzon, of Keddleston, Chancellor of Oxford University, declared that this selection was "among the glories and treasures of mankind …… the purest gold of human eloquence, nay, of eloquence almost divine":

"Fondly do we hope, fervently do we pray, that this mighty scourge of war may speedily pass away. Yet if God wills that it continue until all the wealth piled by the bondsman's two hundred and fifty years of unrequited toil shall be sunk, and until every drop of blood drawn with the lash shall be paid by another drawn with the sword, as was said three thousand years ago, so still it must be said that 'the judgments of the Lord are true and righteous altogether.'

With malice toward none; with charity for all; with firmness in the right, as God gives us to see the right, let us strive on to finish the work we are in; to bind up the nation's wounds; to care for him who shall have borne the battle, and for his widow and his orphan—to do all which may achieve and cherish a just and lasting peace among ourselves, and with all nations."

You have just read, my dear reader, what is, in my opinion, the most beautiful speech ending ever delivered by the lips of mortal man······ Do you agree with my estimate? Where, in all the range of speech literature, will you find more humanity, more sheer loveliness, more sympathy?

"Noble as was the Gettysburg Address," says William E. Barton in *Life of Abraham Lincoln*, "this rises to a still higher level of nobility······ It is the greatest of the addresses of Abraham Lincoln and registers his intellectual and spiritual power at their highest altitude."

"This was like a sacred poem," wrote Carl Schurz. "No American President had ever spoken words like these to the American people. America had never had a president who had found such words in the depths of his heart."

But you are not going to deliver immortal pronouncements as President in Washington or as Prime Minister in Ottawa or Melbourne. Your problem, perhaps, will be how to close a simple talk before a group of business men. How shall you set about it? Let us search a bit. Let us see if we cannot uncover some fertile suggestions.

## SUMMARIZE YOUR POINTS

Even in a short talk of three to five minutes a speaker is very apt to cover so much ground that at the close the listeners are a little hazy about all his main points. However, few speakers realize that. They are misled into assuming that because these points are crystal clear in their own minds, they must be equally lucid to their hearers. Not at all. The speaker has been pondering over his ideas for some time. But his points are all new to the audience; they are flung at the audience like a handful of shot. Some may stick, but the most are liable to roll off in confusion. The hearers are liable, like Iago, to "remember a mass of things but nothing distinctly."

Some anonymous Irish politician is reported to have given this recipe for making a speech: "First, tell them that you are going to tell them; then tell them; then tell them that you have told them." Not bad, you know. In fact, it is often highly advisable to "tell them that you have told them." Briefly, of course, speedily—a mere outline, a summary.

Here is a good example. The speaker is a student of Mr. Bills' class in Public Speaking at the Chicago Central Y. M. C. A. He is also a traffic manager for one of Chicago's railways:

"In short, gentlemen, our own back door yard experience with this block device, the experience in its use in the East, in the West, in the North—the sound operating principles underlying its operation, the actual demonstration in the money saved in one year in wreck prevention, move me most earnestly and unequivocally to recommend its immediate installation on our Southern branch."

You see what he has done? You can see it and feel it without having heard the rest of the talk. He has summed up in a few sentences, in sixty-two words, practically all the points he has made in the entire talk.

Don't you feel that a summary like that helps? If so, make that technique your own.

APPEAL FOR ACTION

The closing just quoted is an excellent illustration of the appeal-for-action ending. The speaker wanted something done: a block device installed on the Southern branch of his road. He based his appeal for it on the money it would save, on the wrecks it would prevent. The speaker wanted action, and he got it. This was not a mere practise talk. It was delivered before the board of directors of a certain railway, and it secured the installation of the block device for which it asked.

Chapter XV will discuss, in detail, the problems that confront the speaker when he attempts to get action, and how to solve them.

## A TERSE, SINCERE COMPLIMENT

"The great state of Pennsylvania should lead the way in hastening the coming of the new day. Pennsylvania, the great producer of iron and steel, mother of the greatest railroad company in the world, third among our agricultural states—Pennsylvania is the keystone of our business arch. Never was the prospect before her greater, never was her opportunity for leadership more brilliant."

With these words, Charles Schwab closed his address before the Pennsylvania Society of New York. He left his hearers pleased, happy, optimistic. That is an admirable way to finish; but, in order to be effective, it must be sincere. No gross flattery. No extravagances. This kind of closing, if it does not ring true, will ring false, very false. And like a false coin, people will have none of it.

## A HUMOROUS CLOSE

"Always leave them laughing," said George Cohan, "when you say good-by." If you have the ability to do it, and the material, fine! But how? That, as Hamlet said, is the question. Each man must do it in his own individual way.

One would hardly expect Lloyd George to leave a gathering of Methodists laughing when he was talking to them on the ultra-solemn subject of John Wesley's Tomb; but note how cleverly he managed it. Note, also, how smoothly and beautifully the talk is rounded off:

"I am glad you have taken in hand the repair of his tomb. It should be honored. He was a man who had a special abhorrence of any absence of neatness or cleanliness. He it was, I think, who said, 'let no one ever see a ragged Methodist.' It is due to him that you never can see one. (Laughter.) It is a double unkindness to leave his tomb ragged. You remember what he said to a Derbyshire girl who ran to the door as he was passing and cried, 'God bless you Mr. Wesley.' 'Young woman,' he answered, 'your blessing would be of more value if your face and apron were cleaner.' (Laughter.) That was his feeling about untidiness. Do not leave his grave untidy. If he passed along, that would hurt him more than anything, Do look after that. It is a memorable and sacred shrine. It is your trust." (Cheers.)

# CLOSING WITH A POETICAL QUOTATION

Of all methods of ending, none are more acceptable, when well done, than humor or poetry. In fact, if you can get the proper verse of poetry for your closing, it is almost ideal. It will give the desired flavor. It will give dignity. It will give individuality. It will give beauty.

Rotarian Sir Harry Lauder closed his address to the American Rotarian delegates at the Edinburgh convention in this fashion:

"And when you get back home, some of you send me a postcard. I will send you one if you do not send me one. You will easily know it is from me because there will be no stamp on it. (Laughter.) But I will have some writing on it, and the writing will be this:

'Seasons may come and seasons may go,
Everything withers in due course, you know,
But there is one thing still blooms as fresh as the dew,
That is the love and affection I still have for you.'"

That little verse fits Harry Lauder's personality, and no doubt it fitted the whole tenor of his talk. Therefore, it was excellent for him. Had some formal and restrained Rotarian used it at the end of a solemn talk, it might have been so out of key as to be almost ridiculous. The longer I teach public speaking, the more clearly I see, the more vividly I feel, that it is impossible to give general rules that will serve on all occasions. So much depends upon the subject, the time, the place, and the man. Everyone must, as Saint Paul said, "work out his own salvation."

Mr. J. A. Abbott, Vice President of the L. A. D. Motors Corporation of Brooklyn, spoke to the employes of his organization on the subject of Loyalty and Cooperation. He closed his address with this ringing verse from Kipling's Second Jungle Book:

"Now this is the Law of the Jungle—as old and as true as the sky;
And the Wolf that shall keep it may prosper, but the Wolf that shall break it must die.
As the creeper that girdles the tree-trunk, the Law runneth forward and back?
For the strength of the Pack is the Wolf, and the strength of the Wolf is the Pack."

If you will go to the public library in your town and

tell the librarian that you are preparing a talk on a certain subject and that you wish a poetical quotation to express this idea or that, she may be able to help you find something suitable in some reference volume such as Bartlett's book of quotations.

## THE POWER OF A BIBLICAL QUOTATION

If you can quote a passage from Holy Writ to back up your speech, you are fortunate. A choice Biblical quotation often has a profound effect. The well known financier, Frank Vanderlip, used this method in ending his address on the Allied Debts to the United States:

"If we insist to the letter upon our claim, our claim will in all probability never be met. If we insist upon it selfishly, we realize in hatreds but not in cash. If we are generous, and wisely generous, those claims can all be paid, and the good we do with them will mean more to us materially than anything we would conceivably be parting with. 'For whosoever will save his life shall lose it; but whosoever shall lose his life for My sake and the Gospel's, the same shall save it.'"

# THE CLIMAX

The climax is a popular way of ending. It is often difficult to manage and is not an ending for all speakers nor for all subjects. But, when well done, it is excellent. It works up to a crest, a peak, getting stronger sentence by sentence. A good illustration of the climax will be found in the close of the prize winning speech on Philadelphia in Chapter III.

Lincoln used the climax in preparing his notes for a lecture on Niagara Falls. Note how each comparison is stronger than the preceding, how he gets a cumulative effect by comparing its age to Columbus, Christ, Moses, Adam, and so on:

"It calls up the indefinite past. When Columbus first sought this continent —when Christ suffered on the cross— when Moses led Israel through the Red Sea —nay, even when Adam first came from the hands of his Maker; then, as now, Niagara was roaring here. The eyes of that species of extinct giants whose bones fill the mounds of America have gazed on Niagara, as ours do now. Contemporary with the first race of men, and older than the first man, Niagara is as strong and fresh today as ten thousand years ago. The Mammoth and Mastodon, so long dead that fragments of their monstrous bones alone testify that they ever lived, have gazed on Niagara—in that long, long time never still for a moment, never dried, never frozen, never slept, never rested."

Wendell Phillips employed this selfsame technique in his address on Toussaint l'Ouverture. The close of it is quoted below. This selection is often cited in books on public speaking. It has vigor, vitality. It is interesting even though it is a bit too ornate for this practical age. This speech was written more than half a century ago. Amusing, isn't it, to note how woefully wrong were Wendell Phillips' prognostications concerning the historical significance of John Brown and Toussaint l'Ouverture "fifty years hence when truth gets a hearing?" It is as hard evidently to guess history as it is to foretell next year's stock market or the price of lard.

"I would call him Napoleon, but Napoleon made his war to empire over broken oaths and through a sea of blood. This man never broke his word. 'No Retaliation' was his great motto and the rule of his life; and the last words uttered to his son in France were these: 'My boy, you will one day go back to Santo Domingo; forget that France murdered your father.' I would call him Cromwell, but

Cromwell was only a soldier, and the state he founded went down with him into his grave. I would call him Washington, but the great Virginian held slaves. This man risked his empire rather than permit the slave-trade in the humblest village of his dominions.

You think me a fanatic tonight, for you read history, not with your eyes, but with your prejudices. But fifty years hence, when Truth gets a hearing, the Muse of History will put Phocion for the Greek, and Brutus for the Roman, Hampden for England, Lafayette for France, choose Washington as the bright, consummate flower of our earlier civilization, and John Brown the ripe fruit of our noonday, then, dipping her pen in the sunlight, will write in the dear blue, above them all, the name of the soldier, the statesman, the martyr, Toussaint L'Ouverture."

## WHEN THE TOE TOUCHES

Hunt, search, experiment until you get a good ending and a good beginning. Then get them close together.

The speaker who does not cut his talk to fit in with the prevailing mood of this hurried, rapid age will be unwelcome and, sometimes, positively disliked.

No less a saint than Saul of Tarsus sinned in this respect. He preached until a chap in the audience, "a young man named Eutychus," went to sleep and fell out of a window and all but broke his neck. Even then he may not have stopped talking. Who knows? I remember a speaker, a doctor, standing up one night at the University Club, Brooklyn. It had been a long banquet. Many speakers had already talked. It was two o'clock in the morning when his turn came. Had he been endowed with tact and fine feeling and discretion, he would have said half a dozen sentences and let us go home. But did he? No, not he. He launched into a forty-five minute tirade against vivisection. Long before he was half way through his audience were wishing that he, like Eutychus, would fall out of a window and break something, anything, to silence him.

Mr. Lorimer, the editor of the *Saturday Evening Post*, told me that he always stopped a series of articles in the *Post* when they were at the height of their popularity, and people were clamoring for more. Why stop then? Why then of all times? "Because," said Mr. Lorimer—and he ought to know? "the point of satiation is reached very soon after that peak of popularity."

The same wisdom will apply, and ought to be applied, to speaking. Stop while the audience is still eager to have you go on.

The greatest speech Christ ever delivered, the Sermon on the Mount, can be repeated in five minutes. Lincoln's Gettysburg address has only ten sentences. One can read the whole story of creation in Genesis in less time than it takes to peruse a murder story in the morning paper······ Be brief! Be brief!

Doctor Johnson, Archdeacon of Nyasa, has written a book about the primitive peoples of Africa. He has lived among them, observed them, for forty-nine years. He relates that when a speaker talks too long at a village gathering or the Gwangwara, the audience silences him with shouts of "Imetosha!" "Imetosha!"- "Enough!" "Enough!"

Another tribe is said to permit a speaker to hold forth only so long as he can stand on one foot. When the toe of the lifted member touches the ground, *finito*. He has come to an end.

And the average white audience, even though they are more polite, more restrained, dislike long speeches as much as do those African negroes.

So be warned by their lot,
Which I know you will not,
And learn about speaking from them.

## SUMMARY

1. The close of a speech is really its most strategic element. What is said last is likely to be remembered longest.
2. Do not end with: "That is about all I have to say on the matter; so I guess I shall stop." Stop, but don't talk about stopping.
3. Plan your ending carefully in advance as Webster, Bright, and Gladstone did. Rehearse. Know almost word for word how you are going to close. Round off your talk.
4. Seven suggested ways of closing:
   a. Summarizing, restating, outlining briefly the main points you have covered.
   b. Appealing for action.
   c. Paying the audience a sincere compliment.
   d. Raising a laugh.
   e. Quoting a fitting verse of poetry.
   f. Using a Biblical quotation.
   g. Building up a climax.
5. Get a good ending and a good beginning; and get them close together. Always stop before your audience wants you to. "The point of satiation is reached very soon after the peak of popularity."

# CHAPTER
# TWELVE

## HOW TO MAKE YOUR MEANING CLEAR

"Nine readers out of ten take a lucid statement for a true one"—Encyclopedia Britannica.

"Study carefully what you have to say, and put it into words by writing or by speaking aloud to an imaginary person. Arrange your points in order. Stick to your order. Divide your time among your points according to their importance. Stop when you are through."—Dr. Edward Everett Hale.

"If speaking on Solomon to a group of business men, refer to him as the J. P. Morgan of his day. If talking to baseball fans about Samson call him the Babe Ruth of his time. When Frank Simonds undertook to describe Foch's strategy in battering down the Hindenburg line he used the figure of pounding at the two hinges of a gate. In a similar manner Hugo used the letter A to illustrate the battlefield of Waterloo, and Elson the horseshoe in describing the battle of Gettysburg. Everyone is acquainted with gates, horseshoes and the alphabet, although not everyone has seen battles."

—Glenn Clark, Self-Cultivation in Extemporaneous Speaking.

# HOW TO MAKE
# YOUR MEANING CLEAR

A famous English bishop, during the war, spoke to some unlettered negro troops at Camp Upton, Long Island. They were on their way to the trenches; but a very small percentage of them had any adequate idea why they were being sent. I know: I questioned them. Yet the Lord Bishop talked to these negroes about "International amity," and "Servia's right to a place in the sun." Why, the half of those negroes did not know whether Servia was a town or a disease. He might as well, as far as results were concerned, have delivered a sonorous eulogy on the Nebular Hypothesis. However, not a single trooper left the hall while he was speaking: the military police with revolvers were stationed at every exit to prevent that consummation.

I do not wish to belittle the bishop. He is every inch a scholar; and before a body of collegiate men he would probably have been powerful; but he failed with these negroes, and he failed utterly: he did not know his audience, and he evidently knew neither the precise purpose of his talk nor how to accomplish it.

What do we mean by the purpose of an address? Just this: every talk, regardless of whether the speaker realizes it or not, has one of four major goals. What are they?

1. To make something clear.
2. To impress and convince.
3. To get action.
4. To entertain.

Let us illustrate these by a series of concrete examples.

Lincoln, who was always more or less interested in mechanics, once invented and patented a device for lifting stranded boats off sand bars and other obstructions. He worked in a mechanic's shop near his law office, making a model of his apparatus. Although the device finally came to naught, he was decidedly enthusiastic over its possibilities. When friends came to his office to view the model, he took no end of pains to explain it. The main purpose of those explanations was clearness.

When he delivered his immortal oration at Gettysburg, when he gave his first and second inaugural addresses, when Henry Clay died and Lincoln delivered an eulogy on his life—on all these occasions, Lincoln's main purpose was impressiveness and conviction. He had to be clear, of course, before he could be convincing; but, in these instances, clearness was not his major consideration.

In his talks to juries, he tried to win favorable decisions. In his political talks, he tried to win votes. His purpose, then, was *action*.

Two years before he was elected President, Lincoln prepared a lecture on Inventions. His purpose was entertainment. At least, that should have been his goal; but he was evidently not very successful in attaining it. His career as a popular lecturer was, in fact, a distinct disappointment. In one town, not a person came to hear him.

But he did succeed and he succeeded famously in the other speeches of his that I have referred to. And why? Because, in those instances, he knew his goal, and he knew how to achieve it. He knew where he wanted to go and how to get there. And because so many speakers don't know just that, they often flounder and come to grief.

For example: I once saw a United States Congressman hooted and hissed and forced to leave the stage of the old New York Hippodrome, because he had—unconsciously, no doubt, but nevertheless, unwisely—chosen clearness as his goal. It was during the war. He talked to his audience about how the United States was *preparing*, The crowd did not want to be instructed. They wanted to be entertained. They listened to him patiently, politely, for ten minutes, a quarter of an hour, hoping the performance would come to a rapid end. But it didn't. He rambled on and on; patience snapped; the audience would not stand for more. Someone began to cheer ironically. Others took it up. In a moment, a thousand people were whistling and shouting. The speaker, obtuse and incapable as he was of sensing the temper of his audience, had the bad taste to continue. That aroused them. A battle was on. Their impatience mounted to ire. They determined to silence him. Louder and louder grew their storm of protest. Finally, the roar of it, the anger of it drowned his words—he could not have been heard twenty feet away. So he was forced to give up, acknowledge defeat, and retire in humiliation.

Profit by his example. Know your goal. Choose it

wisely before you set out to prepare your talk. Know how to reach it. Then set about it, doing it skillfully and with science.

All this requires knowledge, special and technical instruction. And so important is this phase of speech construction that four chapters of this course will be devoted to it. The remainder of this chapter will show you how to make your talks clear. Chapter XIII will indicate how to make them impressive and convincing. Chapter XIV will show how to make them interesting. Chapter XV will demonstrate a scientific method for getting action.

## USE COMPARISONS TO PROMOTE CLEARNESS

As to clearness: do not underestimate the importance of it nor the difficulty. I recently heard a certain Irish poet give an evening of readings from his own poems. Not ten per cent of the audience, half the time, knew what he was talking about. Many talkers, both in public and private, are a lot like that.

When I discussed the essentials of public speaking with Sir Oliver Lodge, a man who has been lecturing to university classes and to the public for forty years, he emphasized most of all the importance, first, of knowledge and preparation; second, of "taking good pains to be clear."

The great General Von Moltke, at the outbreak of the Franco-Prussian War, said to his officers:

"Remember, gentlemen, that any order that *can* be misunderstood, *will* be misunderstood."

Napoleon recognized the same danger. His most emphatic and oft-reiterated instruction to his secretaries was: "Be clear! Be clear!"

When the disciples asked Christ why He taught the public by parables, He answered: "Because they seeing, see not: and hearing, hear not; neither do they understand."

And when you talk on a subject strange to your hearer or hearers, can you hope that they will understand you any more readily than people understood the Master?

Hardly. So what can we do about it? What did He do when confronted by a similar situation? Solved it in the most simple and natural manner imaginable: described the things people did not know by likening them to things they did know. The kingdom of Heaven······ what would it be like? How could those untutored peasant of Palestine know? So Christ described it in terms of objects and actions with which they were already familiar:

"The kingdom of Heaven is like unto leaven, which a woman took, and hid in three measures of meal, till the whole was leavened."

"Again, the kingdom of Heaven is like unto a merchantman seeking goodly pearls······"

"Again, the kingdom of Heaven is like unto a net that was cast into the sea······"

That was lucid; they could understand that. The housewives in the audience were using leaven every week; the fishermen were casting their nets into the sea daily; the merchants were dealing in pearls.

And how did David make clear the watchfulness and loving kindness of Jehovah?

"The Lord is my shepherd, I shall not want. He maketh me to lie down in green pastures, He leadeth me beside the still waters······"

Green grazing grounds in that almost barren country······ still waters where the sheep could drink—those pastoral people could understand that.

Here is a rather striking and half-amusing example of the use of this principle: some missionaries were translating the Bible into the dialect of a tribe living near equatorial Africa. They progressed to the verse: "Though your sins be as scarlet, they shall be white as snow." How were they to translate that? Literally? Meaningless. Absurd. The natives had never scooped off the sidewalk on a February morning. They did not even have a word for snow. They could not have told the difference between snow and coal tar; but they had climbed cocoanut trees many times and shaken down a few nuts for lunch; so the missionaries likened the unknown to the known, and changed the verse to read: "Though your sins be as scarlet, they shall be as white as the meat of a cocoanut."

Under the circumstances, it would be hard to improve on that, wouldn't it?

At the State Teachers' College at Warrensburg, Missouri, I once heard a lecturer on Alaska who failed, in many places, to be either clear or interesting because, unlike those African missionaries, he neglected to talk in terms of what his audience knew. He told us, for example, that Alaska had a gross area of 590,804 square miles, and a population of 64,356.

Half a million square miles—what does that mean to

the average man? Precious little. He is not used to thinking in terms of square miles. They conjure up no mental picture. He does not have any idea whether half a million square miles are approximately the size of Maine or Texas. Suppose the speaker had said that the coast line of Alaska and its islands is longer than the distance around the globe, and that its area more than equals the combined areas of Vermont, New Hampshire, Maine, Massachusetts, Rhode Island, Connecticut, New York, New Jersey, Pennsylvania, Delaware, Maryland, West Virginia, North Carolina, South Carolina, Georgia, Florida, Mississippi and Tennessee. Would not that give everyone a fairly clear conception of the area of Alaska?

He said the population was 64,356. The chances are that not one person in ten remembered the census figures for five minutes—or even one minute. Why? Because the rapid saying of "sixty-four thousand, three hundred and fifty-six" does not make a very clear impression. It leaves only a loose, insecure impression, like words written on the sand of the seashore. The next wave of attention quite obliterates them. Would it not have been better to have stated the census in terms of something with which they were very familiar? For example: St. Joseph was not very far away from that little Missouri town where the audience lived. Many of them had been to St. Joseph; and, Alaska had, at that time, ten thousand less people than St. Joseph. Better still, why not talk about Alaska in terms of the very town where you are speaking? Wouldn't the speaker have been far clearer had he said: "Alaska is eight times as large as the state of Missouri; yet it has only thirteen times as many people as live right here in Warrensburg?"

In the following illustrations, which are the clearer, the *a* statement or the *b*?

(a) Our nearest star is thirty-five trillion miles away.
(b) A train going at the rate of a mile a minute would reach our nearest star in forty-eight million years; if a song were sung there and the sound could travel here it would be three million, eight hundred thousand years before we could hear it. A spider's thread reaching to it would weigh five hundred tons.
(a) St. Peter's, the biggest church in the world, is 232 yards long, and 364 feet wide.
(b) It is about the size of two buildings like the capitol at Washington piled on top of one another.

Sir Oliver Lodge happily uses this method when

explaining the size and nature of atoms to a popular audience. I heard him tell a European audience that there were as many atoms in a drop of water as there were drops of water in the Mediterranean Sea; and many of his hearers had spent over a week sailing from Gibraltar to the Suez Canal. To bring the matter still closer home, he said there were as many atoms in one drop of water as there were blades of grass on all the earth.

Richard Harding Davis told a New York audience that the Mosque of St. Sophia was "about as big as the auditorium of the Fifth Avenue theater." He said Brindisi "looks like Long Island City when you come into it from the rear."

Use this principle henceforth in your talks. If you are describing the great pyramid, first tell four hearers it is 451 feet, then tell them how high that is in terms of some building they see every day. Tell how many city blocks the base would cover. Don't speak about so many thousand gallons of this or so many hundred thousand barrels of that without also telling how many rooms the size of the one you are speaking in could be filled with that much liquid. Instead of saying twenty feet high, why not say one and a half times as high as this ceiling? Instead of talking about distance in terms of rods or miles, is it not clearer to say as far as from here to the union station, or to such and such a street?

## AVOID TECHNICAL TERMS

If you belong to a profession the work of which is technical—if you are a lawyer, a physician, an engineer, or are in a highly specialized line of business—be doubly careful when you talk to outsiders, to express yourself in plain terms and to give necessary details.

I say be doubly careful, for, as a part of my professional duties, I have listened to hundreds of speeches that failed right at this point and failed woefully. The speakers appeared totally unconscious of the general public's widespread and profound ignorance regarding their particular specialties. So what happened? They rambled on and on, uttering thoughts, using phrases that fitted into their experience and were instantly and continuously meaningful to them; but to the uninitiated, they were about as clear as the Missouri River after the June rains have fallen on the newly-plowed corn fields of Iowa and Kansas.

What should such a speaker do? He ought to read and heed the following advice from the facile pen of

Ex-Senator Beveridge of Indiana:

"It is a good practice to pick out the least intelligent looking person in the audience and strive to make that person interested in your argument. This can be done only by lucid statement of fact and clear reasoning. An even better method is to center your talk on some small boy or girl present with parents.

Say to yourself—say out loud to your audience, if you like—that you will try to be so plain that the child will understand and remember your explanation of the question discussed, and after the meeting be able to tell what you have said."

I remember hearing a physician, a student of this course, remark in the course of his talk that "diaphragmatic breathing is a distinct aid to the peristaltic action of the intestines and a boon to health." He was about to dismiss that phase of his talk with that one sentence and to rush on to something else, I stopped him; and asked for a show of hands of those who had a clear conception of how diaphragmatic breathing differs from other kinds of breathing, why it is especially beneficial to physical well-being and what peristaltic action is. The result of the vote surprised the doctor; so he went back, explained, enlarged in this fashion:

"The diaphragm is a thin muscle forming the floor of the chest at the base of the lungs and the roof of the abdominal cavity. When inactive and during chest breathing, it is arched like an inverted washbowl.

In abdominal breathing every breath forces this muscular arch down until it becomes nearly flat and you can feel your stomach muscles pressing against your belt. This downward pressure of the diaphragm massages and stimulates the organs of the upper part of the abdominal cavity—the stomach, the liver, the pancreas, the spleen, the solar plexus.

When you breathe out again, your stomach and your intestines will be forced up against the diaphragm and will be given another massage. This massaging helps the process of elimination.

A vast amount of ill health originates in the intestines. Most indigestion, constipation, and auto-intoxication would disappear if our stomachs and intestines were properly exercised through deep diaphragmatic breathing."

# THE SECRET OF LINCOLN'S CLEARNESS

Lincoln had a deep and abiding affection for putting a proposition so that it would be instantly clear to everyone. In his first message to Congress, he used the phrase "sugar-coated." Mr. Defrees, the public printer, being Lincoln's personal friend, suggested to him that although the phrase might be all right for a stump speech in Illinois, it was not dignified enough for a historical state paper. "Well, Defrees," Lincoln replied, "if you think the time will ever come when the people will not understand what 'sugar-coated' means, I'll alter it; otherwise, I think I'll let it go,"

He once explained to Dr. Gulliver, the President of Knox College, how he developed his "passion" for plain language, as he phrased it:

"Among my earliest recollections I remember how, when a mere child, I used to get irritated when anybody talked to me in a way I could not understand. I don't think I ever got angry at anything else in my life. But that always disturbed my temper, and has ever since. I can remember going to my little bedroom, after hearing the neighbors talk of an evening with my father, and spending no small part of the night walking up and down and trying to make out the exact meaning of some of their, to me, dark sayings. I could not sleep, though I often tried to, when I got on such a hunt after an idea, until I had caught it, and when I thought I had got it I was not satisfied until I had repeated it over and over, until I had put it in language plain enough as I thought for any boy I knew to comprehend. This was a kind of passion with me, and it has since stuck by me."

A passion? Yes, it must have amounted to that, for Mentor Graham, the schoolmaster of New Salem, testified: "I have known Lincoln to study for hours the best way of three to express an idea."

An all too common reason why men fail to be intelligible is this: the thing they wish to express is not clear even to themselves. Hazy impressions! Indistinct, vague ideas! The result? Their minds work no better in a mental fog than a camera does in a physical fog. They need to be as disturbed over obscurity and ambiguity as Lincoln was. They need to use his methods.

## APPEAL TO THE SENSE OF SIGHT

The nerves that lead from the eye to the brain are, as we observed in Chapter IV, many times larger than those leading from the ear; and science tells us that we give twenty-five times as much attention to eye suggestions as we do to ear suggestions.

"One seeing," says an old Japanese proverb, "is better than a hundred times telling about."

So, if you wish to be clear, picture your points, visualize your ideas. That was the plan of the late John H. Patterson, president of the well known National Cash Register Company. He wrote an article for *System Magazine*, outlining the methods he used in speaking to his workmen and his sales forces:

"I hold that one cannot rely on speech alone to make himself understood or to gain and hold attention. A dramatic supplement is needed. It is better to supplement whenever possible with pictures which show the right and the wrong way; diagrams are more convincing than mere words, and pictures are more convincing than diagrams. The ideal presentation of a subject is one in which every subdivision is pictured and in which the words are used only to connect them. I early found that in dealing with men, a picture was worth more than anything I could say.

Little grotesque drawings are wonderfully effec-tive ...... I have a whole system of cartooning or 'chart talks.' A circle with a dollar mark means a piece of money, a bag marked with a dollar is a lot of money. Many good effects can be had with moon faces. Draw a circle, put in a few dashes for the eyes, nose, mouth, and ears. Twisting these lines gives the expressions. The out-of-date man has the corner of his mouth down; the chipper, up-to-date fellow has the curves up. The drawings are homely, but the most effective cartoonists are not the men who make the prettiest pictures; the thing is to express the idea and the contrast.

The big bag and the little bag of money, side by side, are the natural heads for the right way as opposed to the wrong way; the one brings much money, the other little money. If you sketch these rapidly as you talk, there is no danger of people's letting their minds wander; they are bound to look at what you are doing and thus to go with you through the successive stages to the point you want to make. And again, the funny figures put people in good humor.

I used to employ an artist to hang around in the shops with me and quietly make sketches of things that were not being done right. Then the sketches were made into drawings and I called the men together and showed them exactly what they were doing. When I heard of the stereopticon I immediately bought one and projected the drawings on the screen, which, of course, made them even more effective than on paper. Then came the moving picture. I think that I had one of the first machines ever made and now we have a big department with many motion picture films and more than 60,000 colored stereopticon slides."

Not every subject or occasion, of course, lends itself to exhibits and drawings; but let us use them when we can. They attract attention, stimulate interest and often make our meaning doubly clear.

## ROCKEFELLER RAKING OFF THE COINS

Mr. Rockefeller also used the columns of *System Magazine* to tell how he appealed to the sense of sight to make clear the financial situation of the Colorado Fuel and Iron Company:

"I found that they (the employees of the Colorado Fuel and Iron Co.) imagined the Rockefellers had been drawing immense profits from their interests in Colorado; no end of people had told them so. I explained the exact situation to them. I showed them that during the fourteen years in which we had been connected with the Colorado Fuel and Iron Co., it had never paid one cent in dividends upon the common stock.

At one of our meetings, I gave a practical illustration of

the finances of the company. I put a number of coins on the table. I swept off a portion which represented their wages—for the first claim upon the company is the pay roll. Then I took away more coins to represent the salaries of the officers, and then the remaining coins to represent the fees of the directors. There were no coins left for the stockholders. And when I asked: 'Men, is it fair, in this corporation where we are all partners, that three of the partners should get all the earnings, be they large or small—all of them—and the fourth nothing?'

After the illustration, one of the men made a speech for higher wages. I asked him, 'Is it fair for you to want more wages when one of the partners gets nothing?' He admitted that it did not look like a square deal; I heard no more about increasing the wages."

Make your eye appeals definite and specific. Paint mental pictures that stand out as sharp and clear as a stag's horn silhouetted against the setting sun. For example, the word "dog" calls up a more or less definite picture of such an animal—perhaps a cocker spaniel, a Scotch terrier, a St. Bernard, or a Pomeranian. Notice how much more distinct an image springs into your mind when I say "bulldog"—the term is less inclusive. Doesn't "a brindle bulldog" call up a still more explicit picture? Is it not more vivid to say "A black Shetland pony" than to talk of "a horse"? Doesn't "a white bantam rooster with a broken leg" give a much more definite and sharp picture than merely the word "fowl"?

## RESTATE YOUR IMPORTANT IDEAS IN DIFFERENT WORDS

Napoleon declared repetition to be the only serious principle of rhetoric. He knew that because an idea was clear to him was not always proof that it was instantly grasped by others. He knew that it takes time to comprehend new ideas, that the mind must be kept focussed on them. In short, he knew they must be repeated. Not in exactly the same language. People will rebel at that, and rightly so. But if the repetition is couched in fresh phraseology, if it is varied, your hearers will never regard it as repetition at all.

Let us take a specific example. The late Mr. Bryan said:

"You cannot make people understand a subject, unless you understand that subject yourself. The more clearly you have a subject in mind, the more clearly can you present that subject to the minds of others."

The last sentence here is merely a restatement of the idea contained in the first; but when these sentences are spoken, the mind does not have time to see that it is repetition. It only *feels* that the subject has been made more clear.

I seldom teach a single session of this course without hearing one or perhaps half a dozen talks that would have been more clear, more impressive, had the speaker but employed this principle of restatement. It is almost entirely ignored by the beginner. And what a pity!

## USE GENERAL ILLUSTRATIONS AND SPECIFIC INSTANCES

One of the surest and easiest ways to make your points clear is to follow them with general illustrations and concrete cases. What is the difference between the two? One, as the term implies, is general; the other, specific.

Let us illustrate the difference between them and the uses of each with a concrete example. Suppose we take the statement: "There are professional men and women who earn astonishingly large incomes."

Is that statement very clear? Have you a clear-cut idea of what the speaker really means? No, and the speaker himself cannot be sure of what such an assertion will call up in the minds of others. It may cause the country doctor in the Ozark Mountains to think of a family doctor in a small city with an income of five thousand. It may cause a successful mining engineer to think in terms of the men in his profession who make a hundred thousand a year. The statement, as it stands, is entirely too vague and loose. It needs to be tightened. A few illuminating details ought to be given to indicate what professions the speaker refers to and what he means by "astonishingly large."

"There are lawyers, prize fighters, song writers, novelists, playwrights, painters, actors and singers who make more than the President of the United States."

Now, hasn't one a much clearer idea of what the speaker meant? However, he has not individualized. He has used general illustrations, not specific instances. He has said "singers," not Rosa Ponselle, Kirsten Flagstad, or Lily Pons.

So the statement is still more or less vague. We

cannot call up concrete cases to illustrate it. Should not the speaker do it for us? Would he not be clearer if he employed specific examples—as is done in the following paragraph?

"The great trial lawyers Samuel Untermeyer and Max Steuer earn as much as one million dollars a year. Jack Dempsey's annual income has been known to be as high as a half million dollars. Joe Louis, the young, uneducated negro pugilist, while still in his twenties, has earned more than a half million dollars. Irving Berlin's rag-time music is reported to have brought him a half million dollars yearly. Sidney Kingsley has made ten thousand dollars a week royalty on his plays. H. G. Wells has admitted, in his autobiography, that his pen has brought him three million dollars. Diego Rivera has earned, from his paintings, more than a half a million dollars in a year. Katherine Cornell has repeatedly refused five thousand dollars a week to go into pictures. Lawrence Tibbet and Grace Moore are reported to have an annual income of a quarter million dollars."

Now, has not one an extremely plain and vivid idea of exactly and precisely what the speaker wanted to convey?

Be concrete. Be definite. Be specific. This quality of definiteness not only makes for clearness but for impressiveness and conviction and interest also.

## DO NOT EMULATE THE MOUNTAIN GOAT

Professor William James, in one of his talks to teachers, pauses to remark that one can make only one point in a lecture, and the lecture he referred to lasted an hour. Yet I recently heard a speaker, who was limited by a stop watch to three minutes, begin by saying that he wanted to call our attention to eleven points. Sixteen and a half seconds to each phase of his subject! Seems incredible, doesn't it, that an intelligent man should attempt anything so manifestly absurd. True, I am quoting an extreme case; but the tendency to err in that fashion, if not to that degree, handicaps almost every novice. He is like a Cook's guide who shows Paris to the tourist in one day. It can be done, just as one can walk through the American Museum of Natural History in thirty minutes. But neither clearness nor enjoyment results. Many a talk fails to be clear because the speaker seems intent upon establishing a world's record for ground covered in the allotted time. He leaps from one point to another with the swiftness and agility of a mountain goat.

The talks in this course must, owing to the pressure of time, be short; so cut your cloth accordingly. If, for example, you are to speak on Labor Unions, do not attempt to tell us in three or six minutes why they came into existence, the methods they employ, the good they have accomplished, the evil they have wrought, and how to solve industrial disputes. No, no; if you strive to do that, no one will have a very clear conception of what you have said. It will be all confused, a blur, too sketchy, too much of a mere outline.

Wouldn't it be the part of wisdom to take one phase and one phase only of labor unions, and cover that adequately and illustrate it? It would. That kind of speech leaves a single impression. It is lucid, easy to listen to, easy to remember.

However, if you must cover several phases of your topic, it is often advisable to summarize briefly at the end. Let us see how that suggestion operates. Here is a summary of this lesson. Does the reading of it help to make the message we have been presenting more lucid, more comprehensible?

# SUMMARY

1. To be clear is highly important and often very difficult. Christ declared that He had to teach by parables, "Because they (His hearers) seeing, see not; and hearing, hear not; neither do they understand."
2. Christ made the unknown clear by talking of it in terms of the known. He likened the Kingdom of Heaven to leaven, to nets cast into the sea, to merchants buying pearls. "Go thou, and do likewise." If you wish to give a clear conception of the size of Alaska, do not quote its area in square miles; name the states that could be put into it; enumerate its population in terms of the town where you are speaking.
3. Avoid technical terms when addressing a lay audience. Follow Lincoln's plan of putting your ideas into language plain enough for any boy to comprehend.
4. Be sure that the thing you wish to speak about is first as clear as noonday sunshine in your own mind.
5. Appeal to the sense of sight. Use exhibits, pictures, illustrations when possible. Be definite.

Don't say "dog" if you mean "a fox terrier with a black splotch over his right eye."

6. Restate your big ideas; but don't repeat, don't use the same phrases twice. Vary the sentences, but reiterate the idea without letting your hearers detect it.
7. Make your abstract statement clear by following it with general illustrations—and what is often better still—by specific instances and concrete cases.
8. Do not strive to cover too many points. In a short speech, one cannot hope to treat adequately more than one or two phases of a big topic.
9. Close with a brief summary of your points.

# CHAPTER THIRTEEN

## HOW TO BE IMPRESSIVE AND CONVINCING

"The secret of success in life consists in knowing how to change men's minds. It is this power that makes the successful lawyer, grocer, politician or preacher."—Dr. Frank Crane.

"Never was the power of moving men by speech more potent than now, never was it more useful, more admired as an accomplishment."
—Earl Curzon of Kedleston, while Chancellor of the University of Oxford.

"The recipe for perpetual ignorance is be satisfied with your opinions and content with your knowledge." —Elbert Hubbard.

"The public speaker must set forth with power and attractiveness the very same topic which others discuss in such tame and bloodless phraseology."
—Cicero.

# HOW TO BE IMPRESSIVE
# AND CONVINCING

Here is a psychological discovery of tremendous import: "Every idea, concept or conclusion which enters the mind," says Walter Dill Scott, President of Northwestern University, "is held as true unless hindered by some contradictory idea······ If we can give a man any sort of an idea it is not necessary to convince him of the truth of the idea if we can keep conflicting ideas from arising in his mind. If I can get you to read the sentence, 'United States tires are good tires,' you will believe that they are good tires and that too without any further proof if any contradictory ideas do not surge up into your mind."

Dr. Scott is here speaking about suggestion—one of the most powerful influences the public speaker—or private one, too, for that matter—can employ.

Three centuries before the Wise Men of the East

followed the star of Bethlehem on the first Christmas, Aristotle taught that man was a reasoning animal—that he acted according to the dictates of logic. He flattered us. Acts of pure reasoning are as rare as romantic thoughts before breakfast. Most of our actions are the result of suggestion.

Suggestion is getting the mind to accept an idea without offering any proof or demonstration. If I say to you, "Royal Baking Powder is absolutely pure," and do not attempt to prove it, I am using suggestion, If I present an analysis of the product and the testimony of well-known chefs regarding it, I am trying to prove my assertion. Those who are most successful in handling others rely more upon suggestion than upon argument. Salesmanship and modern advertising are based chiefly on suggestion.

It is easy to believe; doubting is more difficult. Experience and knowledge and thinking are necessary before we can doubt and question intelligently. Tell a child that Santa Claus comes down the chimney or a savage that thunder is the anger of the gods and the child and the savage will accept your statements until they acquire sufficient knowledge to cause them to demur. Millions in India passionately believe that the waters of the Ganges are holy, that snakes are deities in disguise, that it is as wrong to kill a cow as it is to kill a person—and, as for eating roast beef······ that is no more to be thought of than cannibalism. They accept these absurdities, not because they have teen proved, but because the suggestion has been deeply imbedded in their minds, and they have not the intelligence, the knowledge, the experience, necessary to question them.

We smile······ the poor benighted creatures! Yet you and I, if we examine the facts closely, will discover that the majority of our opinions, our most cherished beliefs, our creeds, the principles of conduct on which many of us base our very lives, are the result of suggestion, rather than reasoning. To take a concrete illustration from business. We have come to regard Arrow collars, Royal baking powder, Heinz pickles, Gold Medal flour, Ivory soap as among the leading, if not the best, products of their kind. Why? Have we adequate reason for these judgments? Reason? Most of us have none at all. Have we made a careful comparison of the value of these brands and the output of competing firms? No! We have come to believe things for which no proof has been given. Prejudiced, biased, and reiterated assertions, not logic, have formulated our beliefs.

We are creatures of suggestion. There is no denying that. Had you and I been taken from our cradles here in America when we were six months old, and had we been reared by a Hindoo family on the banks of the mighty Brahmaputra, we would have been taught from infancy that cows are holy; we too, would be kissing them when we met them on the streets of Benares; we, too, would look with horror on the "Christian dogs" who ate beefsteak; we, too, would then, be bowing down to monkey gods and elephant gods and gods of wood and stone. So our beliefs are seldom due to reasoning. They are almost all due to suggestion and geography.

Let us take a homely illustration that shows how most of us are being influenced by suggestion every day: You have read many times that coffee is harmful. Let us suppose you intend to abstain from drinking it. You go into your favorite restaurant for dinner. If the waitress is not skilled in the niceties of salesmanship, she may inquire, "Do you wish coffee?" If she does, the arguments for and against it may battle momentarily in your mind, and your self-control perhaps wins. You want good digestion more than you wish the immediate gratification of your palate. However, if she phrases it negatively, "You don't want any coffee, do you?" you find it still simpler to say "no." The idea of refusing what she has put into your mind passes into action. (Haven't you heard many an unschooled and undiscerning salesman greet his prospective customer with just such a negative proposal?) But suppose she asks, "Will you have your coffee now or later?" What happens? She has subtly assumed that there is no question about your wanting it; She concentrates your entire attention on *when* you wish it served; and so she excludes other considerations from your mind, rendering it difficult for contradictory ideas to arise, making it easy for the thought of ordering coffee to pass into action. The result? You say "bring it now," when you really didn't intend to order it at all. This has happened to the writer. It has happened to most of the men who read these lines. It, and a thousand things like it, are happening every day. Department stores train their sales people to inquire, "Will you take it with you?" because they have learned that "Do you wish to have it sent?" increases delivery costs immediately.

Not only does every idea that enters the mind tend to be accepted as true; but it is a well-known psychological fact that it also tends to pass into action. For example, you cannot even think of a letter of the alphabet without moving ever so slightly the muscles used in pronouncing it. You cannot think of swallowing without moving ever so slightly the muscles used in that act. The movement may be imperceptible to you; but there are machines delicate enough to register that muscular reaction. The only reason that you do not do everything you think of is because another idea—the uselessness of it, the expense, the trouble, the absurdity, the danger or some such thought—arises to slay the impulse.

## OUR MAIN PROBLEM

So in the last analysis, our problem of getting people to accept our beliefs or to act upon our suggestions, is just this: to plant the idea in their minds and to keep contradictory and opposing ideas from arising. He who is skilled in doing that will have power in speaking and profit in business.

## HELPS PSYCHOLOGY HAS TO OFFER

Has Psychology any suggestions that will prove helpful to you in this connection? Emphatically, yes. Let us see what they are. First, haven't you noticed that contradictory ideas are much less likely to arise in your mind when the main idea is presented with feeling and contagious enthusiasm? I say "contagious," for enthusiasm is just that. It lulls the critical faculties. It is a veritable "rough-on-rats" to all dissenting, to all negative and opposing ideas. When your aim is impressiveness, remember it is more productive to stir emotions than to arouse thoughts. Feelings are more powerful than cold ideas. To arouse feelings one must be intensely in earnest. Insincerity rips the vitals out of delivery. Regardless of the pretty phrases a man may concoct; regardless of the illustrations he may assemble; regardless of the harmony of his voice, and the grace of his gestures: if he does not speak sincerely, these are hollow and glittering trappings. If you would impress an audience, be impressed yourself. Your spirit, shining through your eyes, radiating through your voice, and proclaiming itself through your manner, will communicate itself to your auditors.

## LIKEN WHAT YOU WISH PEOPLE TO ACCEPT TO SOMETHING THEY ALREADY BELIEVE

An atheist once declared to William Paley that there

was no God, and he challenged the English rector to disprove his contention. Paley very quietly took out his watch, opened the case and showed the works to the unbeliever, saying: "If I were to tell you that those levers and wheels and springs made themselves and fitted themselves together and started running on their own account, wouldn't you question my intelligence? Of course, you would. But look up at the stars. Every one of them has its perfect appointed course and motion—the earth and planets around the sun, and the whole group pitching along at more than a million miles a day. Each star is another sun with its own group of worlds, rushing on through space like our own solar system. Yet there are no collisions, no disturbance, no confusion. All quiet, efficient, and controlled. Is it easier to believe that they just happened or that someone made them so?"

Rather impressive, isn't it? What technique did the speaker use? Let us see. He began on common ground, got his opponent saying "yes," and agreeing with him at the outset, as we advised in Chapter X. Then he went on to show that belief in a deity is as simple, as inevitable, as belief in a watchmaker.

Suppose he had retorted to his antagonist at the outset: "No God? Don't be a silly ass. You don't know what you are talking about." What would have happened? Doubtlessly a verbal joust—a wordy war would have ensued, as futile as it was fiery. The atheist would have risen with an unholy zeal upon him to fight with all the fury of a Fuzzy Wuzzy for his opinions. Why? Because, as Professor Robinson has pointed out, they were *his* opinions, and his precious, indispensable self-esteem would have been threatened; his pride would have been at stake.

Since pride is such a fundamentally explosive characteristic of human nature, wouldn't it be the part of wisdom to get a man's pride working for us, instead of against us? How? By showing, as Paley did, that the thing we propose is very similar to something that our opponent already believes. That renders it easier for him to accept than to reject your proposal. That prevents contradictory and opposing ideas from arising in the mind to vitiate what we have said.

Paley showed delicate appreciation of how the human mind functions. Most men, however, lack this subtle ability to enter the citadel of a man's beliefs arm in arm with the owner. They erroneously imagine that in order to take the citadel, they must storm it, batter it down by a frontal attack. What happens? The moment hostilities commence, the drawbridge is lifted, the great gates are slammed and bolted, the mailed archers draw their long bows—the battle of words and wounds is on. Such frays always end in a draw; neither has convinced the other of anything.

## SAINT PAUL'S SAGACITY

This more sensible method we are advocating is not new. It was used long ago by Saint Paul. He employed it in that famous address of his to the Athenians on Mars Hill—employed it with an adroitness and finesse that compels our admiration across nineteen centuries. He was a man of finished education; and, after his conversion to Christianity, his eloquence made him its leading advocate. One day he arrived at Athens—the post-Pericles Athens, an Athens that had passed the summit of its glory and was now on the decline. The Bible says of it at this period:

"All the Athenians and strangers which were there spent their time in nothing else but either to tell or to hear some new thing."

No radios, no cables, no A. P. dispatches; those Athenians must have been hard put in those days to scratch up something fresh every afternoon. Then Paul came. Here was something new. They crowded about him, amused, curious, interested. Taking him to the Areopagus, they said:

"May we know what this new doctrine, whereof thou speakest, is? For thou bringest certain strange things to our ears: we would know therefore what these things mean."

In other words, they invited a speech; and, nothing loth, Paul agreed. In fact, that was what he had come for. He probably stood up on a block or stone, and, being a bit nervous, as all good speakers are at the very outset, he may have given his hands a dry wash, and have cleared his throat before he began.

However, he did not altogether approve of the way they had worded their invitation; "New doctrines ······ strange things," That was poison. He must eradicate those ideas. They were fertile ground for the propagating of contradictory and clashing opinions. He did not wish to present his faith as something strange and alien. He wanted to tie it up to, liken it to, something they already believed. That would smother dissenting suggestions. But how? He thought a moment; hit upon a brilliant plan; he began his immortal address:

"Ye men of Athens, I perceive that in all things ye are very superstitious."

Some translations read: "ye are very religious." I think that is better, more accurate. They worshipped many gods; they were very religious. They were proud of it. He complimented them, pleased them. They began to warm toward him. One of the rules of the art of public speaking is to support a statement by an illustration. He does just that:

"For, as I passed by, and beheld your devotions, I found an altar with this inscription, TO THE UNKNOWN GOD."

That proves, you see, that they were very religious. They were so afraid of slighting one of the deities that they had put up an altar to the unknown God, a sort of blanket insurance policy to provide against all unconscious slights and unintentional oversights. Paul, by mentioning this specific altar, indicated that he was not dealing in flattery: he showed that his remark was a genuine appreciation born of observation.

Now, here comes the consummate rightness of this

opening:

"Whom therefore ye ignorantly worship, Him declare I unto you."

"New doctrine ······ strange things?" Not a bit of it. He was there merely to explain a few truths about a God they were already worshipping without being conscious of it. Likening the things they did not believe, you see, to something they already passionately accepted—such was his superb technique.

He propounded his doctrine of salvation and resurrection, quoted a few words from one of their own Greek poets; and he was done. The whole speech had consumed less than two minutes. Some of his hearers mocked, but others said:

"We will hear thee again on this matter."

Just in passing, let us note that that is one of the advantages of a two minute talk: you may be asked to speak again, as Paul was. A Philadelphia politician once remarked to me that the main rules to remember in making a speech were: make it short, and make it snappy. Saint Paul, on this occasion, did both.

This technique that Saint Paul used at Athens is employed by the more discriminating business men of today in their selling talks and advertising. For example, here is a paragraph lifted from a sales letter that recently arrived at my desk:

"Old Hampshire Bond costs less than one half cent more per letter than the cheapest paper available. If you write a customer or a prospect ten letters a year, the influence of Old Hampshire will cost you less than a car fare —less than giving your customer a good cigar once every five years."

Who could possibly object to paying a car fare for a customer once a year or offering him a Havana twice in a decade? Surely, no one. And using Old Hampshire Bond would cost no more than that in additional expense? Doesn't that tend to forestall contradictory ideas regarding prohibitive cost?

## MAKING SMALL SUMS APPEAR LARGE AND LARGE SUMS APPEAR SMALL

In much the same way, a large sum can be made to appear small by distributing it over a long period of time and comparing the daily outlay with something that seems trivial. For example, a life insurance president, addressing the sales organization of his company, impressed his men with the low cost of insurance in this fashion:

"A man below thirty can at death leave his family one thousand dollars by cutting out his daily five cent shine, doing the job himself, and investing the sum saved in insurance. The man of thirty-four who smokes a quarter's worth of cigars daily can stay with his family longer, and leave them three thousand dollars more, by spending his cigar money for insurance."

Small sums, on the other hand, can be made to appear huge by reversing this process—by massing them. A telephone company official heaped insignificant minutes together to impress his audience with the vast amount of time lost by New Yorkers neglecting to answer telephones promptly:

"Out of each one hundred telephone connections made, seven show a delay of more than a minute before the person called answers. Every day 280,000 minutes are lost in this way. In the course of six months, this minute's delay in New York is about equal to all the business days that have elapsed since Columbus discovered America."

# HOW TO MAKE FIGURES IMPRESSIVE

Mere numbers and amounts, taken by themselves, are never very impressive. They have to be illustrated; they ought, if possible, to be put in terms of our experiences, our recent experiences and our feeling experiences. For example, Alderman Lambeth used this technique when he was addressing the Borough Council of London anent labor conditions. He stopped abruptly in the middle of his speech, took out his watch, and stood staring in blank silence at the audience for one minute and twelve seconds. The other members of the Borough Council twisted in their seats uneasily, looked questioningly at the speaker, at one another. What was wrong? Had Alderman Lambeth suddenly lost his mind? Resuming his speech, he declared: "You have just sat through and fidgeted through the seventy-second eternity of time which it takes the average workman to lay one brick,"

Was this method of doing it effective? It was so effective that it was cabled to all parts of the world, printed in newspapers across the seas. It was so effective that the Amalgamated Union of Building Trades at once called a strike "in protest against this insult to our dignity."

Which of the two following statements drives the point home with the greater force?

1. The Vatican has 15,000 rooms.
2. The Vatican has so many rooms that one might occupy a different one every day for forty years without having lived in them all.

Which of the following methods gives you a more impressive conception of the incredible amount of money that Great Britain spent during the world war?

1. Great Britain spent approximately seven billion pounds sterling or about thirty-four billion dollars during the war.
2. Would you be surprised to learn that Great Britain spent, during the four and a half years of the world war, a sum equal to thirty-four dollars for every minute that has passed night and day since the Pilgrim Fathers landed at Plymouth Rock? The sum is even more stupendous than that. Great Britain spent in the World War thirty-four dollars for every minute that has passed, night and day, since Columbus discovered America. The sum is even more colossal than that. Great Britain spent during the world war, thirty-four

dollars for every minute that has passed night and day since William, Duke of Normandy, came over and conquered England in 1066. The sum is even more fabulous than that. Great Britain spent during the world war a sum equal to thirty-four dollars for every minute that has passed night and day since Christ was born. In other words, Great Britain spent thirty-four billion dollars; and there have been approximately only a billion minutes elapsed since the birth of Christ.

## WHAT RESTATEMENT WILL DO

Restatement is another club that we can use to prevent contradictory and dissenting ideas from arising to challenge our assertions. "It is not by advancing a political truth once or twice, or even ten times, that the public will take it up and adopt it," declared Daniel O'Connell, the famous Irish orator. O'Connell had had a lot of experience with audiences and the public. His testimony ought to merit consideration. "Incessant repetition," he continued, "is required to impress political truths upon the mind. Men, by always hearing the same thing, insensibly associate them with truisms. They find the facts at last quietly reposing in a corner of their minds, and no more think of doubting them than if they formed a part of their religious beliefs."

Hiram Johnson knew the truth O'Connell expressed. That was why he went up and down the state of California for seven months, ending almost everyone of his addresses with this same prediction:

"Remember this, my friends, I am going to be the next Governor of California; and, when I am, I am going to kick out of this government William F. Herrin and the Southern Pacific railroad—Good night."

John Wesley's mother knew the truth O'Connell expressed. That is why, when her husband asked her why she repeated the same truths to her sons twenty times, she replied: "Because they have not learned the lesson when I have repeated it nineteen times."

Woodrow Wilson knew the truth O'Connell expressed. That is why he used it in his addresses.

Note that he merely reiterates and rephrases in the last two sentences, the idea he had stated in the first.

"You know that the pupils in the colleges in the last several decades have not been educated. You know that with all of our teaching we train nobody. You know that with all of our instructing, we educate nobody."

However, in spite of all that we have said in praise of the principle of restatement, we ought to be warned that in the hands of an inexpert speaker, it may prove to be a dangerous tool. Unless he has a fairly rich phraseology, his restatement may deteriorate into an unadorned and all-too-evident repetition. That is deadly. If the audience catches you at that, they will begin twisting in their seats, looking at their watches.

## GENERAL ILLUSTRATIONS AND SPECIFIC INSTANCES

There is little danger, however, of boring people when you employ general illustrations and specific instances. Interesting, easy to pay attention to, they are extremely valuable when the purpose of your talk is to impress and convince. They help to keep contradictory ideas from rising.

For example, Dr. Newell Dwight Hillis, in one of his addresses, declared that "disobedience is slavery; obedience is liberty." He felt that such a statement, unless it was illustrated, would not be either clear or impressive; so he continued: "Disobedience to the law of fire or water or acid is death. Obedience to the law of color gives the artist his skill; obedience to the law of eloquence gives the orator his force; obedience to the law of iron gives the inventor his tools."

Those illustrations help; they impress, don't they? Could we have given still more life and vitality to his statement by citing concrete cases? Let us see. "Obedience to the law of color gave Leonardo da Vinci his Last Supper; obedience to the law of eloquence gave Henry Ward Beecher his Liverpool address; obedience to the law of iron gave McCormick his reaper."

Isn't that better? People like to have a speaker give names and dates—something they can examine for themselves if they wish. That kind of procedure is frank, honest. It wins confidence. It impresses.

For example, suppose I say, "Many wealthy men lead very simple lives." I have not been impressive. The statement is too vague, isn't it? It does not leap off the page and strike you between the eyes. It will soon drop out of your mind. It is neither clear nor interesting nor convincing. Memories of newspaper reports to the contrary will probably arise to cast doubt upon the assertion.

If I believe that many rich men lead simple lives, how did I reach that conclusion? Through observing several concrete cases; so the best way—to make you believe as I do, is to exhibit those specific instances to you. If I can show you what I have seen, you may arrive at the same conclusion that I have arrived at; and you will probably do it without any urging on my part.

A conclusion that I let you discover for yourself from concrete cases and evidence that I supply, will have twice, three, five times the force of a ready made conclusion that I might hand you on a platter. To illustrate:

John D. Rockefeller, Sr., had a leather couch in his office at 26 Broadway, and took a midday nap each day.

The late J. Ogden Armour used to retire at nine o'clock, and get up at six.

George F. Baker, who controlled at one time more corporations than any other man, never tasted a cocktail. He began to smoke only a few years before his death.

The late John H. Patterson, President of the National Cash Register Company, neither smoked nor drank.

Frank Vanderlip, at one time the president of the largest bank in America, eats only two meals a day.

Milk and old fashioned ginger wafers constituted Harriman's midday meal.

Jacob H. Schiff used to lunch on a glass of milk.

Andrew Carnegie's favorite dish was oatmeal and cream.

Cyrus H. Fortis, owner of the *Saturday Evening Post* and the *Ladies Home Journal*, loves no food better than baked beans.

What is the effect of these specific instances on your mind? Do they dramatize the statement that rich men often lead simple lives? Do they impress you with the truth of it? As you listen to them, isn't it very unlikely that contradictory ideas will arise in your mind?

## THE PRINCIPLE OF CUMULATION

Do not expect a hurried reference to one or possibly two specific instances to have the desired effect.

"There must be," says Professor Phillips in *Effective Speaking*, "a succession of impressions all emphasizing the first. Over and over again must the mind have its attention riveted upon the thought; experience upon experience must be piled up until the very weight imbeds the thought deep in the tissues of the brain. Then it becomes a part of him and neither time nor events can rub it out. And the working principle that does this is Cumulation."

Note how this principle of cumulation was used in marshalling an array of specific instances on page 396 to prove that rich men often lead simple lives. Note how it was employed on pages 77 and 80 to prove that Philadelphia is "the greatest workshop of the world." Note how Senator Thurston employed it in the following paragraph to prove that humanity has been able to right the wrongs of injustice and oppression only by force. What would have been the result had two-thirds of these specific references been omitted?

"When has a battle for humanity and liberty ever been won except by force? What barricade of wrong, injustice, and oppression has ever been carried except by force?

Force compelled the signature of unwilling royalty to the great Magna Charta; force put life into the Declaration of Independence and made effective the Emancipation Proclamation; force beat with naked hands upon the iron gateway of the Bastile and made reprisal in one awful hour for centuries of kingly crime; force waved the flag of revolution over Bunker Hill and marked the snows of Valley Forge with blood-stained feet; force held the broken line of Shiloh, climbed the flame-swept hill at Chattanooga, and stormed the clouds on Lookout Heights; force marched with Sherman to the sea, rode with Sheridan in the valley of the Shenandoah, and gave Grant victory at Appomattox; force saved the Union, kept the stars in the flag, made 'niggers' men."

## GRAPHIC COMPARISONS

Many years ago, a student of this course at the Brooklyn Central Y. M. C. A., told in a speech the number of houses that had been destroyed by fire during the previous year. He further said that, if these burned buildings had been placed side by side, the line would have reached from New York to Chicago, and that if the people who had been killed in those fires had been placed half a mile apart, that gruesome line would reach back again from Chicago to Brooklyn.

The figures he gave I forgot almost immediately; but ten years have passed, and, without any effort on my part, I can still see that line of burning buildings stretching from Manhattan Island to Cook County, Illinois.

Why is that so? Because ear impressions are hard to retain. They roll away like sleet striking the smooth bark of a beech tree. But eye impressions? I saw, a few years ago, a cannon ball imbedded in an old house standing on the banks of Danube—a cannon ball that

Napoleon's artillery had fired at the battle of Ulm. Visual impressions are like that cannon ball: they come with a terrific impact. They imbed themselves. They stick. They tend to drive out all opposing suggestions as Bonaparte drove away the Austrians.

The power of William Paley's reply to the atheist was due in no small degree to the fact that it was visual. Burke used this technique when, in denouncing the taxation of the American colonies, he declared with prophetic vision: "We are shearing, not a sheep, but a wolf."

## CALL IN AUTHORITY TO BACK YOU UP

As a boy in the middle west, I used to amuse myself by holding a stick across a gateway that the sheep had to pass through. After the first few sheep had jumped over the stick, I took it away; but all the other sheep leaped through the gateway over an imaginary barrier. The only reason for their jumping was that those in front had jumped. The sheep is not the only animal with that tendency. Almost all of us are prone to do what others are doing, to believe what others are believing, to accept, without question, the testimony of prominent men.

The student in the New York Chapter of the American Institute of Banking who began his talk on thrift in this manner had a distinct advantage:

"James J. Hill said: 'If you want to know whether you are going to succeed, the test is easy. Are you able to save money? If not, drop out. You will surely lose. You may not think it, but you will lose as sure as you live.'"

That was the next best thing to having James J. Hill himself there. His words impressed. Their influence tended to prevent opposing ideas from arising.

However, in quoting authorities, bear these four Points in mind.

1. *Be Definite*

Which of these statements is the more impressive and convincing?

(a) Statistics show that Seattle is the healthiest city in the world.

(b) "According to the official federal mortality statistics, Seattle's annual death rate for the last fifteen years has been 9.78 per thousand: Chicago's, 14.65: New York's, 15.83; New Orleans', 21.02."

Beware of beginning "statistics show ……" What

statistics? Who gathered them and why? Be careful! "Figures won't lie, but liars will figure."

The usual phrase? "many authorities declare"—is ridiculously vague. Who are the authorities? Name one or two. If you do not know who they are, how can you be sure of what they said?

Be definite. It wins confidence. It demonstrates to the audience that you know whereof you speak. Even Theodore Roosevelt thought he could not afford to be vague. In an address at Louisville, Kentucky, during the administration of Woodrow Wilson, he said:

"Mr. Wilson's promises before election, both those made in his own speeches and those made in the platform, have been so well nigh invariably broken that the breaking of them has become a subject for jest even among his own friends. One of Mr. Wilson's prominent Democratic supporters in Congress stated with refreshing frankness the exact truth about Mr. Wilson's pre-election promises and those made on his behalf when, in answer to some charge of inconsistency, he responded by saying that 'our platform was made to get into office on—and we have won.' *You will find this remark on page 4618 of the Congressional Record, the third session of the Sixty-second Congress.*"

## 2. *Quote a Popular Man.*

Our likes and dislikes have more to do with our beliefs than most of us would care to admit. I once saw Samuel Untermyer hissed while he was engaged in a socialistic debate at Carnegie Hall, New York. What he said was polite enough, and, it seemed to me, in all truth, harmless enough, quiet enough. But most of the audience were socialists. They despised him. They would almost have been inclined to question the veracity of the multiplication table had he but quoted it.

On the other hand, the James J. Hill quotation referred to previously was especially appropriate before a chapter of the American Institute of Banking, for the bewhiskered railroad builder stood well with the banking fraternity.

## 3. *Quote Local Authorities.*

If you are speaking in Detroit, quote a Detroit man. Your hearers can look him up, can investigate the matter. They will be more impressed with his testimony than with the words of some unknown individual away off in Spokane or San Antonio.

## 4. *Quote Someone Qualified to Speak.*

Ask yourself such questions as these: Is this person

generally recognized as an authority on this subject? Why? Is he a prejudiced witness? Has he any selfish ends to serve?

The student at the Brooklyn Chamber of Commerce who opened his talk on *Specialization* with the following quotation from Andrew Carnegie chose wisely. Why? Because the business men in his audience had an abiding respect for the great steel magnate. Besides, Mr. Carnegie was being quoted on business success, a subject on which a lifetime of experience and observation had qualified him to speak.

"I believe the true road to pre-eminent success in any line is to make yourself master in that line. I have no faith in the policy of scattering one's resources, and in my experience I have rarely if ever met a man who achieved preeminence in money-making —certainly never one in manufacturing—who was interested in many concerns. The men who have succeeded are the men who have chosen one line and stuck to it."

## SUMMARY

"Every idea, concept or conclusion which enters the

mind is held as true unless hindered by some contradictory idea." Our problem then, when the purpose of our talk is impressiveness and conviction, is twofold: first, to set forth our own ideas; second, to prevent opposing ideas from arising to render them null and void. Here are eight suggestions that will aid in achieving that consummation:

1. Convince yourself before you attempt to convince others. Speak with contagious enthusiasm.
2. Show how the thing you want people to accept is very similar to something they already believe. (Illustrations: Paley and the atheist, Saint Paul in Athens, Old Hampshire Bond.)
3. Restate your ideas. (Illustrations: Hiram Johnson, "I am going to be the next governor of California……" Woodrow Wilson, "We educate nobody……")
   When restating figures, illustrate them. For example, Great Britain spent thirty-four billion dollars during the world war—a sum equal to thirty-four dollars for every minute that has passed night and day since Christ was born.
4. Use general illustrations. (Illustration: Dr. Hillis, "Obedience to the law of color gives the artist his

skill······")

5. Use specific instances, cite concrete cases. (Illustrations: "Many wealthy men lead very simple lives······ Frank Vanderlip eats only two meals a day······," etc.)

6. Use the principle of cumulation. "Experience upon experience must be piled up until the very weight imbeds the thought deep in the tissues of the brain." (Illustrations: "Force compelled the signature of unwilling royalty to the great Magna Charta······," and so on.)

7. Use graphic comparisons. Ear impressions are easily obliterated. Visual impressions stick like an imbedded cannon ball. (Illustration: The line of burning buildings stretching from Brooklyn to Chicago.)

8. Back up your statements with unprejudiced authority. Be definite as Roosevelt was in his quotation. Quote a popular man. Quote a local man. Quote someone qualified to speak.

# CHAPTER FOURTEEN

# HOW TO INTEREST YOUR AUDIENCE

"There is in all communication—written or spoken—a certain dead line of interest. If we can cross that dead line, we have the world with us—temporarily at least. If we cannot cross it, we may as well retire. The world will have none of us."
—H. A. Overstreet, in *Influencing Human Behavior*.

"Always have something to say. The man who has something to say, and who is known never to speak unless he has, is sure to be listened to. Always know before what you mean to say. If your own mind is muddled, much more will the minds of your hearers be confused. Always arrange your thoughts in some sort of order. No matter how brief they are to be, they will be better for having a beginning, a middle, and an end. At all hazards, be clear. Make your meaning, whatever it is, plain to your audience. In controversial speaking, aim to anticipate your adversary's argument. Reply to his jests seriously and to his earnestness by jest. Always reflect before hand upon the kind of audience you are likely to have……Never, if you can help it, be dull."—Lord Bryce.

**HOW TO INTEREST YOUR AUDIENCE**

If you were invited to dine at the home of a rich man in certain sections of China, it would be proper to toss chicken bones and olive seeds over your shoulder onto the floor. You pay your host a compliment when you do that. You show that you realize that he is wealthy, that he has plenty of servants to tidy up after the meal. And he likes it.

You can be reckless with the remains of your sumptuous meal in a rich man's home; but in some parts of China the poorer people must save even the water they bathe in. To heat water costs so much that they must buy it at a hot water shop. After they have bathed in it, they can take it back and sell it second hand to the shopkeeper from whom they purchased it. When the second customer has soiled it, the water still retains a market value, although the price has softened a bit.

Have you found these facts about Chinese life interesting? If so, do you know why? Because those are very unusual aspects of very usual things. They are strange truths about such commonplace events as dining out and bathing.

That is what interests us—something new about the old.

Let us take another illustration. This page you are reading now, this sheet of paper you are looking at—it is very ordinary, isn't it? You have seen countless thousands of such pages. It seems dull and insipid now; but if I tell you a strange fact about it, you are almost sure to be interested. Let us see! This page seems like solid matter as you look at it now. But, in reality, it is more like a cobweb than solid matter. The physicist knows it is composed of atoms. And how small is an atom? We learned in Chapter XII that there are as many atoms in one drop of water as there are drops of water in the Mediterranean sea, that there are as many atoms in one drop of water as there are blades of grass in all the world. And the atoms that make this paper are composed of what? Still smaller things called electrons and protons. These electrons are all rotating around the central proton of the atom, as far from it, relatively speaking, as the moon is from the earth. And they are swinging through their orbits, these electrons of this tiny universe, at the inconceivable speed of approximately ten thousand miles a second. So the electrons that compose this sheet of paper you are holding, have moved, since you began reading this very sentence, a distance equal to that which stretches between New York and Tokio……

And only two minutes ago you may have thought this piece of paper was still and dull and dead; but, in reality, it is one of God's mysteries. It is a veritable cyclone of energy.

If you are interested in it now, it is because you have learned a new and strange fact about it. There lies one of the secrets of interesting people. That is a significant truth, one that we ought to profit by in our every day intercourse. The entirely new is not interesting; the entirely old has no attractiveness for us. We want to be told something new about the old. You cannot, for example, interest an Illinois farmer with a description of the Cathedral at Bourges, or the Mona Lisa. They are too new to him. There is no tie-up to his old interests. But you can interest him by relating the fact that farmers in Holland till land below the level of the sea and dig ditches to act as fences and build bridges to serve as gates. Your illinois farmer will listen open-mouthed while you tell him that Dutch farmers keep the cows, during the winter, under the same roof that houses the family, and sometimes the cows look out through lace curtains at driving snows. He knows about cows and fences—new slants, you see, on old things. "Lace curtains! For a cow!" he'll exclaim. "I'll be doggoned!" And he will retail that story to his friends.

Here is a talk delivered by a New York City student of this course. As you read it, see if it interests you. If it does, do you know why?

## HOW SULPHURIC ACID AFFECTS YOU

"Most liquids are measured by the pint, quart, gallon or barrel. We ordinarily speak of quarts of wine, gallons of milk, and barrels of molasses. When a new oil gusher is discovered, we speak of its output as so many barrels per day. There is one liquid, however, that is manufactured and consumed in such large quantities that the unit of measurement employed is the ton. This liquid is sulphuric acid.

It touches you in your daily life in a score of ways. If it

were not for sulphuric acid, your car would stop, and you would go back to "old Dobbin" and the buggy, for it is used extensively in the refining of kerosene and gasoline. The electric lights that illuminate your office, that shine upon your dinner table, that show you the way to bed at night, would not be possible without it.

When you get up in the morning and turn on the water for your bath, you use a nickel-plated faucet, which requires sulphuric acid in its manufacture. It was required also in the finishing of your enameled tub. The soap you use has possibly been made from greases or oils that have been treated with the acid …… Your towel has made its acquaintance before you made the acquaintance of your towel. The bristles in your hair-brush have required it, and your celluloid comb could not have been produced without it. Your razor, no doubt, has been pickled in it after annealing.

You put on your underwear; you button up your outer garments. The bleacher, the manufacturer of dyes and the dyer himself used it, The button-maker possibly found the acid necessary to complete your buttons. The tanner used sulphuric acid in making the leather for your shoes, and it serves us again when we wish to polish them.

You come down to breakfast. The cup and saucer, if they be other than plain white, could not have come into being without it. It is used to produce the gilt and other ornamental colorings. Your spoon, knife and fork have seen a bath of sulphuric acid, if they be silver-plated.

The wheat of which your bread or rolls are made has possibly been grown by the use of a phosphate fertilizer, whose manufacture rests upon this acid. If you have buckwheat cakes and syrup, your syrup needed it······

And so on through the whole day, its work affects you at every turn. Go where you will, you cannot escape its influence. We can neither go to war without it nor live in peace without it. So it hardly seems possible that this acid, so essential to mankind, should be totally unfamiliar to the average man······But such is the case."

## THE THREE MOST INTERESTING THINGS IN THE WORLD

What would you say they are—the three most interesting subjects in the world? Sex, property and religion. By the first we can create life, by the second we maintain it, by the third we hope to continue it in the world to come.

But it is *our* sex, *our* property, *our* religion that interests us. Our interests swarm about our own egos.

We are not interested in a talk on How to Make

Wills in Peru; but we may be interested in a talk entitled: How to Make Our Wills. We are not interested—except, perhaps, out of curiosity—in the religion of the Hindoo; but we are vitally interested in a religion that insures *us* unending happiness in the world to come.

When the late Lord Northcliffe was asked what interests people, he answered with one word—and that word was "themselves." Northcliffe ought to have known for he was the wealthiest newspaper owner in Great Britain.

Do you want to know what kind of person you are? Ah, now we are on an interesting topic. We are talking about *you*. Here is a way for *you* to hold the mirror up to your real self, and see *you* as *you* really are. Watch your reveries. What do we mean by reveries? Let Professor James Harvey Robinson answer. We are quoting from *The Mind in the Making*:

"We all appear to ourselves to be thinking all the time during our waking hours, and most of us are aware that we go on thinking while we are asleep, even more foolishly than when awake. When uninterrupted by some practical issue we are engaged in what is now known as a *reverie*. This is our spontaneous and favorite kind of thinking. We allow our ideas to take their own course and this course is determined by our hopes and fears, our spontaneous desires, their fulfillment or frustration; by our likes and dislikes, our loves and hates and resentments. *There is nothing else anything like so interesting to ourselves as ourselves.* All thought that is not more or less laboriously controlled and directed will inevitably circle about the beloved Ego. It is amusing and pathetic to observe this tendency in ourselves and in others. We learn politely and generously to overlook this truth, but if we dare to think of it, it blazes forth like the noontide sun.

Our reveries form the chief index of our fundamental character. They are a reflection of our nature as modified by often hidden and forgotten experiences⋯⋯ The reverie doubtless influences all our speculations in its persistent tendency to self-magnification and self-justification, which are its chief preoccupations."

So remember that the people you are to talk to spend most of their time when they are not concerned with the problems of business, in thinking about and justifying and glorifying themselves. Remember that the average man will be more concerned about the cook leaving than about Italy paying her debts to the United States. He will be more wrought up over a dull razor blade than over a revolution in South America. His own toothache will distress him more than an earthquake in Asia destroying half a million lives. He would rather listen to you say some nice thing about him than hear you discuss the ten greatest men in history.

## HOW TO BE A GOOD CONVERSATIONALIST

The reason so many people are poor conversationalists is because they talk about only the things that interest them. That may be deadly boring to others. Reverse the process. Lead the other person into talking about *his* interests, *his* business, *his* golf score, *his* successor, if it is a mother, *her* children. Do that and listen intently and you will give pleasure; consequently you will be considered a good conversationalist—even though you have done very little of the talking.

Mr. Harold Dwight of Philadelphia recently made an extraordinarily successful speech at a banquet which marked the final session of a public speaking course. He talked about each man in turn around the entire table, told how he had talked when the course started, how he had improved; recalled the talks various members had made, the subjects they had discussed;

he mimicked some of them, exaggerated their peculiarities, had everyone laughing, had everyone pleased. With such material, he could not possibly have failed. It was absolutely ideal. No other topic under the blue dome of Heaven would have so interested that group. Mr. Dwight knew how to handle human nature.

## AN IDEA THAT WON TWO MILLION READERS

A few years ago, the *American Magazine* enjoyed an amazing growth. Its sudden leap in circulation became one of the sensations of the publishing world. The secret? The secret was the late John M. Siddall and his ideas. When I first met Siddall he had charge of the Interesting People Department of that periodical. I had written a few articles for him; and one day he sat down and talked to me for a long time:

"People are selfish," he said. "They are interested chiefly in themselves. They are not very much concerned about whether the government should own the railroads; but they do want to know how to get ahead, how to draw more salary, how to keep healthy. If I were editor of this magazine," he went on, "I would tell them how to take care of their teeth, how to take baths, how to keep cool in summer, how to get a position, how to handle employees, how to buy homes, how to remember, how to avoid grammatical errors, and so on. People are always interested in human stories, so I would have some rich man tell how he made a million in real estate. I would get prominent bankers and presidents of various corporations to tell the stories of how they battled their ways up from the ranks to power and wealth."

Shortly after that, Siddall was made editor. The magazine then had a small circulation, was comparatively a failure. Siddall did just what he said he would do. The response? It was overwhelming. The circulation figures climbed up to two hundred thousand, three, four, half a million······ Here was something the public wanted. Soon a million people a month were buying it, then a million and a half, finally two millions. It did not stop there, but continued to grow for many years. Siddall appealed to the selfish interests of his readers.

# HOW DR. CONWELL INTERESTED MILLI-ONS OF HEARERS

What was the secret of the world's most popular lecture, "Acres of Diamonds?" Just the thing we have been talking about. John M. Siddall discussed this lecture in the conversation I have just referred to; and I think that its enormous success had something to do with determining the policy of his magazine.

It was never a static lecture. Dr. Conwell made it personal to each town where he spoke. That was of immense importance. The local references made it appear fresh and new. They made that town, that audience, seem important. Here is his own story of how he did it:

"I visit a town or city, and try to arrive there early enough to see the postmaster, the barber, the keeper of the hotel, the principal of the schools, and the ministers of some of the churches, and then go into some of the factories and stores, and talk with the people, and get into sympathy with the local conditions of that town or city and see what has been their history, what opportunities they had and what they had failed to do—and every town fails to do something—and then go to the lecture and talk to those people about the subjects which apply to their locality. Acres of Diamonds—the idea—has continuously been precisely the same. The idea is that in this country of ours, every man has the opportunity to make more of himself than he does in his own environment, with his own skill, with his own energy, and with his own friends."

## THE KIND OF SPEECH MATERIAL THAT ALWAYS HOLDS ATTENTION

You may possibly bore people if you talk about things and ideas, but you can hardly fail to hold their attention when you talk about people. Tomorrow there will be millions of conversations floating over fences in the backyards of America, over tea tables and dinner tables—and what will be the predominating note in most of them? Personalities. He said this. Mrs. So-and-so did that. I saw her doing this, that and the other. He is making a "killing," and so on.

I have addressed many gatherings of school children in the United States and Canada; and I soon learned by experience that in order to keep them interested I had to tell them stories about people. As soon as I became general and dealt with abstract ideas, Johnny became restless and wiggled in his seat, Tommy made a face at someone, Billy threw something across the aisle.

True, these were audiences of children; but the intelligence tests used in the army during the war revealed the startling fact that 49% of the people in the United States have a mental age of about 13. So one can hardly go wrong in making a generous use of human interest stories. Our magazines that are read by millions, periodicals such as the *American, Cosmopolitan, Saturday Evening Post*, are filled with them.

I once asked a group of American business men in Paris to talk on *How to Succeed*. Most of them praised the homely virtues, preached at, lectured to, and bored their hearers. (Incidentally, I recently heard one of the most prominent business men in America make this identical mistake in a radio talk on this identical topic.)

So I halted this class, and said something like this: "We don't want to be lectured to. No one enjoys that. Remember you must be entertaining or we will pay no attention whatever to what you are saying. Also remember that one of the most interesting things in the world is sublimated, glorified gossip. So tell us the stories of two men you have known. Tell why one succeeded and why the other failed. We will gladly listen to that, remember it and possibly profit by it. It will also, by the way, be far easier for you to deliver than are these wordy, abstract preachments."

There was a certain member of that course who invariably found it difficult to interest either himself or his audience. This night, however, he seized the human story suggestion; and told us of two of his classmates in college. One of them had been so conservative that he had bought shirts at the different stores in town, and made charts showing which ones laundered best, wore longest and gave the most service per dollar invested. His mind was always on pennies; yet, when he was graduated—it was an engineering college—he had such a high opinion of his own importance that he was not willing to begin at the bottom and work his way up, as the other graduates were doing. Even when the third annual reunion of the class came, he was still mating laundry charts of his shirts, while waiting for some extraordinarily good thing to come his way. It never came. A quarter of a century has passed since then, and this man, dissatisfied and soured on life, still holds a minor position.

The speaker then contrasted with this failure the story of one of his classmates who had surpassed all expectations. This particular chap was a good mixer.

Everyone likes him. Although he was ambitious to do big things later, he started as a draughtsman. But he was always on the lookout for opportunity. Plans were then being made for the Pan-American exposition in Buffalo. He knew engineering talent would be needed there; so he resigned from his position in Philadelphia and moved to Buffalo. Through his agreeable personality, he soon won the friendship of a Buffalo man with considerable political influence. The two formed a partnership, and engaged immediately in the contracting business. They did considerable work for the telephone company, and this man was finally taken over by that concern at a large salary. Today he is a multi-millionaire, one of the principal owners of Western Union.

We have recorded here only the bare outline of what the speaker told. He made his talk interesting and illuminating with a score of amusing and human details······ He talked on and on—this man who could not ordinarily find material for a three minute speech—and he was surprised beyond words to learn when he stopped that he had held the floor on this occasion for half an hour. The speech had been so interesting that it seemed short to everyone. It was this student's first real triumph.

Almost every student can profit by this incident. The average speech would be far more appealing if it were rich and replete with human interest stories. The speaker ought to attempt to make only a few points and to illustrate them with concrete cases. Such a method of speech building can hardly fail to get and hold attention.

If possible, these stories ought to tell of struggles, of things fought for and victories won. All of us are tremendously interested in fights and combats. There is an old saying that all the world loves a lover. It doesn't. What all the world loves is a scrap. It wants to see two lovers struggling for the hand of one woman. As an illustration of this fact, read almost any novel, magazine story, or go to see almost any film drama. When all the obstacles are removed and the reputed hero takes the so-called heroine in his arms, the audience begins reaching for their hats and coats. Five minutes later the sweeping women are gossiping over their broom handles.

Almost all magazine fiction is based on this formula. Make the reader like the hero or heroine. Make him or her long for something intensely. Make that something seem impossible to get. Show how the hero or heroine fights and gets it.

The story of how a man battled in business or profession against discouraging odds, and won, is always inspiring, always interesting. A magazine editor once told me that the real, inside story of any person's life is entertaining. If one has struggled and fought—and who hasn't?—his story, if correctly told, will appeal. There can be no doubt of that.

## BE CONCRETE

The writer once had in the same course in public speaking, a Doctor of Philosophy and a rough-and-ready fellow who had spent his youth thirty years ago in the British Navy. The polished scholar was a university professor; his classmate from the seven seas was the proprietor of a small side street moving-van establishment. Strange to say, the moving-van man's talks during the course would have held a popular audience far better than the talks of the college professor. Why? The college man spoke in beautiful English, with a demeanor of culture and refinement, and with logic and clearness; but his talks lacked one essential, *concreteness*. They were too vague, too general. On the other hand, the van owner possessed hardly enough power of cerebration to generalize.

When he talked he got right down to business immediately. He was definite; he was concrete. That quality, coupled with his virility and his fresh phraseology, made his talks very entertaining.

I have cited this instance, not because it is typical either of college men or moving-van proprietors, but because it illustrates the interest-getting power that accrues to the man —regardless of education—who has the happy habit of being concrete and definite in his speaking.

This principle is so important that we are going to use several illustrations to try to lodge it firmly in your mind. We hope you will never forget it, never neglect it.

Is it, for example, more interesting to state that Martin Luther, as a boy, was "stubborn and intractable," or is it better to say that he confessed that his teachers had flogged him as often as "fifteen times in a forenoon"?

Words like "stubborn and intractable" have very little attention value. But isn't it easy to listen to the flogging count?

The old method of writing a biography was to deal in a lot of generalities which Aristotle called, and rightly called, "The refuge of weak minds." The new method is to deal with concrete facts that speak for themselves. The old fashioned biographer said that John Doe was born of "poor but honest parents." The new method would say that John Doe's father couldn't afford a pair of overshoes, so when the snow came, he had to tie gunny sacking around his shoes to keep his feet dry and warm; but, in spite of his poverty, he never watered the milk and he never traded a horse with the heaves as a sound animal. That shows that his parents were "poor but honest," doesn't it? And doesn't it do it in a way that is far more interesting than the "poor but honest" method?

If this method works for modern biographers it will work also for modern speakers.

Let us take one more illustration. Suppose you wished to state that the potential horse power wasted at Niagara every day was appalling. Suppose you said just that, and then added, that if it were utilized and the resulting profits turned to purchasing the necessities of life, crowds could be clothed and fed. Would that be the way to make it interesting and entertaining? No— No. Isn't this far better? We are quoting from Edwin E. Slosson in the *Daily Science News Bulletin*:

"We are told that there are some millions of people in

poverty and poorly nourished in this country, yet here at Niagara is wasted the equivalent of 250,000 loaves of bread an hour. We may see with our mind's eye 600,000 nice fresh eggs dropping over the precipice every hour and making a gigantic omelet in the whirlpool. If calico were continuously pouring from the looms in a stream 4,000 feet wide like Niagara River, it would represent the same destruction of property. If a Carnegie Library were held under the spout it would be filled with good books in an hour or two. Or we can imagine a big department store floating down from Lake Erie every day and smashing its varied contents on the rocks 160 feet below. That would be an exceedingly interesting and diverting spectacle, quite as attractive to the crowd as the present, and no more expensive to maintain. Yet some people might object to that on the ground of extravagance who now object to the utilization of the power of the falling water."

## PICTURE-BUILDING WORDS

In this process of interest-getting, there is one aid, one technique, that is of the highest importance; yet it is all but ignored. The average speaker does not seem to be aware of its existence. He has probably never consciously thought about it at all. I refer to the process of using words that create pictures. The speaker who is easy to listen to is the one who sets images floating before your eyes. The one who employs foggy, commonplace, colorless symbols sets the audience to nodding.

Pictures. Pictures. Pictures. They are as free as the air you breathe. Sprinkle them through your talks, your conversation; and you will be more entertaining, more influential.

To illustrate: let us take the excerpt just quoted from the *Daily Science News Bulletin* regarding Niagara. Look at the picture words. They leap up and go scampering away in every sentence, as thick as rabbits in Australia: "250,000 loaves of bread, 600,000 eggs dropping over the precipice, gigantic omelette in the whirlpool, calico pouring from the looms in a stream 4,000 feet wide, Carnegie library held under the spout, books, a big department store floating, smashing, rocks below, falling water."

It would be almost as difficult to ignore such a talk or article as it would be to pay not the slightest attention to the scenes from a film unwinding on the silver screen of the motion picture theater.

Herbert Spencer, in his famous little essay on the *Philosophy of Style*, pointed out long ago the superiority of terms that call forth bright pictures:

"We do not think," says he, "in generals but in particulars ······ We should avoid such a sentence as

In proportion as the manners, customs and amusements of a nation are cruel and barbarous, the regulations of their penal code will be severe.

And in place of it, we should write:

In proportion as men delight in battles, bull fights and combats of gladiators, will they punish by hanging, burning and the rack."

Picture-building phrases swarm through the pages of the Bible and through Shakespeare like bees around a cider mill. For example, a commonplace writer would have said that a certain thing would be superfluous, like trying to improve the perfect. How did Shakespeare express the same thought? With a picture phrase that is immortal: "To gild refined gold, to paint the lily, to throw perfume on the violet."

Did you ever pause to observe that the proverbs that are passed on from generation to generation are almost all visual sayings? "A bird in the hand is worth two in the bush." "It never rains but it pours." "You can lead a horse to water but you can't make him drink." And you will find the same picture element in almost all the similes that have lived for centuries and grown hoary with too much use: "Sly as a fox." "Dead as a door nail" "Flat as a pancake." "Hard as a rock."

Lincoln continually talked in visual terminology. When he became annoyed with the long, complicated, red-tape reports that came to his desk in the White House, he objected to them, not with a colorless phraseology, but with a picture phrase that it is almost impossible to forget. "When I send a man to buy a horse," said he, "I don't want to be told how many hairs the horse has in his tail. I wish only to know his points."

## THE INTEREST GETTING VALUE OF CONTRASTS

Listen to the following condemnation of Charles I by Macaulay. Note that Macaulay not only uses pictures, but he also employs balanced sentences. Violent contrasts almost always hold our interests; violent contrasts are the very brick and mortar of this paragraph:

"We charge him with having broken his coronation oath; and we are told that he kept his marriage vow! We accuse him of having given up his people to the merciless inflictions of the most hot-headed of prelates; and the defense is that he took his little son on his knee and kissed him! We censure him for having violated the articles of the Petition of Right, after having, for good and valuable consideration, promised to observe them; and we are informed that he was accustomed to hear prayers at six o'clock in the morning! It is to such considerations as these, together with his Vandyke dress, his handsome face and his peaked beard, that he owes, we verily believe, most of his popularity with the present generation."

## INTEREST IS CONTAGIOUS

We have been discussing so far the kind of material that interests an audience. However, one might mechanically follow all the suggestions made here and speak according to Cocker, and yet be vapid and dull. Catching and holding the interest of people is a delicate thing, a matter of feeling and spirit. It is not like operating a steam engine. No book of precise rules can be given for it.

Interest, be it remembered, is contagious. Your hearers are almost sure to catch it if you have a bad case of it yourself. A short time ago, a gentleman rose during a session of this course in Baltimore and warned his audience that if the present methods of catching rock fish in Chesapeake Bay were continued the species would become extinct. And in a very few years! He felt his subject. It was important. He was in real earnest about it. Everything about his matter and manner showed that. When he arose to speak, I did not know that there was such an animal as a rock fish in Chesapeake Bay. I imagine that most of the audience shared my lack of knowledge and lack of interest. But before the speaker finished, all of us had caught something of his concern. All of us would probably have been willing to have signed a petition to the legislature to protect the rock fish by law.

I once asked Richard Washburn Child, then American Ambassador to Italy, the secret of his success as an interesting writer. He replied: "I am so excited about life that I cannot keep still. I just have to tell people about it." One cannot keep from being enthralled with a speaker or writer like that.

# SUMMARY

1. We are interested in extraordinary facts about ordinary things.
2. Our chief interest is ourselves.
3. The person who leads others to talk about themselves and their interests and listens intently will generally be considered a good conversationalist, even though he does very little talking.
4. Glorified gossip, stories of people, will almost always win and hold attention. The speaker ought to make only a few points and to illustrate them with human interest stories.
5. Be concrete and definite. Do not belong to the "poor-but-honest" school of speakers. Do not merely say that Martin Luther was "stubborn and intractable" as a boy. Announce that fact. Then follow it with the assertion that his teachers flogged him as often as "fifteen times in a forenoon." That makes the general assertion clear, impressive and interesting.
6. Sprinkle your talks with phrases that create pictures, with words that set images floating before your eyes.

7. If possible use balanced sentences and contrasting ideas.
8. Interest is contagious. The audience is sure to catch it if the speaker himself has a bad case of it. But it cannot be won by the mechanical adherence to mere rules.

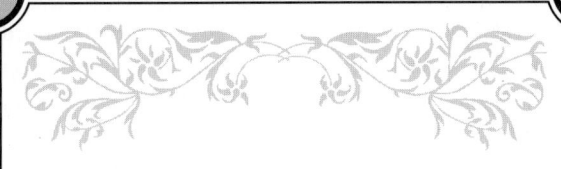

**CHAPTER
FIFTEEN**

**HOW TO GET ACTION**

"The truly effective speakers never have enthroned blind impulse as their god. They have controlled and directed it with the judgment born of a careful study of the laws governing action and belief."
—Effective Speaking, by Arthur Edward Phillips.

"Every business talk, whether it is selling a stove or putting a factory policy up for vote, has a definite end to gain—a decision to win—a product or an idea to sell. It is therefore as much dependent upon an appeal to 'you' interests as a business letter or an advertisement on the billboard across the street. The talk that is so planned and directed is as sure to win against unplanned conversation, as is the carefully prepared and tested advertisement."
—How To Talk Business to Win.

"The great end of life is not knowledge but action." —Huxley.

"Action is the distinguishing characteristic of greatness." —E. St. Elmo Lewis.

## HOW TO GET ACTION

If you could have the power of any talent that you now possess doubled and trebled for the mere asking, which one would you select to have this mighty boon conferred upon? Wouldn't you very likely designate your ability to influence others, to get action? That would mean additional power, additional profit, additional pleasure.

Must this art—so essential to our success in life—remain forever a hit and miss affair with most of us? Must we blunder along depending upon our instinct, upon rule of thumb methods only? Or is there a more intelligent way to set about achieving it?

There is, and we shall discuss it at once—a method based on the rules of common sense, on the rules of human nature, your nature and mine, a method that the writer has frequently employed himself, a method that he has trained others to use successfully.

The first step in this method is to gain interested attention. Unless you do that, people will not listen closely to what you say.

How to do this was dealt with at length in Chapters IX and XIV. Would it not be well to review them in this connection?

The second step is to gain the confidence of your hearers. Unless you do that, they will have no faith in what you say. And here is where many a speaker falls down. Here is where many an advertisement fails, many a business letter, many an employe, many a business enterprise. Here is where many an individual fails to make himself effective within his own human environment.

## WIN CONFIDENCE BY DESERVING IT

The prime way to win confidence is to deserve it. The elder J. Pierpont Morgan said that character was the biggest element in obtaining credit. It is also one of the biggest elements in obtaining the confidence of an audience. I have noticed time without number that facile and witty speakers —if those are their chief qualities —are not nearly as effective as those who are less brilliant but more sincere.

A certain member of a course that the author was recently conducting had been blessed with a striking appearance; and when he stood up to speak, he possessed an admirable fluency of thought and language. When he had finished; however, people said: "clever chap." He made a ready, surface impression; but it was only on the surface, it never amounted to much. In that same group, there was an insurance representative, a man small of stature, a man who groped sometimes for a word, a man lacking grace of diction; but his deep sincerity shone through his eyes and vibrated in his voice. His hearers listened intently to what he said, had faith in him, warmed to him without being conscious of why they did it.

"No Mirabeau, Napoleon, Burns, Cromwell, no man adequate to do anything," said Carlyle in *Heroes and Hero Worship*, "but is first of all in right earnest about it; what I call a sincere man. I should say sincerity, a great deep, genuine sincerity, is the first characteristic of all men in any way heroic. Not the sincerity that calls itself sincere; ah, no, that is a very poor matter indeed —a shallow braggart, conscious sincerity, oftenest self-conceit mainly. The great man's sincerity is of the kind he cannot speak of —is not conscious of."

There died a few years ago, one of the most brilliant and accomplished speakers of his generation. In his youth sanguine hopes were raised, mighty things were prophesied of him; but he passed on without achieving them. He had less heart than head; he prostituted his undeniable talents, spoke for whatever cause brought him a momentary advantage and financial profit. He gained a reputation of insincerity. His public career was ruined.

There is, as Webster said, no use trying to pretend a sympathy or sincerity that one does not feel. It won't work. It must be genuine. It must have the right ring.

"The profoundest feeling among the masses," says the well known Indiana speaker, Albert J. Beveridge, "the most influential element in their character is the religious element. It is as instinctive and elemental as the law of self-preservation. It informs the whole intellect and personality of the people. And he who would greatly influence the people by uttering their unformed thoughts, must have this great and unanalyzable bond of sympathy with them."

Lincoln had this sympathy with the people. He was seldom dazzling. I do not think anyone called him "an orator." In his debates with Judge Douglas, he lacked the grace and smoothness and rhetoric of his opponent. People christened Douglas "The Little Giant." And what did they call Lincoln? "Honest Abe."

Douglas had a charming personality, and he was a man of extraordinary spirit and vitality; but he was a man who tried to carry water on both shoulders, he put policy above principle, expediency above justice. That was his final undoing.

And Lincoln? Well, when he spoke, there was a certain rugged flavor that emanated from the man and doubled the power of his words. People felt his honesty and sincerity and his Christ-like character. As far as knowledge of law is concerned, scores of other men outstripped him; but few of them had more influence with a jury. He was not much concerned about serving Abe Lincoln. He was a thousand times more concerned about serving justice and eternal truth. And people felt it when he spoke.

## SPEAK OUT OF YOUR OWN EXPERIENCE

The second way to gain the confidence of the audience is to speak discreetly out of your own experience. That helps immensely. If you give opinions, people may question them. If you relate hearsay or repeat what you have read, the thing may have a second-hand flavor. But what you yourself have gone through and lived through, that has a genuine ring, a tang of truth and veracity: and people like it. They believe it. They recognize you as the world's leading authority on that particular topic.

## BE PROPERLY INTRODUCED

Many a speaker fails to gain the attention of his audience immediately because he is not introduced properly.

An introduction—that term was fashioned from two Latin words, *intro*, to the inside, and *ducere*, to lead—so an introduction ought to lead us to the inside of the topic sufficiently to make us want to hear it discussed. It ought to lead us to the inside facts regarding the speaker, facts that demonstrate his fitness for discussing this particular topic. In other words, an introduction ought to "sell" the topic to the audience and it ought to "sell" the speaker. And it ought to do these things in the briefest amount of time possible.

That is what it ought to do. But does it? Nine times out of ten—no—emphatically *no*. Most introductions are poor affairs—feeble and inexcusably inadequate.

For example, I heard a well known speaker —a man who ought to have known better—introduce the Irish poet, W. B. Yeats. Yeats was to read his own poetry. Three years prior to that he had been awarded the Nobel prize in literature, the highest distinction that can be bestowed upon a man of letters. I am confident that not ten percent of that particular audience knew of either the award or its significance. Both ought, by all means, to have been mentioned. They ought to have been announced even if nothing else were said. But what did the chairman do? He utterly ignored these facts, and wandered off into talking about mythology and Greek poetry. He was doubtlessly entirely unconscious of the fact that his own ego was prompting him to impress the audience with his own knowledge, his own importance.

That chairman, in spite of the fact that he is known internationally as a speaker and had been introduced a thousand times himself, was a total failure in introducing another. If a man of his caliber makes such a faux pas, what can we expect of the average chairman?

And what are we going to do about it? With all due humility of soul and meekness of spirit, go to the chairman beforehand and ask him if he would like a few facts to use in his introduction. He will appreciate your suggestions. Then tell him the things you would like to have mentioned, the things that show why you are in a position to talk about this particular subject, the simple facts that the audience ought to know, the facts that will win you a hearing. Of course, after being told only once, the chairman is going to forget half of them and get the other half all mixed up; so it is a good plan to hand them to him, just a sentence or two, type-written, hoping that he will refresh his mind before he introduces you. But will he? Probably not. And that is that.

## BLUE GRASS AND HICKORY WOOD ASHES

One autumn the author was conducting courses in public speaking at various Y. M. C. A.'s in greater New York. The star salesman of one of the best known selling organizations in the city was a member of one of those courses, and one evening he made the preposterous statement that he had been able to make blue grass grow without the aid of seed or roots. He had, according to his story, scattered hickory wood ashes over newly-plowed ground. Presto! Blue grass had appeared. He firmly believed that the hickory wood ashes and the hickory wood ashes alone were responsible for the blue grass.

In criticizing his talk, I smilingly pointed out to him that his phenomenal discovery would, if true, make him a millionaire, for blue grass seed was worth several dollars a bushel. I also told him that it would make him immortal, that it would make him the outstanding scientist of all history. I informed him that no man, living or dead, had ever been able to perform the miracle he claimed to have performed, no man had ever been able to produce life from an inanimate substance.

I told him that very quietly, for I felt that his mistake was so palpable, so absurd, as to require no emphasis in the refutation. When I had finished, every other member of the course saw the folly of his assertion; but he did not see it, not for a second. He was in earnest about his contention, deadly in earnest. He leaped to his feet and informed me that he was *not* wrong. He had not been relating theory, he protested, but personal experience. He *knew* whereof he spoke. He continued to talk, enlarging on his first remarks, giving additional information, piling up additional evidence, a rugged sincerity and honesty shining through his voice.

Again I informed him that there was not the remotest hope in the world of his being right or even approximately right or within a thousand miles of the truth. In a second he was on his feet once more, offering to bet me five dollars and to let the U.S. Department of Agriculture settle the matter.

I noticed that he had soon won over several members of the course to his way of thinking. Marveling at their credulity, I inquired why they had now come to believe in his contention. His earnestness—that was the only explanation they could give—earnestness.

Earnestness: The power of it is incredible—especially with a popular audience.

Very few people have the capacity for independent thought. It is as rare as the topaz of Ethiopia. But all of us have feelings and emotions, and all of us are influenced by the speaker's feeling. If he *believes* a thing *earnestly enough*, and *says* it *earnestly enough*, even though he claims he can produce blue grass from dust and ashes, he will gain some adherents, he will win some disciples. He can do that even among supposedly sophisticated and unquestionably successful business men in the city of New York.

After you have won the audience's interested

attention and their confidence, the real work begins. The third step then is to state the facts, to

## EDUCATE PEOPLE REGARDING THE MERITS OF YOUR PROPOSITION

This is the very heart of your talk, the meat. This is where you will need to devote most of your time. Now you will need to apply all you have learned in Chapter XII about Clearness, all you have learned in Chapter XIII about Impressiveness and Conviction.

Here is where your preparation will count. Here is where the lack of it will rise up like Banquo's ghost and mock you.

Here you are on the firing line. And "a battle field," says Marshal Foch, "does not give an opportunity for study. One does what he can to apply what he already knows, therefore it is necessary that he should know thoroughly and be able to use his knowledge quickly."

Here is where you need to know a score of times more about your topic than you can possibly use. When the White Knight in *Alice Through the Looking Glass* started out on his journey, he prepared for every possible contingency: he took a mouse trap lest he should be troubled with mice at night, and he carried a bee hive in case he should find a stray swarm of bees. If the White Knight had prepared public talks like that, he would have been a winner. He would have been able to overwhelm with a torrent of information every objection that could be brought forth. He would have known his subject so well and he would have planned it so thoroughly that he could hardly have failed.

## HOW PATTERSON ANSWERED OBJECTIONS

If you are addressing a business group on some proposal that affects them, you should not only educate them; but you should let them educate you. You should ascertain what is in their minds—otherwise you may be dealing with something entirely beside the point. Let them express their minds; answer their objections; then they will be in a more placid state to listen to you. Here is the way the late John H. Patterson, the first president of the National Cash Register Company, handled a situation of that kind. We are quoting from his article in *System Magazine*:

"It became necessary to raise the prices of our cash registers. The agents and sales managers protested; they said that our business would go, that prices had to be kept where they were. I called them all in to Dayton and we had a meeting. I staged the affair. Back of me on the platform I had a great sheet of paper and a sign painter.

I asked the people to state their objections to the increasing of prices. The objections came ripping out from the audience like shots from a machine gun. As fast as they came, I had the sign man post them on the big sheet. We spent all of the first day gathering objections. I did nothing but exhort. When the meeting closed we had a list of at least a hundred different reasons why the prices should not be raised. Every possible reason was up there before the men, and it seemed conclusively settled in the minds of the audience that no change should be made. Then the meeting adjourned.

On the next morning, I took up the objections one by one and explained by diagrams and words exactly why each was unsound. The people were convinced. Why? Everything that could be said contra was up in black and white and the discussion centered. No loose ends were left. We settled everything on the spot.

But in a case such as this one it would not have been enough, in my mind, merely to have settled the point in dispute. A meeting of agents should break up with all of the audience filled with a new lot of enthusiasm; perhaps the points of the register itself might have been a little blurred in the discussion. That would never do. We had to have a dramatic climax. I had arranged for that and just before the close of the conference, I had a hundred men march, one by one, across the stage; each bore a banner and on that banner was a picture of a part of the latest register and just what it did. Then when the last man passed across, they all came back into a kind of grand finale —the complete machine. The meeting ended with the agents on their feet and cheering wildly!"

## SETTING ONE DESIRE TO FIGHTING ANOTHER

The fourth step in this method is to appeal to the motives that make men act.

This earth and all things in it and on it and in the waters underneath it, are run, not haphazardly, but according to the immutable law of cause and effect.

"For the world was made in order,
And the atoms march in tune."

Everything that ever has happened or ever will happen has been, or will be, the logical and inevitable effect of something that preceded it, the logical and inevitable cause of something that follows. This principle, like the laws of the Medes and Persians, changeth not. It is as true of earthquakes and Joseph's coat of many colors, and the honking of wild geese and jealousy and the price of baked beans, and the Kohinoor diamond, and the beautiful harbor in Sydney—it is as true of those things as it is of putting a nickel in a slot and getting a package of gum······ When one recognizes this, he understands, once and for all, why superstition is unspeakably silly—for how can the unchangeable laws of nature be stopped or altered or affected in the slightest by thirteen people sitting at a table or because one breaks a mirror?

Every conscious and deliberate act we perform is caused by what? By some desire. The only people to whom this does not apply are incarcerated in insane asylums. The things that actuate us are not many. We are ruled hour by hour, dominated day and night, by a surprisingly small number of longings.

All that means just this: if one knows what these motives are and can appeal to them with sufficient force, he will have extraordinary power. The wise speaker attempts to do precisely that. But the blunderer gropes his way blindly and to no purpose.

For example, a father finds that his young son has

been smoking cigarettes surreptitiously. He grows irate, fumes, scolds, commands the boy to have done with the pernicious habit, warns him that it will ruin his health.

But suppose that the boy is not concerned about his health, that he loves the flavor and adventure of smoking a cigarette more than he fears physical consequences. What will happen? The father's appeal will prove futile. Why? Because the parent was not shrewd enough to play upon a motive that touched his son. The parent played only on the motives that actuated himself. He did not get over on the boy's side of the fence at all.

However, it is quite probable that that boy longs with all his heart to make the track team at school, to compete for the hundred yard dash, to excel at athletics. So if the father will only cease unloading his own feelings, and show his son that smoking is going to impede and interfere with his cherished athletic ambitions, the father will probably get the desired action, get it smoothly and completely, and get it by the eminently sensible process of putting a stronger desire against a weaker one. This is precisely what does happen in one of the biggest sporting events in the world—the Oxford-Cambridge boat race. The oarsmen deny themselves the use of tobacco all during their training. Compared to the winning of the race, every other desire is secondary.

One of the most serious problems that mankind faces today is the battle with insects. A few years ago, the Oriental fruit moth was imported into this country on some cherry trees which were forwarded at the instance of the Japanese government and were used to ornament the borders of a lake at our national capital. This moth spread and threatened the fruit crop of some of the eastern states. Spraying seemed to have no effect, so finally, the government was obliged to import another insect from Japan, and turn it loose here to prey upon this moth. So our agricultural experts are fighting one pest with another.

The man skilled in getting action employs similar tactics. He sets one motive to war against another. This method is so sensible, so simple, so utterly apparent that one might imagine that the use of it was all but universal. Far from it. One often sees exhibitions that make him inclined to suspect that the use of it is very rare.

To cite a concrete case: the writer recently attended a noonday luncheon club in a certain city. A golf party was being organized to play over the country club course of a neighboring city. Only a few members had put down their names. The president of the club was displeased; something he was behind was about to fall; his prestige was at stake. So he made what he imagined was an appeal for more members to go. His talk was woefully inadequate; he based his urge very largely on the fact that *he wanted them to go*. That was no appeal at all. He was not handling human nature skillfully; he was merely unloading his own feelings. Like the irate father with the cigarette-smoking son, he neglected entirely to talk in terms of the desires of his hearers.

What should he have done? He should have used a generous supply of common sense; he should have had a little quiet talk with himself before he spoke to the others; and he should have addressed himself somewhat in this fashion: "Why aren't more of these men going on this golfing party? Some probably imagine they cannot spare the time; others may be thinking of the railway fare and various expenses. How can I overcome these objections? I will show them that recreation is not lost time, that grinds are not the most successful men, that one can do more in five days when he is fresh than he can in six when his batteries need recharging. Of course, they know this already; but they need to be reminded of it. I will play up things that they ought to want more than they want to save the small expense connected with this party. I will show them that it is an investment in health and pleasure. I will stir their imaginations, make them see themselves out on the course, the west wind in their faces, the green sward under their feet, feeling sorry for those back in the hot city who live for nothing but money."

Would such a procedure, in your opinion, have been more likely to succeed than the mere "I-want-you-to-go" appeal that the speaker used?

## THE DESIRES THAT DETERMINE OUR ACTIONS

What, then, are these basic and human longings that should mold our conduct and make us behave like human beings? If an understanding of them and a playing upon them is so essential to our success, then out with them. Let us have the light upon them, let us examine and dissect and analyze them.

We shall devote the rest of this chapter to discussing and telling a few stories about them. That, you will agree, is the way to make them clear, the way to make them convincing, the way to engrave them deep upon the walls of your memory.

One of the very strongest of these motives is—what would you say? You are right: the desire for gain. That will be largely responsible for a few hundred million people getting out of bed tomorrow morning two or three hours earlier than they would otherwise arise without this spur. Is it necessary to discourse further upon the potency of this well-known urge?

And even stronger than the money motive is the desire for self-protection. All health appeals are based on that. For example, when a city advertises its healthful climate, when a food manufacturer features the purity and strength-giving qualities of his product, when a patent medicine vendor enumerates all the ills that his nostrums will alleviate, when a dairymen's league tells us that milk is rich in vitamines, a product indispensable to the maintenance of life, when a speaker for an anticigarette society tells us that about 3% of all tobacco is nicotine and that one drop of nicotine will kill a dog and eight drops will destroy a horse—all of these people are appealing to our innate desire to preserve life.

To make the appeal to this motive strong, make it personal. Don't, for example, quote statistics to show that cancer is on the increase. No. Tie it right down to the people who are listening to you, e.g., "There are thirty people in this room. If all of you live to be forty-five, three of you, according to the law of medical averages, will die of cancer. I wonder if it will be you, or you, or you over there."

As strong as the desire for money—in fact, in many people it is far stronger—is the wish to be thought well of, to be admired. In other words, pride.

Pride, what crimes have been committed in thy name! For many years thousands and thousands of young girls suffered excruciating pains in China, screamed with it and did it willingly because the dictates of pride said that their feet must be bound and not allowed to grow. At this very moment, thousands of native women in certain parts of Central Africa are wearing wooden discs in their lips. Incredible as it may seem, these discs are as large as the plate on which you ate breakfast this morning, When the little girls in these tribes reach eight years of age, a slit is made in the outer portion of their lips and a disc is inserted. As the seasons pass, one disc is replaced by another progressively larger. Finally the teeth have to be removed to make room for this much-prized ornament. These cumbersome appendages render it impossible for these ebony belles to utter an intelligible sound. The rest of the tribe can seldom understand their attempts at talking. But all this is endured, even silence is endured by these women, in order that they may appear beautiful, in order that they may be admired, in order that they may stand high in their own estimation, in order that their pride may be appeased.

Although we don't go quite that far in Melbourne, on Montreal, or Cleveland, nevertheless,

"The colonel's lady and Judy O'Grady,
Are sisters under the skin."

So the appeal to pride, if done skillfully, has a force only a trifle less potent than T. N. T.

Ask yourself why you are taking this course. Were you influenced, to some extent, by the wish to make a better impression? Did you covet the glow of inward satisfaction that comes from making a creditable talk? Won't you feel a very pardonable pride in the power, leadership, and distinction, that naturally pertain to the public speaker?

The editor of a mail order journal recently stated in a public address that of all the appeals that one could put in a sales letter, none were so effective as the appeals to pride and profit.

Lincoln won a lawsuit once by a clever appeal to this pride motive. It was in the Tazewell County Court in 1847. Two brothers by the name of Snow had purchased two yokes of oxen and a prairie plow from a Mr. Casc. In spite of the fact that they were minors, he accepted their joint note for two hundred dollars. When it fell due, and he tried to collect it, he got laughter, not cash. It wasn't promising laughter, either; so he employed Lincoln and had them into court. The Snow brothers pleaded that they were minors and that Case knew they were minors when he accepted the note. Lincoln admitted everything they claimed and the validity of the minor act. "Yes, gentlemen, I reckon that is so," he said to point ofter point. It seemed as if he had given his entire case away. However, when his turn came, he addressed the twelve good men and true, in this fashion: "Gentlemen of the jury, are you willing to allow these boys to begin life with this shame and disgrace attached to their character? The best judge of human character that ever wrote has left these words —

"'Good name in man or woman, dear my Lord,
Is the immediate jewel of their souls:

Who steals my purse, steals trash; 'tis something, nothing;
'Twas mine, 'tis his, and has been slave to thousands;
But he that filches from me my good name
Robs me of that which not enriches him
And makes me poor indeed!'"

Then he pointed out that these boys might never have stooped to this villainy had it not been for the unwise counsel of their attorney. Showing how the noble profession of law was sometimes prostituted to prevent rather than to promote justice, he turned and scathingly rebuked the opposing attorney. "And now, gentlemen of the jury," he continued, "you have it in *your* power to set these boys right before the world." Surely these men would not lend their names nor their influence to shielding patent dishonesty? They could not be true to their ideals and do it—such was his plea. He appealed to their pride, you see: and, without leaving their seats, the jury voted that the debt must be paid.

Lincoln in this instance appealed also to the jury's innate love of justice. It is native to almost all of us. We will stop on the street to take the part of a small boy who is being mistreated by a larger one.

We are creatures of feeling, who long for comforts and pleasures. We drink coffee and wear silk socks and go to the theater and sleep on the bed instead of the floor, not because we have reasoned out that these things are good for us, but because they are pleasant. So show that the thing you propose will add to our comforts and increase our pleasures, and you have touched a powerful spring of action.

When Seattle advertised that its death rate was the lowest of any large city in the United States and that a child born there had the best chances of surviving and living long, to what motive was the city appealing? A very strong one, one that is responsible for much of the conduct of the world—affection. Patriotism is also based on the motives of affection and sentiment.

Sometimes an appeal to the sentiments will produce action when all others fail. That was the experience of the well-known real estate auctioneer of New York City, Joseph P. Day. He closed the largest sale of his life by such an appeal. Here is his own story of how he did it.

"Expert knowledge is not the all of selling. In my largest single sale I used no technical knowledge whatsoever. I had been negotiating with Judge Gary for the sale to the

United States Steel Corporation of the building at 71 Broadway, which has always contained its offices. I thought I had closed the sale when, calling upon Judge Gary, he said very quietly but very decisively:

'Mr. Day, we have had the offer of a much more modern building near here and it would seem to answer our purpose better. It is, 'pointing to the woodwork,' a better-finished building. This building is too old-fashioned; you know it is a very old structure. Some of my associates here think that, all in all, the other building will answer our purposes more adequately than this one.'

There was a $5,000,000 sale drifting out of the window! I did not answer for a moment, and Judge Gary did not go on. He had given his decision. If a pin had dropped to the floor it would have sounded like a bomb. I did not attempt to answer. Instead, I asked:

'Judge Gary, where was your first office when you came to New York?'

'Right here,' he said, 'or rather in the room on the other side.'

'Where was the Steel Corporation organized?'

Why, right here in these offices,' he mused rather than answered. And then, of his own accord: 'Some of the younger executives have from time to time had more elaborate offices than this. They have not been quite satisfied with the older furniture. But,' he added, 'none of those men are with us now.'

The sale was over. The next week we formally closed.

Of course, I knew what building had been offered to him, and I might have compared the structural merits of the two. Then I should have Judge Gary arguing —with himself if not with me— over material points of construction. Instead I appealed to sentiment."

## RELIGIOUS MOTIVES

There is another powerful group of motives that influence us mightily. Shall we call them religious motives? I mean religious, not in the sense of orthodox worship or the tenets of any particular creed or sect. I mean rather that broad group of beautiful and eternal truths that Christ taught: justice and forgiveness and mercy, serving others and loving our neighbors as ourselves.

No man likes to admit, even to himself, that he is not good and kind and magnanimous. So we love to be appealed to on these grounds. It implies a certain nobleness of soul. We take pride in that.

For a great many years, C. S. Ward was a secretary of the International Committee of the Y. M. C. A., devoting all of his time to conducting campaigns to raise funds for Association buildings. It does not mean self-preservation or an increase of property or power for a man to write a check for a thousand dollars to the local Y. M. C. A.; but many men will do it out of a desire to be noble and just and helpful.

Setting up a campaign in a northwestern city, Mr. Ward approached a well-known business executive who had never been identified with the church or with social movements. What? Was he expected to neglect his business for a week to raise funds for a Y. M. C. A. building? The idea was preposterous. He finally consented to come to the opening meeting of the campaign; and was so moved there by Mr. Ward's appeal to his nobleness and altruism that he devoted an entire week to an enthusiastic money-raising campaign. Before the week was over, this man who had been noted for his constant use of profanity, was praying for the success of the undertaking.

A group of men once called upon the late James J. Hill to persuade him to establish Y. M. C. A.'s along his railroad lines in the Northwest. Money was required, a considerable outlay of it; and, knowing Hill to be a shrewd business man they unwisely based their principal arguments upon his desire for gain. These

Associations, they pointed out, would make for happy, contented workmen, and would enhance the value of his property.

"You have not yet mentioned," Mr. Hill replied, "the thing that will really lead me to establish these Y. M. C. A.'s — that is the desire to be a force for righteousness and to build Christian character."

A long-standing dispute over some frontier territory had, in 1900, brought Argentine and Chile to the brink of war. Battleships had been built, armaments amassed, taxes increased, and costly preparations made to settle the issue by blood. On Easter day, 1900, an Argentine bishop made a passionate appeal for peace in the name of Christ. Across the Andes, the Chilean bishop reechoed the message. The bishops went from village to village appealing for peace and brotherly love. At first, their audiences were only women; but finally this appeal stirred the entire nations. Popular petitions and public opinion forced the governments to arbitrate and to reduce their armies and navies. The frontier fortresses were dismantled, and the guns melted and cast into a huge bronze figure of Christ. Today high in the lofty Andes, guarding the disputed frontiers, towers this statue of the Prince of Peace holding the cross. On the pedestal is written:

"These mountains themselves shall fall and crumble to dust before the peoples of Chile and the Argentine Republic shall forget their solemn covenant sworn at the feet of Christ."

Such is the power of the appeal to the religious emotions and convictions.

## SUMMARY

So much for the method we have been discussing.

First, get interested attention.

Second, win confidence by deserving it, by your sincerity, by being properly introduced, by being qualified to speak on your subject, by telling the things that your experience has taught you.

Third, state your facts, educate your audience regarding the merits of your proposal, answer their objections.

Fourth, appeal to the motives that make men act: the desire for gain, self-protection, pride, pleasures, sentiments, affections, and religious ideals, such as justice, mercy, forgiveness, love.

This method, if used wisely, will not only help the speaker in public; it will help him also in private. It will help him in the writing of sales letters, in constructing advertisements, in managing business interviews.

## HAS THE AUTHOR USED SUCCESSFULLY THE METHOD HE HAS BEEN DESCRIBING?

First step: Did the writer gain your interested attention by emphasizing the importance of this matter of influencing human nature and by declaring that there was a scientific method of going about it and that we would discuss it forthwith?

Second step: Did the writer gain your confidence by telling you that this system was based upon the rules of common sense, that he himself had employed it and had taught thousands of others to do it?

Third step: Did the writer state the facts clearly, did he educate you regarding the working and the merits of the method?

Fourth step: Did the writer convince you that the use of this method will bring you additional influence and profit? Will you, as a result of reading this chapter, endeavor to use this method? In other words, has the writer gotten action?

PUBLIC SPEAKING AND
INFLUENCING MEN IN BUSINESS
Dale Carnegie

# Words & Phrases

# CHAPTER 1

**phraseology** 어구, 표현
[fréiziáləd‍ʒi]

**gathering** 모임, 회합
[gǽðəriŋ]

**fussed** 안절부절못하다
[fʌsid]

**sidestep** 회피하다
[sáidstèp]

**trustee** (대학 등 법인의) 이사, 평의원
[trʌstíː]

**sanguine** 낙천적인, 자신만만한
[sǽŋgwin]

**gratifying** 만족을 주는, 유쾌한
[grǽtəfàiiŋ]

**Baptist** 침례교, 침례교인
[bǽptist]

**premier** 수상
[primíər]

**forge ahead** 서서히 선두로 나서다, 빠르게 진척되다

**banquet** 연회, 축하연
[bǽŋkwit]

**toastmaster** 연회의 사회자, 건배를 제안하는 사람
[tóustmæ̀stər]

**hygiene** 위생, 위생학
[háidʒiːn]

**paralyze** 마비시키다
[pǽrəlàiz]

**dead** 전적인, 완전한
[ded]

**subside** 가라앉다, 진정되다
[səbsáid]

**stump** 유세하며 다니다, 선거 운동하다
[stʌmp]

**bestow** 주다, 수여하다
[bistóu]

**perpendicular** 수직의, 직립한
[pə̀ːrpəndíkjələr]

**abiding** 오래 지속되는, 영구적인
[əbáidiŋ]

**outset** 시초, 발단
[àutsèt]

**battle-marked** 역전의, 많은 전투를 겪은
[bǽtlmɑːrkt]

**locomotor ataxia** 보행성 운동 실조증

**tongue-tied** 말문이 막힌, 말을 하지 않는
[tʌ́ŋtàid]

**figure of speech** 수사적 표현

**clove** (cleave의 과거형) 붙다, 점착하다
[klouv]

**emancipation** 해방
[imæ̀nsəpéiʃən]

**bolster** 기운 나게 하다, 튼튼하게 하다
[bóulstər]

**cavalry** 기병대
[kǽvəlri]

**charge** 돌격, 진군
[tʃɑːrdʒ]

**inauspicious** 불길한, 조짐이 나쁜
[ìnɔːspíʃəs]

**take heart** 용기를 내다

**flutter** 두근거림, 심장의 박동
[flʌ́tər]

**agitation** 동요, 흥분
[æ̀dʒətéiʃən]

**thoroughbred** 순혈종의 말, 서러브레드
[θə́ːroubrèd]

**bit** 재갈
[bit]

**baudeville** 보드빌(뮤지컬, 서커스, 마술, 텀블링 등을 모아 놓은 공연)
[bɔːdvíl]

**sketch** 풍자극
[sketʃ]

**legitimate** 정통의, 정규의
[lidʒítəmit]

**padded** 방음이 된
[pǽdid]

**mop** (눈물, 땀 등을) 닦다
[map]

**perspiration** 땀, 발한 작용
[pə̀ːrspəréiʃən]

**diffidence** 자신이 없음, 기가 죽음
[dífidəns]

**piping** (목소리가) 새된, 높고 날카로운
[páipiŋ]

**dispatch** 신속
[dispǽtʃ]

**flabby** 연약한, 박약한
[flǽbi]

**accrue** 생기다, 발생하다
[əkrúː]

**terrestrial** 지구의
[təréstriəl]

**downright** 솔직한, 전적인
[dáunràit]

**whip** 때리다, 매질하다
[hwip]

**wayside** 길가, 노변
[wéisàid]

  fall by the wayside 중도에서 단념하다, 낙오하다

**legion** 군단
[líːdʒən]

**legislature** 입법부, 주의회
[lédʒislèitʃər]

**paraphrase** 바꾸어 말하다, 부연 설명하다
[pǽrəfrèiz]

**sovereign** 최상의, 탁월한
[sávərin]

**fit** (감정, 행동의) 격발(激發)
[fit]

**briskly** 힘차게, 씩씩하게
[brískli]

**buoy** 띄우다, 기운을 북돋우다
[búːi]

**Peuhl** 풀라니족의

**flagellation** 채찍질, 태형
[flæ̀dʒəléiʃən]

**foregather** 모이다
[fɔːrgǽðər]

**tomtom** 북, 북소리
[tamtam]

**stride** 성큼성큼 걷다
[straid]

**lash** 채찍으로 때리다
[læʃ]

**flog** 채찍질하다
[flag]

**welt** 채씩 사국, 부푼 자리
[welt]

**scourge** 채찍질, 매
[skəːrdʒ]

Words & Phrases 473

**aspirant** 지망자
[ǽspərənt]

**paean** 승리의 노래, 찬가
[píːən]

**wiggle** 흔들다
[wígəl]

**prowess** 용기, 용맹
[práuis]

**man-of-war** 군함
[mǽnəvɔ́ːr]

**take a grip on oneself**

  분발하다

**dint** 힘
[dint]

**grizzly bear** 회색곰
[grízli bɛər]

**mean** (개, 말 등이) 다루기 힘든,
[miːn]

  사나운

**gunfighter** (미국 서부 개척 시대
[gʌ́nfàitər]

  의) 사격의 명수, 총잡이

**Western Union** 기업간의 전신

  서비스인 텔렉스를 제공한 회사

**sine quo non** 필수조건

**buck** 수사슴
[bʌk]

**self-mastery** 극기, 자제
[sélfmǽstəri]

### CHAPTER 2

**enumerate** 열거하다
[injúːmərèit]

**bearing** 관계, 관련, 의미
[bɛ́əriŋ]

**yoke** 멍에
[jouk]

**subdue** 정복하다, 억누르다
[səbdjúː]

**cohort** 패거리, 한 무리
[kóuhɔːrt]

**ammunition** 탄약, 무기
[æ̀mjuníʃən]

**canned** 통조림으로 된, 판에 박힌
[kænd]

**hemlock** 북미산 솔송나무
[hémlɑk]

**assimilate** 자기 것으로 흡수하다,
[əsíməlèit]

  이해하다

**surfeit** 과다, 홍수, 범람
[sɔ́ːrfit]

**mint** 조폐국
[mint]

**fortnight** 2주일
[fɔ́ːrtnàit]

**colossal** 놀랄 만한, 어마어마한
[kəlɑ́səl]

**eulogize** 찬양하다, 칭송하다
[júːlədʒàiz]

**glean** 줍다, 수집하다
[gliːn]

**booster** 후원자
[búːstər]

  booster booklet 후원 책자, 광고

  책자

**nigh** = near
[nai]

**fine** 벌금을 물리다
[fain]

**ire** 분노
[áiər]

**part and parcel** 본질적인(중요한) 부분

**foolproof** [fúːlprùːf] 바보라도 할 수 있는, 아주 간단한

**dispense** [dispéns] 분배하다, 베풀다

**Psalm** [sɑːm] 성서의 시편

**text** [tekst] 성경의 원구, 성구(聖句)

**forenoon** [fɔ́ːrnùːn] 오전, 아침 나절

**foolscap** [fúːlzkæ̀p] 풀스캡 판, 대판양지

**garble** [gɑ́ːrbəl] 왜곡하다, 마음대로 뜯어 고치다

**milk** [milk] 젖을 짜다

**go about** 부지런히 …하다

**peeved** [piːv] 심술 난, 고집불통의

**jerk** [dʒəːrk] 갑자기 움직이다

**stalk** [stɔːk] 으스대며 걷다, 활보하다

**stow away** 집어넣다, 치우다, 감추다

**dingy** [díndʒi] 우중충한, 음산한, 초라한

**lick** [lik] 한 번의 수고, 일거리

**clog** [klɑg] 움직임을 방해하다, 막다

**take to**… 습관이 붙다, 적응하다

**rap** [ræp] 톡톡 두드림

**retire** [ritáiər] 잠자리에 들다

**forge ahead** (서서히) 선두로 나서다

**set about** …하기 시작하다, 착수하다

**surefire** [ʃúərfaiər] 틀림없는, 틀림없이 성공할

**labor** [léibər] 노동자, 노동계급

**dry** [drai] (우물이) 말라붙은, (소의) 젖이 안 나오는

**canvasser** [kǽnvəs] 방문판매원, 집집마다 주문 받으러 다니는 사람

**food chart** 식품 영양표

**carbohydrate** [kɑ̀ːrbouháidreit] 탄수화물

**ash** [æʃ] 회분(灰分)

**concern** [kənsə́ːrn] 회사

**confide** [kənfáid] 털어놓다, 고백하다

**kick oneself** 자신의 행동을 후회하다, 자책하다

**plethora** [pléθərə] 과잉, 과다

**Airedale** 에어데일 테리어종(種)
[ɛ́ərdéil]
의 개

**impromptu** 즉흥의, 즉석에서,
[imprάmptju:]
준비 없이

**sundry** 가지가지의, 잡다한
[sʌ́ndri]

### CHAPTER 3

**carload** 화차 한 대분(의 분량)
[kάːrlòud]

**slosh** 출렁거리다
[slɑʃ]

**crate** 나무상자(에 채워 넣다)
[kreit]

**hodgepodge** 뒤범벅, 뒤죽박죽
[hάdʒpὰdʒ]

**red herring** 훈제 청어
[red hériŋ]

**flat car** 무개화차
[flæt kɑːr]

**scrap iron** 고철
[skræp άiərn]

**fiasco** 큰 실수, 대실패
[fiǽsˈkou]

**harrow** 괴롭히다, 고민하게 하다
[hǽrou]

**positive** 실재(實在)의, 현실의
[pάzətiv]

**vicarious** 대리의, 대행의
[vaikɛ́əriəs]

**flounder** 버둥거리다, 허우적거리다
[flάundər]

**chart** 계획하다, 진로를 정하다
[tʃɑːrt]

**emphatically** 결단코, 단연코
[imfǽtikəli]

**Irish stew** 아이리시스튜(양고기,
[άiriʃ stju:]
감자, 양파, 당근 등이 재료)

**arrangement** 준비
[əréindʒmənt]

**infallible** 오류 없는, 절대 확실한
[infǽləbəl]

**real estate** 부동산
[ríːəl istéit]

**board** 위원회, 위원, 부(部)
[bɔːrd]

**workshop** 작업장, 일터
[wə́ːrkʃὰp]

**army** 대군(大群), 대집단
[άːrmi]

**knit goods** 편물, 편성제품
[nit gudz]

**textile** 직물
[tékstail]

**felt hat** 펠트 모자, 중절모
[felt hæt]

**storage battery** 축전지
[stɔ́ːridʒ bǽtəri]

**steel ship** 강선(鋼船)
[stiːl ʃip]

**street car** 시내전차
[striːt kɑːr]

**hosiery** 양말, 메리야스
[hóuʒəri]

**mill** 공장
[mil]

**rug** 러그(카펫과 비슷하나 방의 일
[rʌg]
부만 덮음)

**clearings** 어음 교환액
[klíəriŋ]

**Liberty Bond** 자유[전시] 공채(1
[líbərti bɑnd]
차 대전 중 모집)

**clear** 충분히, 완전히
[kliər]

**IWW** 세계산업노동자동맹

(Industrial Workers of the World)

**fertile** 비옥한, 풍요로운
[fə́ːrtl]

**anarchy** 무정부상태, 혼란, 무질서
[ǽnərki]

**fountain head** 원천(源泉), 근원
[fáuntin hed]

**relic** 유물, 유적
[rélik]

**the Liberty Bell** 자유의 종

**wild geese** 기러기
[waild giːs]

**on the wing** 날고 있는, 출발하려 하는

**dawdle** 빈둥거리다
[dɔ́ːdl]

**trite** 진부한
[trait]

**make a mark** 주목 받다

**drive home** 납득시키다

**muddle** 혼란시키다, 어리둥절케 하다
[mʌ́dl]

**steam** 증기로 나아가다, 빠른 속도로 움직이다
[stiːm]

**swerve** 빗나가다, 벗어나다
[swəːrv]

**steel trap** 강철 올가미[덫]

**nil** 무(無)
[nil]

**establish** 수립하다, 입증하다
[istǽbliʃ]

**slur** 경시하다, 간과하다
[sləːr]

**slight** 경시하다, 등한히 하다
[slait]

**material fact** 중대한 사실관계

**build up** 서서히 고조되다

**home stretch** 최후의 직선코스, 최종 단계

**denounce** 비난하다, 탄핵하다
[dináuns]

**lay down** 버리다, 던지다

**come to grief** 재난을 당하다, 실패하다

**campaigner** (사회, 정치) 운동가
[kæmpéinər]

**painstaking** 공들인, 고생스러운
[péinztèikiŋ]

**marshal** 정리(정돈)하다
[máːrʃəl]

**shorthand** 속기
[ʃɔ́ːrthænd]

**dig** 탐구하다, 찾아내다, 캐내다
[dig]

**finding** 조사 결과, 평결
[fáindiŋ]

**dictaphone** 구술 녹음기
[díktəfòun]

**disillusion** 환상을 깨다
[dìsilúːʒən]

**chasten** 단련시키다, 벌하여 바로
[tʃéisən]

잡다

**wholesome** [hóulsəm] 건전한, 유익한

**plain** [plein] 평이한, 단조로운

**peruse** [pərúz] 정독하다, 숙독하다, 읽다

**odd** [ɑd] 낱권의

**Spectator** [spékteitər] 스펙테이터. 영국의 시사 주간지

**measure** [méʒər] 운율, 선율, 박자

**rhyme** [raim] 운, 각운, 압운

**solitaire** [sɑ́litɛ̀ər] 혼자 하는 놀이(카드, 장기 등)

**chaff** [tʃæf] 왕겨, 쭉정이

**coach** [koutʃ] 객차

**Pullman coach** (기차) 풀먼식 침대차

**state papers** [steit péipərs] 정부공식문서

**smashup** [smǽʃʌp] 추락, 전복

**wreck** [rek] 충돌, 파괴

**ample** [ǽmpl] 충분한, 넓은

**tangent** [tǽndʒənt] 직선도로

shoot off at a tangent (행동, 생각 등이) 갑자기 옆으로 빗나가다

**drift off track** 길에서 벗어나다

**flounder** [fláundər] 허우적거리다, 버둥거리다

**morass** [mərǽs] 습지, 늪지, 곤경

**verbatim** [vərbéitim] 축어적으로, 글자 그대로

**court** [kɔːrt] 초래하다

**tumble** [tʌ́mbəl] 구르다, 구르듯 뛰어나가다

**get off** 일에서 해방되다, 퇴근하다

**scaffold** [skǽfəld] 단두대, 교수형

**bravado** [brəvάːdou] 허세, 허장성세

**facility** [fəsíləti] 재주, 솜씨, 유창함

**fool** [fuːl] 농담하다, 빈둥거리다

**lampshade** [lǽmpʃèid] 전등갓

**get through** 마치다, 끝내다, 통과하다

**let oneself go** 열광하다, 열중하다

### CHAPTER 4

**mandate** [mǽndeit] 명령, 지시

**distraction** [distrǽkʃən] 정신이 흩어짐, 주의산만

**moon** 멍하니 보내다(바라보다)
[muːn]

**cherry tree** 벚나무
[tʃéri triː]

**copybook** 습자책, 습자 교본
[kápibùk]

**split** 토막, 동강, 얇은 나무 판
[split]

**blab** 수다, 수다쟁이
[blæb]

**ungainly** 꼴사나운, 볼품없는
[ʌngéinli]

**retentive** 보유력이 있는, 기억력
[riténtiv]
이 좋은

**unstriking** 눈에 띄지 않는, 이목
[ʌnstráikiŋ]
을 끌지 못하는

**take hold** 달라붙다, 뿌리 내리다

**mislay** 둔 곳을 잊다
[misléi]

**sprawl** 몸을 쭉 펴고 눕다(앉다)
[sprɔːl]

**jamb** 문설주
[dʒæm]

**wild boar** 멧돼지
[waild bɔːr]

**den** 굴, 동굴, 우리
[den]

**regular** 완전한, 순전한, 진짜의
[régjələr]

**leavening** 효모, 발효소
[lévəniŋ]

**horn of plenty** 풍요의 뿔

**wren** 굴뚝새
[ren]

**sen-sen** 센센(구취제거제 상표명)

**mediocre** 보통의, 평범한
[mìːdióukər]

**feat** 묘기, 재주, 곡예
[fiːt]

**go over** 복습하다, 되읽다

**by rote** 기계적으로 외워서

**judicious** 현명한, 적절한
[dʒuːdíʃəs]

**peculiarity** 특색, 독특함
[pikjùːliǽrəti]

**look to** 기대하다

**contiguous** 인접하는, 접촉하는
[kəntígjuəs]

**inveterate** 만성의, 뿌리 깊은
[invetərit]

**Savior** 구세주
[séivjər]

**court plaster** 반창고
[kɔːrt plǽstər]

**piddle** 빈둥거리며 시간 낭비하다
[pídl]

**subscription** 구독 신청
[sʌbskrípʃən]

**Bastille** (파리의) 바스티유 감옥
[bæstíːl]

**outing** 소풍, 피크닉
[áutiŋ]

**hors de combat** 전투력을 잃은

**jumble** 뒤범벅, 허접쓰레기
[dʒʌmbl]

**balk** 방해하다, 좌절시키다
[bɔːk]

**blind** 막다른, 출구가 없는
[blaind]

**scintillating** 기지가 번뜩이는
[síntəlèitiŋ]

**without a hitch** 거침없이, 술술

Words & Phrases **479**

**demarcation** 구분, 경계
[dimá:rkéiʃən]

**off the top of one's mind(head)**

즉석에서, 잘 생각하지 않고

**resuscitate** 소생시키다, 부활시키다
[risʌ́sətèit]

**desiliconize** 실리콘을 제거하다
[disílikənìz]

**pig iron** 선철, 무쇠
[pigáiərn]

### CHAPTER 5

**geyser** 간헐천
[gáizər]

**puddle** 웅덩이
[pʌ́dl]

**Second Chronicles** 역대기 하편

**lumberjack** 벌목하는 사람
[lʌ́mbərdʒæ̀k]

**wax flower** 왁스플라워

**Hoyle** 카드 놀이법
[hɔil]

according to Hoyle 규칙대로, 공정하게

**palpitate** 가슴이 뛰다, 두근두근하다
[pǽlpətèit]

**lackadaisical** 기력이 없는, 열의 없는
[lækədéizikəl]

**Leghorns** 레그혼종 (닭)
[légə:rn]

**plight** 곤궁, 고난
[plait]

**League of Nations** 국제연맹

(1920-46) UN의 전신

**myriad** 무수히 많음
[míriəd]

**note** 악보, 음표
[nout]

**condone** 묵과하다, 용서하다
[kəndóun]

**stutter** 말을 더듬다
[stʌ́tər]

**squeal** 깩깩거리다
[skwi:l]

**Zulu** 줄루 족, 줄루 사람
[zú:lu:]

**gas log** (통나무 모양의) 가스난로 파이프

**powder** 화약
[páudər]

**inertia** 무력증, 이완, 타성
[inə́:rʃ(i)ə]

**Probate Court** (유언) 검인 법원

**ring** (이야기의) 느낌
[riŋ]

**terra firma** 대지

**coax** 구슬러서 얻어내다
[kouks]

**Becky Sharp** 새커리의 소설

(Vanity Fair)의 여주인공

**taxidermist** 박제사
[tǽksidə́:rmist]

**turn** 적대하다, 반항하다
[tə:rn]

**fleece** 속여 빼앗다, 강탈하다
[fli:s]

**defendant** 피고(인)
[diféndənt]

**right** 바로잡다
[rait]

**skin** 껍질을 벗기다, 호되게 혼내다
[skin]

**verdict** (배심원의) 평결, 답신
[və́:rdikt]

**surety** (채무) 보증인
[ʃúərti]

**Def't** 피고

**Pl'ff** 원고

**bob** 위아래로 움직이다
[bɑb]

**housetop** 지붕, 평지붕
[háustɑ̀p]

**commencement address** 대학 졸업 축사

**usher** 안내인, 의전관
[ʌ́ʃər]

**prod** 찌르다, 자극하다
[prɑd]

**tome** 크고 묵직한 책, 학술서
[toum]

**limber** 유연하게 하다
[límbər]

**court** 구하다, 얻으려고 애쓰다
[kɔ:rt]

**wing** (무대) 양 옆(의 빈칸)
[wiŋ]

**pummel** 주먹으로 연달아 때리다
[pʌ́məl]

**preface** …으로 시작하다
[préfis]

**thoroughbred** 순혈마, 서러브레드
[θə́:roubrèd]

**plunge** 뛰어듦, 다이빙하는 곳
[plʌndʒ]

**rubdown** 신체마찰, 마사
[rʌ́bdàun]

**hickory trees** 히코리 나무

**recuperative** 회복시키는, 회복력이 있는
[rikjú:pərèitiv]

**catapult** 쇠뇌, 노포, 투석기
[kǽtəpʌ̀lt]

**weasel** 족제비
[wí:zəl]

**ignoramus** 무지한 사람들
[ìgnəréiməs]

**vitiate** 가치를 떨어뜨리다, 해치다
[víʃièit]

## CHAPTER 6

**stick-to-itiveness** 끈기

**sinew** 힘줄, 근육
[sínju:]

**jerk** 경련, 발작적인 움직임
[dʒə:rk]

**stationary** 정체된, 꼼짝도 않는
[stéiʃənəli]

**plateau** 고원(高原)
[plætóu]

**stall** 지연시키다
[stɔ:l]

**grit** 용기, 기개
[grit]

**knack** 기교, 솜씨, 요령
[næk]

**fidget** 안절부절못하다, 조바심 내다
[fídʒit]

**cuff** (와이셔츠) 커프스, 소매 끝동
[kʌf]

**bashful** 수줍어하는, 부끄럼 타는
[bǽʃfəl]

**involved** 복잡한, 뒤얽힌
[inválvd]

**likeness** 초상, 사진
[láiknis]

**prop** 기대 세우다, 놓다
[prɑp]

**incipient** 시작의, 초기의
[insípiənt]

**hinge on** …에 달려있다, …에 따라 정해진다

**run** (사람, 물건의) 보통의 것
[rʌn]

**Baedeker** 베데커 여행안내서
[béidikər]

**bungling** 서투른
[bʌ́ŋɡliŋ]

**essay** 시도하다, …하려고 하다
[ései]

**gunboat** 포함(砲艦)
[ɡʌ́nbòut]

**crown** 정수리, 머리
[kraun]

**veer** 방향을 바꾸다, 갑자기 계획을 바꾸다
[viər]

**coral insect** 산호충
[kɔ́:rəl ínsekt]

**chrysalis** 번데기, 과도기
[krísəlis]

**demoralize** 사기를 꺾다
[dimɔ́:rəlàiz]

**chaplain** 군목, 예배당 목사
[tʃǽplin]

**gumption** 적극성, 근성
[ɡʌ́mpʃən]

**bang** 똑바로
[bæŋ]

**boil** 종기, 부스럼
[bɔil]

**raw deal** 부당한 대우, 가혹한 처사

**buck up** 기운을 내다

**plug** 꾸준히 일하다, 공부하다
[plʌɡ]

**piker** 조심성 많은 사람
[páikər]

**pard** 동료, 짝패
[pɑ:rd]

**crawfish** 꽁무니 빼다, 변절하다
[krɔ́:fiʃ]

**crawl** 기어가다, 아첨하다
[krɔ:l]

**gruel** 녹초가 되게 하다, 크게 혼내다
[ɡrú:əl]

**bout** 한판 승부, 한 차례의 일
[baut]

### CHAPTER 7

**stand** (의견, 주장 등이) 확실히 서 있다
[stænd]

**rostrum** 설교단, 강단
[rɑ́strəm]

**rendition** 연주, 공연
[rendíʃən]

**outlying** 멀리 떨어진, 외딴
[áutlàiiŋ]

**cum grano salis** 좀 에누리하여, 줄잡아

**shuffle** 이리저리 움직이다
[ʃʌfl]

**drove** 떼 지어 가는 무리(인파)
[drouv]

**tallow** 수지(獸脂), 짐승 기름, 우지(牛脂)
[tǽlou]

**the long and short of it** 요점, 요지, 본질

**twaddle** 쓸데없는 소리, 군소리
[twάdəl]

**elocution** 연설법, 웅변술
[èləkjúːʃən]

**vogue** 대유행, 성행
[voug]

**the year of grace** 그리스도 기원, 서기

**prospector** 시굴자(試掘者), 탐광자
[prάspektər]

**for one** 개인으로서는, 나로서는

**iron out** (문제 등을)제거하다

**rail splitter** (통나무로) 울타리용 가로장을 만드는 사람

**dollars to doughnuts** 거의(십중팔구) 확실함

**stilted** 죽마를 탄, 형식적인
[stíltid]

**snapplng turtle** 무는 서북(북미산 민물 거북)

**Hebrews** (신약성서의) 히브리서
[híːbruːz]

**hobo** 부랑자, 뜨내기 일꾼
[hóubou]

**ironclad** 어길 수 없는, 엄한, 철칙의
[áiərnklǽd]

**cinch** 아주 확실한 일, 식은 죽 먹기
[sintʃ]

**Anon** 익명의, 작자 불명의
[ənάn]

**alkali** 알칼리, 알칼리성의
[ǽlkəlài]

**note** 주의, 주목
[nout]

**goose eggs** 영점
[guːseg]

**knock the cover off the ball** 세게 치다, 장타를 날리다

**plate** 타석, 본루, 투수판
[pleit]

**publicity** 광고, 선전, 홍보
[pʌblísəti]

**Christendom** 기독교계, 기독교국, 전 세계
[krísmdəm]

## CHAPTER 8

**beck** 끄덕임, 손짓
[bek]

**violet** 제비꽃
[váiəlit]

**tralt** 이목구비, 생김새
[treit]

**predilection** 기호, 편애
[prìːdəlékʃən]

**sap** 약화시키다, 해치다
[sæp]

**repast** 식사
[ripǽst]

**sweetbread** (송아지) 내장
[swíːtbrèd]

**filet de sole aux pommes nature** 사과를 곁들인 가자미 요리

**dull** 둔하게 하다, 무디게 하다
[dʌl]

**infallibility** (교황) 무류성(無謬性), 무오류설
[infæ̀ləbíləti]

**well groomed** 몸차림이 단정한

**immaculate** 오점이 없는, 깨끗한
[imǽjəlit]

**baggy** 헐렁헐렁한, 불룩한
[bǽgi]

**bulge** 부풀다, 불룩하게 하다
[bʌldʒ]

**sloppy** 지저분한, 너절한
[slápi]

**unkempt** 빗질하지 않은, 텁수룩한
[ʌnkémpt]

**private** 병사, 이등병
[práivit]

**stand of bees** 양봉상자

**plains** 초원, 대평원
[plein]

**perfunctory** 마지못해 하는, 할 마음이 없는
[pərfʌ́ŋktəri]

**contagious** 전염성의, 옮기 쉬운
[kəntéidʒəs]

**scowl** 얼굴을 찌푸리다, 못마땅한
[skaul]
얼굴을 하다

**fluster** 어리둥절하다, 정신 못 차리게 하다
[flʌ́stər]

**Like begets like** 유유상종(類類相從)

**brazen** 뻔뻔스러운, 철면피한
[bréizən]

**dampen** (열기를) 꺾다, 축축하게 하다
[dǽmpən]

**larynx** 후두(喉頭)
[lǽriŋks]

**pharynx** 인두(咽頭)
[fǽriŋks]

**epiglottis** 후두개(喉頭蓋)
[èpəglátis]

**pulchritude** (여자의) 몸매의 아름다움, 육체미
[pʌ́lkrətjùːd]

**flood tide** 밀물, 최고조
[flʌdtaid]

**blustering** 세차게 몰아치는, 호통 치는
[blʌ́stəriŋ]

**spiritualism** 강신(降神)술, 심령술
[spíritʃuəlìzəm]

**quail** 메추라기, 소녀, 아가씨
[kweil]

**thermos** 보온병, 서모스(상표)
[θə́ːrməs]

**trumpery** 겉보기만 좋은 물건, 싸구려 물건
[trʌ́mpəri]

**pinch** 조금, 한 자밤
[pintʃ]

**saliva** 타액, 침
[səláivə]

**impedimenta** 방해물, (방해가 되는) 수하물
[impèdəméntə]

**clutter** 어지르다, 혼란스럽게 하다
[klʌ́tər]

**appointed** …한 설비를 갖춘
[əpɔ́intid]

**concern** 영업, 사업, 회사
[kənsə́:rn]

**slovenly** 단정치 못한, 게으른, 부주의한
[slʌ́vənli]

**janitor** 수위, 관리인, 잡역부
[dʒǽnətər]

**twiddle** 회전시키다, 만지작거리다, 가지고 놀다
[twidl]

**foxhound** 여우 사냥개, 폭스하운드
[fákshàund]

**flop** 털썩 주저앉다
[flɑp]

**unhampered** 구속 받지 않은, 방해 받지 않은
[ʌ̀nhǽmpərd]

**fastidious** 까다로운, 세심한
[fæstídiəs]

**stupendous** 엄청난, 굉장한
[stju:péndəs]

**automaton** 자동인형, 기계적으로 행동하는 사람
[ɔ:támətən]

**disrepute** 악평, 불명예
[dìsripjú:t]

**dinner jacket** (약식) 야회복
[dínər dʒǽkit]

**colic** 산통(疝痛), 배앓이
[kálik]

**vim** 활력, 기운
[vi:m]

**combustible** 가연성의, 타기 쉬운
[kəmbʌ́stəbəl]

**rend** 째다, 찢다, 나누다
[rend]

**tatter** 헝겊, 넝마, 누더기
[tǽtər]

**execration** 증오, 저주
[eksikréiʃən]

**trample** 짓밟다, 밟아 뭉개다
[trǽmpəl]

**rant** 외치다, 고함치다
[rænt]

**thud** 쿵, 쿵 하는 소리
[θʌd]

**summum bonum** 최고 선(善)

**get it across** 호소하다, 이해시키다

**bung** 마개, 통 주둥이
[bʌŋ]

**caper** 신나게 뛰놀다, 희롱거리다
[kéipər]

## CHAPTER 9

**apropos** ~에 관하여
[æprəpóu]

**austerity** 엄격, 내핍, 긴축
[ɔːstériti]

**ponder** 숙고하다, 곰곰이 생각하다
[pándər]

**cerebration** 대뇌작용, 사고
[sìərbréiʃən]

**expedient** 수단, 방편
[ikspí:diənt]

Words & Phrases **485**

**pitfall** 함정
[pítfɔːl]

**gin** (사냥용) 덫
[dʒin]

**buggy** 2륜(4륜) 경마차
[bʌ́gi]

**niche** 벽감(壁龕), 틈
[nitʃ]

**usurp** 빼앗다, 강탈하다
[juːsə́ːrp]

**make over** 변경하다, 고쳐 만들다

**dog days** 침체기, 정체기

**succinctness** 간결함
[səksíŋktnis]

**veracity** 진실성, 정직
[vərǽsəti]

**boo** 피 하다, 야유하다
[buː]

**give a person the hook** ~을 해

고하다

**predilection** 애호, 편애
[priːdəlékʃən]

**whoop** 고함지르다
[hu(ː)p]

**risibility** 웃음의 감각, 유머, 잘
[rìzəbíləti]
　　　웃는 성질

**anent** ~에 관하여
[ənént]

**tripe** 반추동물의 위, 내장; 하찮은 것
[traip]

**forger** 위조자, 날조자
[fɔ́ːrdʒər]

**embezzler** 횡령자
[embézəl]

**take it from me** 내 말을 믿게

**crooked** 구부러진; 부정직한
[krúkid]

**trepidation** 공포, 전율, 당황
[trèpidéiʃən]

**half-tight** 반쯤 술에 취한

**egregious** 지독한, 엄청난
[igríːdʒəs]

**chamois** 샤무아(영양의 일종)
[ʃǽmi]

**genus homo** 사람속(屬)

**potentate** 유력자, 주권자, 군주
[póutənteit]

**pique** (호기심, 흥미를) 돋우다
[piːk]

**foolproof** 잘못될 수 없는
[fúːlprùːf]

**punctuate** 중단시키다
[pʌ́ŋktʃueit]

**half-wit** 얼빠진 놈, 반편
[hǽfwìt]

**the colored man in the cordwood**

　장작다발 속의 유색인; 숨은(불온

　한) 사실, 결점(예전에 자유주로

　탈출을 시도한 노예들이 장작더

　미 속에 숨어 있곤 했었다.)

**harangue** 장광설, 열변
[hərǽŋ]

**stupendously** 엄청나게, 굉장하게
[stjuːpéndəsli]

**injunction** 명령, 훈령, 지령
[indʒʌ́ŋkʃən]

**jar** 깜짝 놀라게 하다
[dʒɑːr]

**chief justice** 재판장, 법원장
[tʃíːfdʒʌ́stis]

**jurisprudence** 법률(리)학
[dʒùərisprúːdəns]

**requisite** 필요한, 필수적인
[rékwəzit]

**nil** 무, 영
[nil]

**vitiate** 가치를 떨어뜨리다, 손상시키다
[víʃièit]

**emaciate** 수척케(여위게) 하다
[iméiʃièit]

**majority** 성년
[mədʒɔ́(ː)rəti]

**justice of the peace** 치안판사

**smack** ~의 기미가 있다
[smæk]

**smell of the lamp** (문학, 작품 등이) 밤새도록 애쓴 흔적이 보이다

**reek** 냄새가 나다, 기미가 있다
[riːk]

**consequence** 중요성
[kánsikwèns]

**wade** 맹공격하다, 힘차게 착수하다
[weid]

**icing** 당의, 설탕옷
[áisiŋ]

### CHAPTER 10

**extort** 무리하게 강요하다, 강제로 탈취하다
[ikstɔ́ːrt]

**Orangeman** 오렌시 낭원
[ɔ́(ː)rindʒmən]

**double** (주먹을) 쥐다
[dʌ́bəl]

**concern** 사업, 회사
[kənsə́ːrn]

**red-letter day** 기념일, 추억에 남을 날
[rédlétər dei]

**element** 집단, 분자
[éləmənt]

**ringleader** 주모자, 두목
[ríŋliːdər]

**interloper** 남의 일에 참견하는 사람, 불법 침입자
[íntərlóupər]

**be disposed to V** ~할 생각 있는

**gallant** 씩씩한, 의협심 강한
[gǽlənt]

**desperado** 불량자, 무법자
[dèspəréidou]

**finesse** 기교, 솜씨
[finés]

**prohibition** 금주법
[pròuhəbíʃən]

**china shop** 도자기점
[tʃáinəʃap]

**once and for all** 단호하게

**glandular** 선(腺)의
[glǽndʒələr]

**bristle** 털을 곤두세우다, 벌컥 화내다
[brísəl]

**bungle** 망치다, 실수하다
[bʌ́ŋgəl]

**salutation** 인사(말)
[sæ̀ljətéiʃən]

**efficacious** 효험(능) 있는
[èfəkéiʃəs]

**relent** 누그러지다
[rilént]

**imputation** 비난, 비방
[impjutéiʃən]

**pertinent** 타당한, 적절한
[pə́ːrtənənt]

**white heat** 백열, 극도의 긴장
[hwait hiːt]

**moment** 중요성
[móumənt]

**magnitude** 중대(성)
[mǽgnətjùːd]

**revere** 숭배하다
[riviər]

**number** 패, 동아리, 동료
[nʌ́mbər]

**funeral oration** 조사, 추도사
[fjúːnərəl ɔːréiʃən]

**rostrum** 연단, 강단
[rástrəm]

**rabble** 구경꾼, 폭도, 대중
[rǽbəl]

**plebeian** 평민, 서민
[plibíːən]

**mutiny** 폭동, 반란
[mjúːtəni]

**unobtrusively** 주제넘지 않게, 삼가
[ʌ̀nəbtrúːsivli]

**whip up** 자극하다, 흥분시키다

**ransom** (포로의) 몸값, 배상금
[rǽnsəm]

**abide** (죄의 대가를) 치르다
[əbáid]

**parchment** 양피지
[páːrtʃmənt]

**meet** 적당한
[miːt]

**overshoot oneself** 도를 지나치다

**hearse** 관
[həːrs]

**muffle** 싸다, 덮다
[mʌ́fəl]

**vesture** 옷, 의복
[véstʃər]

**ruffle** 교란하다, 성나게 하다
[rʌ́fəl]

**arbor** 정자, 나무그늘
[áːrbər]

**brand** 불이 붙은 나무막대, 타다 남은 나뭇조각
[brænd]

**pluck** 잡아 뜯다, 잡아당기다
[plʌk]

**form** (건축용으로 쓰인) 나무틀
[fɔːrm]

## CHAPTER 11

**round out** 마지막 마무리를 하다

**ominous** 불길한
[ámənəs]

**leave-taking** 작별, 고별
[líːvtèikiŋ]

**coign of vantage** (관찰, 행동 따위에) 유리한 지위

**round off** 완성하다, 마무르다

**discernment** 식별(력), 통찰
[disə́ːrnmənt]

**part company with** ~와 헤어지다, 갈라지다

**thrash** 몸부림치다, 뒹굴다
[θræʃ]

**phraseology** 말씨, 어법, 표현
[frèiziálədʒi]

**materially** [mətíəriəli] 크게, 현저하게

**sputter** [spʌ́tər] 뚝뚝 소리내다, 빠른 말로 지껄이다

**lunge** [lʌndʒ] (펜싱 따위) 찌르기, 돌진

**jerkily** [dʒə́ːrkili] 갑자기, 돌연

**mill** [mil] 떼를 지어 마구 돌아다니다

**forbear** [fɔːrbɛ́ər] 억제하다, 삼가다

**hearthstone** [háːθstòun] 노변, 가정

**ragged** [rǽgid] 누덕누덕한, 거친

**jagged** [dʒǽgid] 깔쭉깔쭉한, 다듬어지지 않은

**blatant** [bléitənt] 뻔뻔스런

**at the beck and call** (~가) 시키는 대로

**apotheosis** [əpàθióusis] 신격화, 숭배, 미화

**bondsman** [bándzmən] 노예, 농노

**unrequited** [ʌ̀nrikwáitid] 보답 없는

**lash** [læʃ] 채찍질

**unequivocally** [ʌ̀nikwívəkəli] 명료하게, 솔직하게

**terse** [təːrs] 간결한, 생동감 있는

**abhorrence** [əbhɔ́ːrəns] 혐오, 증오

**rotarian** [routɛ́əriən] 로터리클럽 회원

**tenor** [ténər] 방침, 방향, 취지

**out of key** 조화하지 않는

**eulogize** [júːlədʒàiz] 칭찬(칭송)하다, 기리다

**abide** [əbáid] 머무르다

**creeper** [kríːpər] 덩굴식물

**girdle** [gə́ːrdl] 띠를 두르다, 에워싸다

**to the letter** 글자 그대로, 엄밀히

**part with** 내놓다, 헤어지다

**cumulative** [kjúːmjəleitiv] 축적의, 누적하는

**mound** [maund] 흙무덤, 작은 언덕

**selfsame** [sélfsèim] 꼭 같은, 동일한

**prognostication** [prɑgnɑ̀stikéiʃən] 예측, 예언

**get a hearing** 발언할 기회를 얻다

**consummate** [kánsəmèit] 완성된, 완전한

**tirade** [táireid] 긴 연설, 장광설

**vivisection** [vívəsékʃən] 생체해부

**satiation** [séiʃiéiʃən] 물리게 함, 포만

**archdeacon** [áːrtʃdíːkən] 부감독, 부주교

**member** [mémbər] 신제의 일부(특히 손발)

Words & Phrases

# CHAPTER 12

**birdshot** 새잡는 산탄
[báːrdʃɑt]

**unlettered** 배우지 못한, 문맹의
[ʌnlétərd]

**a place in the sun** 누구나 받을 수 있는 것에 대한 몫; 유리한 지위, 양지

**sonorous** 낭랑한, 당당한
[sənɔ́ːrəs]

**eulogy** 찬사, 칭송
[júːlədʒi]

**Nebular Hypothesis** (태양계의) 성운설
[nébjələr haipɑ́θəsis]

**flounder** 버둥거리다, 허둥대다
[fláundər]

**hoot** 야유하다, 우우하다
[huːt]

**ramble** 장황하게 지껄이다
[ræmbəl]

**obtuse** 둔한, 무딘
[əbtúːs]

**leaven** 효모, 누룩; 발효시키다, 부풀리다
[lévən]

**meat** 속, 살, 알맹이
[miːt]

**obliterate** 지우다, 말소하다
[əblítəreit]

**bring the matter home** 그 문제를 충분히 납득시키다

**blade** 잎
[bleid]

**rod** 로드(길이의 단위: 5.0292m)
[rɑd]

**uninitiated** 충분한 경험(지식)이 없는, 풋내기의
[ʌniníʃièitid]

**facile** (혀, 펜이) 잘 돌아가는, 날랜, 유창한
[fǽsil]

**diaphragmatic** 횡경막의
[dàiəfræmǽtik]

**peristaltic action** 연동 운동
[pèrəstǽltik ǽkʃən]

**abdominal cavity** 복강
[æbdɑ́mənəl kǽvəti]

**pancreas** 췌장
[pǽŋkriəs]

**spleen** 비장, 지라
[spliːn]

**solar plexus** 태양 신경총, 명치
[sóulər plέksəs]

**elimination** 배설
[ilìmənéiʃən]

**constipation** 변비
[kɑ̀nstəpéiʃən]

**auto-intoxication** 자가 중독
[ɔ́ːtou intɑ̀ksikéiʃən]

**proposition** 서술, 진술, 주장
[prɑ̀pəzíʃən]

**stump speech** 가두연설
[stʌmp spiːtʃ]

**state paper** 정부 문서, 공문서

**chart talk** 도표, 그림
[tʃɑːrt tɔːk]

**moon face** 둥근 얼굴

**chipper** 기운찬, 활기찬
[tʃípər]

**stereopticon** 실체(입체)환등기
[stèriɑ́ptikən]

**square deal** 공정한 거래

**cocker spaniel** 코커스패니얼(사
[kákər spǽnjəl]
냥, 애완용 개)

**Scotch terrier** 스카치테리어(다
[skatʃ tériər]
리가 짧은 테리어 품종의 개)

**Pomeranian** 포메라니아 종의 작
[pàməréiniən]
은 개

**brindle** 얼룩무늬
[brindl]

**Shetland pony** 셰틀랜드 종의
[ʃétlənd póuni]
조랑말

**bantam rooster** 밴텀 종의 수탉
[bǽntəm rúːstər]

**couch** 말로 표현하다
[kautʃ]

**prize fighter** 프로권투선수
[praiz fáitər]

**pugilist** 권투선수, 프로복서
[pjúːdʒəlist]

**make for** 도움 되다, 이바지하다

**fox terrier** 폭스테리어 종의 개

**splotch** 오점, 반점, 얼룩
[splatʃ]

---

**CHAPTER 13**

**tame** 무기력한, 단조로운
[teim]

**bloodless** 생기 없는
[blʌ́dlis]

**quicken** 자극하다, 고무하다
[kwíkən]

**import** 의미, 취지
[impɔ́ːrt]

**demur** 반대하다, 이의를 말하다
[dimə́r]

**imbed**=embed 끼워 넣다, 깊이 새
[imbed]
겨두다

**benighted** 어리석은, 미개한
[bináitid]

**nicety** 정확, 미묘(한 점), 미세한 점
[náisəti]

**lull** 달래다, 진정시키다
[lʌl]

**veritable** 진실의, 틀림없는
[vérətəbəl]

**rough-on-rats** 원래는 쥐약 브

랜드로 '비소가 든 쥐약'을 의미하

며, 여기서는 은유적으로 '쥐를 없

애듯 모든 대립되는 생각들을 박

멸하는 요소'를 가리킨다.

**concoct** 혼합(조합)하다
[kɑnkɑ́kt]

**works** (시계 등의) 장치, 구조
[wəːrk]

**Fuzzy Wuzzy** 수단의 흑인 전사

를 경멸하여 부르는 말

**citadel** 성채, 요새
[sítədl]

**drawbridge** 도개교, 적교
[drɔ́ːbridʒ]

**mail** 쇠미늘 갑옷을 입히다, 무장
[meil]

Words & Phrases **491**

시키다

**fray** 소동, 싸움
[frei]

**draw** 비김, 무승부
[drɔ:]

**sagacity** 총명, 명민
[səgǽsəti]

**give one's hands a dry wash** 손을 비비다

**clear one's throat** 헛기침하다

**smother** 덮어 가리다, 묵살시키다, 질식시키다
[smʌ́ðər]

**blanket insurance policy** 총괄 보험증서(계약)

**propound** 제출하다, 제의하다
[prəpáund]

**snappy** 재빠른
[snǽpi]

**discriminating** 식별력 있는
[diskrímənèitiŋ]

**forestall** 앞질러 방해하다
[fɔ:rstɔ́:l]

**prohibitive** 엄청나게 비싼
[prouhíbətiv]

**outlay** 비용, 경비
[áutlèi]

**drive ~ home** (견해, 사실을) 납득시키다, (일의) 핵심을 찌르다

**stupendous** 엄청난, 굉장한
[stju:péndəs]

**club** 곤봉
[klʌb]

**truism** 자명한 이치, 뻔한 소리
[trú:izəm]

**reaper** 수확기
[rí:pər]

**rivet** 고정시키다, 집중시키다
[rívit]

**Emancipation Proclamation**
[imænsəpéiʃən pràkləméiʃən]
노예해방령

**storm** 습격하다
[stɔ:rm]

**artillery** 포, 대포, 포병대
[a:rtíləri]

**shear** 베다, (털을) 깎다
[ʃiər]

**veracity** 진실, 정확성(도)
[vərǽsəti]

**multiplication table** 구구표

**bewhiskered** 구레나룻을 기른
[biʰwískərd]

**stand well with** ~에게 평판(인기)이 좋다

**fraternity** 협동단체, 친목회, 동업자들
[frətə́:rnəti]

**magnate** 고관, 거물, ~왕
[mǽgneit]

## CHAPTER 14

**at all hazards** 만난을 무릅쓰고, 기어이

**insipid** 맛없는, 무미건조한
[insípid]

**cobweb** 거미집(줄), 엷은 옷
[kábwèb]

**slant** 관점, 견지
[slænt]

**doggoned** 저주할, 괘씸한; 빌어먹을
[dɔ́(:)gɔ́(:)nd]

**sulphuric acid** 황산
[sʌlfjúərik æsid]

**molasses** 당밀
[məlǽsiz]

**gusher** 쏟아져 나오는 것, 분유정
[gʌ́ʃər]

**Dobbin** 농사말, 짐말
[dábin]

**pickle** 묽은 산 용액으로 닦다
[píkəl]

**anneal** 달구었다가 천천히 식히다
[əní:l]

**tanner** 제혁업자
[tǽnər]

**gilt** 입힌 금, 금박
[gilt]

**phosphate fertilizer** 인산비료
[fásfeit fɔ́:rtəlàizər]

**buckwheat cake** 메밀 팬케이크
[bʌ́kʰwi:t keik]

**reverie** 환상, 공상
[révəri]

**work up** (흥미, 열의를) 불러일으키다

**ranks** 일반 사원(당원)
[ræŋk]

**make a killing** 돈을 많이 벌다

**wiggle** (몸을) 뒤흔들다(움직이다)
[wígəl]

**make a face** 얼굴을 찌푸리다

**draughtsman** 제도공, 도안가
[dræftsmən]

**hold the floor** 발언권을 가지고 있다

**scrap** 다툼, 싸움
[skræp]

**rough-and-ready** 거칠지만 유능한, 정력적인

**moving-van** 가구 운반차, 이삿짐 트럭
[mú:viŋ væn]

**demeanor** 처신, 거동, 품행
[dimí:nər]

**virility** 사나이다움, 정력
[viríləti]

**intractable** 억지(고집)스러운
[intrǽktəbəl]

**flog** 채찍질하다, 체형을 가하다
[flɔg]

**overshoes** 덧신
[óuvərʃù:]

**gunny sacking** 굵은 삼베 자루

**heaves** (말의) 천식, 폐기종
[hi:vs]

**calico** 순면직물, 무명베
[kǽlikòu]

**loom** 베틀, 직기
[lu:m]

**spout** 배수구, 방수관
[spaut]

**scamper** 뛰어 돌아다니다
[skǽmpər]

**penal code** 형법
[pí:nəl koud]

**rack** 고문(대)
[ræk]

**superfluous** 여분의, 불필요한
[su:pərfluəs]

**hoary** 백발의, 고색창연한
[hɔ́:ri]

**terminology** 용어, 용어법
[tə̀:rmənálədʒi]

**infliction** 형벌, 고통
[inflíkʃən]

**prelate** 고위 성직자
[prélit]

**vapid** 맛없는, 김빠진
[vǽpid]

**case** 병증, 환자
[keis]

**rock fish** (어류) 볼락

### CHAPTER 15

**address oneself** 본격적으로 착수하다, 전념하다

**hit and miss** 되는대로 하는, 마구잡이의

**rule of thumb** 주먹구구, 눈어림, 경험법칙

**in this connection** 이와 관련하여

**braggart** 허풍선이, 자랑꾼
[brǽgərt]

**elemental** 기본적인, 본질적인
[èləméntl]

**christen** 이름 붙이다, 명명하다
[krísn]

**carry water on both shoulders** 서로 양립할 수 없는 일들을 동시에 추진하다

**expediency** 편의(주의), 방편, 편법
[ikspí:diənsi]

**undoing** 파멸(의 원인)
[ʌndú:iŋ]

**emanate** 발산하다, 나오다
[émənèit]

**outstrip** 앞지르다, 능가하다
[áutstríp]

**tang** 특유한 맛, 특성, 특질
[tæŋ]

**caliber** (인물의) 국량, 관록
[kǽləbər]

**faux pas** 실수, 과실

**that is that** 그것으로 끝이다

**hickory** 히코리(북미산 호두나무과의 나무)
[híkəri]

**preposterous** 상식을 벗어난, 터무니없는
[pripástərəs]

**palpable** 명백한
[pǽlpəbəl]

**refutation** 논박, 반박
[rèfjutéiʃən]

**firing line** 사선, 최전선
[fáiəriŋ lain]

**contingency** 우연(성), 우발사건
[kəntíndʒənsi]

**ascertain** 확인하다, 알아내다
[æ̀sərtéin]

**rip out** 거칠게 말하다

**contra** 반대하여
[kántrə]

**loose end** 미결부분
[luːs end]

**break up** 해산하다, 끝나다

**haphazardly** 우연히
[hæphæzərdli]

**immutable** 불변의
[immjúːtəbəl]

**honk** (기러기) 울다
[hɔːŋk]

**incarcerate** 투옥하다, 감금하다
[inkάːrsəreit]

**insane asylum** 정신병원
[inséin əsáiləm]

**surreptitiously** 은밀하게
[sə̀ːrəptíʃəsli]

**irate** 성난, 노한
[áireit]

**fume** 노발대발하다
[fjuːm]

**pernicious** 유해한, 유독한
[pəːrníʃəs]

**forward** 전송하다, 보내다
[fɔ́ːrwərd]

**at the instance of** ~의 의뢰로, 제의로

**grind** 공부벌레
[graind]

**sward** 초지, 잔디
[swɔːrd]

**play upon** 이용하다

**nostrum** 묘약, 만능약
[nάstrəm]

**excruciating** 몹시 고통스런, 참기 어려운
[ikskrúːʃièitiŋ]

**cumbersome** 성가신, 귀찮은
[kʌ́mbərsəm]

**appendage** 부가물, 부속물
[əpéndidʒ]

**ebony** 흑단의, 칠흑의
[ébəni]

**under the skin** 한꺼풀 벗기면, 내심(심중)은

**pertain** ~에 속하다
[pəːrtéin]

**filch** 훔치다
[filtʃ]

**stoop** 굽히다
[stuːp]

**villainy** 악행
[víləni]

**scathingly** 냉혹하게, 통렬하게
[skéiðiŋli]

**patent** 명백한
[pǽtənt]

**tenet** 주의, 교의
[ténət]

**identify** 행동(사상)을 같이하다, 관계하다
[aidéntəfài]

**profanity** 신성모독, 불경
[prəfǽnəti]

**pedestal** 받침대, 대좌
[pédəstl]

**forthwith** 곧, 즉시
[fɔ́ːrθwiθ]